Rabindranath Tagore's *The*

Anthem South Asian Studies
Series Editor: Crispin Bates

Other titles in the series:

Brosius, Christiane *Empowering Visions* (2005)

Mills, Jim (ed) *Subaltern Sports* (2005)

Joshi, Chitra *Lost Worlds: Indian Labour and its Forgotten Histories* (2005)

Dasgupta, Biplab, *European Trade and Colonial Conquest* (2005)

Kaur, Raminder *Performative Politics and the Cultures of Hinduism* (2005)

Rosenstein, Lucy *New Poetry in Hindi* (2004)

Shah, Ghanshyam, *Caste and Democratic Politics in India* (2004)

Van Schendel, Willem *The Bengal Borderland: Beyond State and Nation in South Asia* (2004)

Rabindranath Tagore's
The Home and the World

A Critical Companion

Edited by
Pradip Kumar Datta

Anthem Press

Anthem Press
An imprint of Wimbledon Publishing Company
75-76 Blackfriars Road, London SE1 8HA
or
PO Box 9779, London SW19 7ZG
www.anthempress.com

This edition first published by Anthem Press 2005

First published in India Permanent Black 2002

British Library Cataloguing in Publication Data
A catalogue record for this book is available from the British Library.

Library of Congress Cataloging in Publication Data
A catalog record for this book has been requested.

1 3 5 7 9 10 8 6 4 2

ISBN 1 84331 099 6 (Hbk)
ISBN 1 84331 100 3 (Pbk)

Cover Photograph:

Typeset by Footprint Labs Ltd, London
www.footprintlabs.com

Printed in India

Dedication

This collection is dedicated to the memory of the many living and dead Mirjans, Panchus and Nikhileshes, whose lives have been smashed up by the communal violence that continues from the days of Tagore to ours especially the recent one in Gujarat.

My heart is thorn-filled with longing for Gujarat
Restless, frantic, flame-wrapped in the spring
On earth there exists no balm for its wound
My heart split asunder by the dagger of separation.

Vali Gujrati, Sufi saint poet.
Born 1650. Died 1707. Tomb razed 2002.

(from 'How has the Gujarat massacre affected minority women? Fact finding by a Women's Panel'.)

Acknowledgements

This book has been fashioned in many deep and silent ways by my memories of John Mason, R.R. Gupta and Professor A.N. Kaul, three teachers who opened out literature as a window to things I am still discovering. And for teaching me the importance of values, debate and self-forgetting.

I wish to thank Shirsendu Chakravarty, Professor Sisir Das, Professor Bikash Bhattacharya, Sibaji Bandopadhyay, Aijaz Ahmad, Jayanti Bandopadhyay for their encouragement at the initial stages of this book. That some of them were not able to contribute to this collection is a matter of deep regret. I want to specially thank Shirsendhu and Prof. Das for discussing the project and for the information they readily imparted, and Aijaz for the efforts he made despite the problems it caused. Anuradha has been a patient editor. Tanika and Sumit, as always, have provided endless encouragement and zest. I want to particularly thank Tanika for getting me started on this collection.

There are many others I wish to thank. I remember my M.Phil batch of 1981 who provided the stimulation and thoughtfulness to break out of the mould of Eng. Lit. studies as we had inherited it. The most important memory I will cherish, along with some others, was their patience and loyalty. My students have been ever a source of exasperation and everyday inspiration. I am grateful, in particular, to my Sri Venkateswara students for they made me experience and realise— in situations that were sometimes agonising for both parties—something that I had (till I encountered them) simply mouthed and tried desperately to believe: that teaching was creative. The teachers who devised the current undergraduate English syllabus need a special mention for boldly entering new academic territories and doing this in an exemplary spirit of democratic exchange.

Lalkaku and Chotopishi have given me many things, not least of all making it a pleasure to work in Calcutta. Above all, for providing me with all the warmth and comforts of home without its backdrop of authority and familial responsibility.

Contents

Introduction

P.K. DATTA

I

i

To say that Rabindranath Tagore (1861–1941) is a Bengali icon would raise no eyebrows today. Children, housing colonies, underground stations (and the list can stretch a long way) derive their names from either his person or his works. To an extent this devotion is explicable by the stunning range of personalities Tagore combined in himself: artist (poet, fiction writer, playwright, essayist, composer, painter) landlord, pedagogue, statesperson, lover, rural activist. He had already become an icon in his lifetime, especially after the award of the Nobel Prize in 1913, a consecration deepened by tributes, among others, from Einstein who called him a 'seer'[1] and Gandhi, 'The Great Sentinel'. And, for a time, when he was alive, he even became a sort of popular idol in Europe.[2]

Tagore has been so firmly canonised that it is easy to forget that he was once a controversial, even iconoclastic figure, who was constantly stirring up customary ways of thinking and engaging in provocation and debate. His most controversial moment perhaps was his questioning of the swadeshi movement—the first popular anti-colonial movement in India that took place in Bengal, from 1905 to 1908—when it became clear that along with stirring up nationalist energies it was also provoking communal tension. Committed to what he called 'Truth', Tagore questioned all forms of fixed, constricting and authoritarian frameworks of thought. This made him a lifelong critic of Hindu orthodoxy, often leading him to bitter exchanges with representatives of neo-orthodoxy such as the critic Chandranath Basu who inherited and deepened the revivalist ideas of Bankim Chattopadhyay's later phase. Indeed, Tagore's novel *Gora* (1910) shows the caste system as defended by the neo-orthodox, as responsible for oppression, social fragmentation and narrow mental horizons.

Interestingly, Rabindranath became more radical as he grew older. In 1914, when he was already past fifty—when most people resign themselves to a pragmatic acceptance of the status quo—Rabindranath became closely involved with the *avant garde* journal *Sabuj Patra* (The Green Leaves) edited by Pramatha Chaudhury, his close relative and intimate friend. The aesthetic programme of *Sabuj Patra*, in Rabindranath's words, was to 'really jolt the readers mind and shake it' and not 'merely excite it'.[3] It was in this phase of his literary career, in 1915–16, that Rabindranath published *Ghare Baire*, the Bengali original of *The Home and the World*, serially in *Sabuj Patra*.

Accompanying his provocativeness was a related quality common to his family. This was a certain outsiderliness, more accurately, a position of social distance. His family was extremely rich and influential. However, unlike a comparable wealthy family like the Rajas of Sovabazar,[4] they were Pirali Brahmins, who were ritually subordinate since one of their ancestors had come into intimate contact with a Muslim. Moreover, while the Tagores were wealthy (having made use of their business contacts with British traders), they had not become bland and conservative. Indeed, the history of their family indicates that they converted their financial audacity into cultural and spiritual intrepidity. Debendranath, Rabindranath's father, inherited little since his father, the grand Raja Dwarkanath Tagore, had zealously accumulated wealth but spent it with greater gusto. Debendranath's interests were different from his father's: he was leader of the Brahmo Samaj, a religio-social reform movement that sought a removal of intermediaries such as priests, the use of reason to understand the nature of the divine, and social reform related to women and caste. While the Brahmo Samaj eventually became a respectable part of upper-caste Hindu society, at the time of Rabindranath's youth it certainly was not. In 1901, Rabindranath wrote to his wife, 'We are totally different from other

Bengalis in everything—in education and culture, in language, in temperament and habit.'[5]

Rabindranath's childhood too was a lonely one. Motherless, and distant from other members of his family, he lived under what he called 'servocracy', that is, the guardianship of servants.[6] The young boy filled his loneliness with stories and fancies of his imagination—desires to live in other worlds. One finds the impress of this in his later zest for travelling—inside Bengal, in the country and internationally. Given the problems of travelling a century ago, it is startling to think that in the period of nine months or so when he was writing *Ghare Baire*, he had stayed in Calcutta, Santiniketan, in his estates in East Bengal (where he also travelled in houseboats), Kashmir and nearly went to Japan!

Nevertheless one should be careful not to overstress Tagore's outsiderliness. After all, in different ways, his social and domestic life was also a success story. The Tagores were well on their way to becoming the 'first family' of Bengal. Rabindranath's brothers and sisters were highly accomplished and at least one achieved great success. Satyendranath was the first Indian to be admitted to the Indian Civil Service. Nor did Rabindranath's childhood isolation last. His precocity earned him attention: he wrote a historical ballad on Prithviraj at the age of eleven, and had translated (possibly parts of) *Macbeth* as well as passages from Sanskrit by his teens. He was much in demand from the women of his family to read out the Ramayan in the original Sanskrit that he had learned from his father.[7] Clearly, the reasons for Tagore's commitment to provocation had to do with the nature of his convictions.

ii

The composition of *Ghare Baire* can be located at the intersection of two sets of preoccupations—one global/national and the other local—that came together in Rabindranath's life at the time when *Ghare Baire* was being written and serialized (between roughly *baisakh* to *falgun* 1322, May 1915 to February 1916). These concerns suggest a context for locating the key social and political themes of the novel itself.

The first concern was with nationalism, the dangers of which became evident to Rabindranath in the World War that was then raging in Europe.[8] Questions about nationalism had begun to plague Rabindranath's mind even in the *fin de siecle*,[9] years when Rabindranath was a convinced nationalist. Like many other intellectuals of the nineteenth century such as Bankimchandra who had envisioned the country as a Hindu goddess in his song 'Bande Mataram' and in other works,[10] Rabindranath began as a Hindu nationalist. From 1901 especially, Rabindranath sought to revive the ancient glories of Hinduism to counter the authority of British rule. It was with this mindset that he threw himself unreservedly into the swadeshi movement that sought to abrogate the partition of Bengal by Lord Curzon's administration in 1905. He addressed meetings, wrote the popular song *'Banglar mati Banglar jal'* (Bengal's soil, Bengal's water) and initiated the ritual of *rakhi bandhan* as a gesture of social solidarity. Communal riots broke out barely a year later following attempts by middle-class swadeshi activists to compel peasants and petty traders to boycott cheaper foreign goods. Mainstream opinion simply blamed the violence on Muslim mullas in the pay of the Nawab of Dacca and British manipulation. Rabindranath dissented and became the movement's most trenchant critic, calling on it to introspect on its high-handedness and Hindu biases. 'Satan,' Rabindranath said in a famous declaration, 'cannot enter till he finds a flaw . . .'[11]

Rabindranath's break with swadeshi reawakened his earlier muted reservations about nationalism, prompting him to elaborate them. His novel *Gora* marks a major step in this critique through the realisation of the eponymous hero that the idea of a 'pure' national identity (based on indigenous culture and the *shastras*) was an unreal and unachievable thing (Gora discovers he is Irish and not Brahmin as he thought himself to be) and that it prevented him from identifying with the poor and humiliated. The World War led Rabindranath to a more passionate analysis. In lectures given in Japan and America in 1916, Rabindranath argued that war and nationalism were twins. He suggested that nationalism sprang from the greed and competition that defined the industrial culture of the West. It made people convert themselves and their social institutions into machines; they banded together as nations in order to earn wealth and power more efficiently. This process brought competing nations into conflict with each other, making people forget the universal values of truth, justice and human relationships.

As a counter, Rabindranath advocated internationalism, the seeds of which he believed lay in the culture of diversity and coexistence which

India had evolved. Rabindranath's internationalism did not call for a synthesis of cultures or the internalisation of foreign cultures alone. His was a more dynamic vision of changing and recharging each culture by contact with others. In his letter to Thomas Sturge Moore in 1914, Rabindranath declared that the value of literature lay in its ability to introduce new, 'foreign' ideas and dispositions into one's own culture, initiate self-division or a 'bifurcation' in the 'mental system which is so needful for all life growth'.[12]

Rabindranath's opposition to war and nationalism made him unpopular globally. In Japan the response to his lectures was lukewarm; in Seattle he had to cut short his trip in 1916 after the American press launched a vicious attack on his lectures. In Bengal he was criticised by Chittaranjan Das (later an all-India Congress leader who opposed Gandhi in the 1920s) and Bepin Chandra Pal (an extremist leader of swadeshi and an old critic of Tagore). However, much to the surprise of many of his critics who had tried to dismiss the power of his arguments by accusing him of collaboration and pointing to the knighthood he received in 1915 as evidence, Rabindranath soon returned to a sustained criticism of British authority from 1917.

What critics had overlooked was that Rabindranath's belief in the universal principles of truth and justice, which had made him a critic of nationalism, also led him to indict colonial oppression and force. This phase began with his condemnation of the internment of Annie Besant, an Englishwoman, who had asked for Home Rule. It culminated in the renunciation of his knighthood as soon as news of General O'Dwyer's massacre of innocent civilians at Jallianwalla Bagh began to leak out in 1919. In his letter to Lord Chelmsford, Tagore wrote that the 'badge of honour' had become shameful to him and that 'I for my part wish to stand, shorn of all special distinctions, by the side of those of my countrymen who for their so-called insignificance are liable to suffer a degradation not fit for human beings.'[13] Rabindranath's gesture was one of the first public responses that set into motion an escalating chain of reactions culminating in the Non-cooperation/Khilafat Movement, the first all-India movement against the British.

The second preoccupation that frames *Ghare Baire* arose from the series of trips he made to his estates in Selaidaha and Patisar in East Bengal when he was writing *Ghare Baire* (a large part of which was

written in Selaidaha). These trips brought back to him the dire condition
of the peasantry, the reality of poverty and the need for intervention,
concerns which he had first developed when he had begun visiting his
estates in the nineteenth century. It was a fraught period then. A major
peasant rebellion had taken place in Pabna in 1873 when Rabindranath
was ten years old and by the time he began to visit his estates regularly
at a more mature age, the countryside was alive with debates and disputes
about the provisions of the Bengal Tenancy Amendment Bill of 1885
which gave some rights of tenure to eligible peasants. It was in these
years that he developed his belief in benevolent paternalism. He did
not wish the system of landlordism to disappear, but wanted landlords
to help in bettering the conditions of the peasants and making them
self-sufficient.

In 1915 Rabindranath returned to his estates to find the peasants in
a sorry plight. Jute prices, crucial to their well-being, had crashed because
of the disruptions of the World War. Rabindranath felt guilty for having
neglected his relationship with the peasants, but he also experienced a
sense of homecoming. He wrote to C.F. Andrews that, 'It was a great
event of my life when I first dwelt among my own people here, for thus
I came into contact with the reality of life.'[14] He energetically began
starting and running banks, cooperatives, schools and so on. He invested
the larger part of his Nobel Prize money in the local Patisar Cooperative
Bank because he believed it would help uplift the condition of villages.
Rabindranath's preoccupation with rural upliftment formed the hub of
a larger concern with solving national problems. In a letter to his friend
Kalimohon Ghosh, Rabindranath observed that the area concentrated
in itself all the problems of the nation, for it was poorly developed and
peopled by poor, illiterate, indebted Hindus, Muslims and low-caste
Namasudras.[15]

However benevolent, there was in all of this the inevitable attitude
of the patron. He writes in the same letter, 'They [the peasants] must
be made into human beings.' But sometimes, in language and imagination, benevolence could slip into empathy and his paternalistic concern approach the spirit of solidarity: '. . . one has to be a helper to be
a real man', he says in the letter to Andrews cited above, 'for then you
share your life with your fellow-beings and not merely your ideas.' It
will be worth recalling these words when we look at the depiction of
Panchu and Mirjan's lives.

iii

Buddhadeb Basu, a major poet and novelist himself, observes that with *Sabuj Patra*, Rabindranath leaves behind his nineteenth-century literary legacy, inaugurating a more dynamic phase in his artistic life.[16] Basu's assertion may seem extreme. There are clear traces of the nineteenth century in *Ghare Baire*. Its multi-confessional form—which seems to be its most obvious novelty—is borrowed from Bankimchandra's *Rajani* published in 1878.[17] The concerns with domesticity and gender relations are key preoccupations in the nineteenth-century novel. The nineteenth-century setting of the novel emerges quite palpably in the design of interiors, objects, clothes and so on in Satyajit Ray's film version.

Nevertheless, Basu's assertion retains a substantial validity. This is so, not because Basu's statement can be applied to this feature or that of *Ghare Baire* (or for that matter, other works of Rabindranath), but because of a more substantive change in the notion of art and culture of which *Ghare Baire* is a product. This concerns the self-conscious emphasis on newness.

Put thus baldly, the concern may seem unoriginal, given that nineteenth-century intellectuals had borne the creatively faced the challenges the British introduced through their institutions, cultural values, and corresponding social and economic processes. But nineteenth-century cultural efforts at newness never lost sight of tradition. Indeed the culturally original was seen as a rediscovery of past traditions or at least continuous with them. This is true for the Brahmo Samaj which claimed to recover the ancient truths of the Upanishads; it also applies to the invention of a Bengali grammar and prose which did not lose sight of its Sanskritic lineage. Even the novel, which was a completely new phenomenon, did not attract charges of Western influence, possibly because the dominant form was that of the historical romance which came close to the more familiar modes of myth and legend.

Sabuj Patra marks an attempt to shift the ground for producing culture. One may recall the metaphors with which *Sabuj Patra* sought to describe its aims, that is, of 'shocking' and 'jolting' (the reader's minds). Clearly, what it forefronted was discontinuity and rupture with established relationships, a stance inimical to the preservation of tradition. In the letter to Sturge Moore cited above, Rabindranath insisted on the value of poets such as Byron and Shelley, despite what he regarded as their 'fanatic impetuosity', precisely because they introduced what was 'vivid and forceful', elements that could shock and introduce breaks rather than allow absorption into a more long-standing tradition. If the nineteenth century introduced the culture of modernity, *Sabuj Patra* made possible a radical variant of it. It set in motion a cultural process that was shaped by the norms of change and the production of alternate literary worlds. It is a comment on the importance of this shift that the Kallol group of litterateurs who targeted Rabindranath as their literary antagonist, did so in the belief that his presence was an impediment to change.[18]

Sabuj Patra introduced two specific innovations. The first was the use of the more colloquial *chalitbhasha* instead of the formal, Sanskritised *sadhubhasha*. Rabindranath had used chalitbhasha earlier, but interestingly, had employed it in only personalised forms such as diaries and letters.[19] The first piece of fiction in which he deployed it was a controversial epistolary short story called *Streer Patra* (The Wife's Letter). The story was about the rejection of her insensitive husband and his family by Mrinal, the protagonist. For Rabindranath chalitbhasha was identified with the individual voice capable of asserting its distinctiveness against the authority of an unjust tradition. In *Ghare Baire*, which is written in the diary form, chalitbhasha carries a more ambitious significance. Its forms are used to explore what Supriya Chaudhuri, in this volume, identifies as the making of the self.[20]

The second innovation concerned the intensification of a preoccupation already present in Rabindranath. This was the attention to gender, specifically relating to questions of women's choices and desires. These formed the stuff of the short stories that Rabindranath contributed to *Sabuj Patra*.[21] Rabindranath inherited his concern with women's condition from his Brahmo background. Its early manifestations took the instrumentalist path of encouraging women's self-assertion to help build the nation. Paradoxically, even in the midst of the ultra nationalist phase of his life, Rabindranath wrote 'Nastanid' (Broken Nest) in 1903, a novella that talks of the desires for self-expression in the wife of a kind, paternal, nationalist zamindar who takes her presence for granted. This trend in Rabindranath's literary thought was developed and intensified in the *Sabuj Patra* years. Most of the stories that

Rabindranath wrote for that journal dealt with women as individual subjects engaged in negotiating with problematic relationships in their marriages and with their husbands' households, but also women who created alternate lives, some of which involved being single.

Interestingly, while Tagore's short stories have often been praised, his novels never attract much enthusiasm. A possible reason for their lack of popularity and even critical respect, is their complexity. Both his poetry and short stories, for instance, are immediately accessible. Rabindranath's novels have the quality of intense, looming depth that are a feature of his paintings especially his portraits, even as they detail nuances of feeling and feature intellectual deliberations. At the same time, the novels lack the resonances of his poetry which evoke a multiplicity of genres including medieval bhakti verse, the 'plebeian' poetry of Kabir and the Bauls, English poetry especially that of the Romantics, Sanskrit verse and the rhythms of children's poetry. The novel form could not obviously contain this range of resonances simply because it was still too new.

Bankimchandra Chattopadhyay had been the real originator of the novel in Bengal and the Indian subcontinent. He had left behind a legacy of two kinds of fiction. The first and more popular kind was that of historical romance, such as *Anandamath* and *Debi Chaudhurani*. He also wrote domestic romances, which often featured triangular love plots that critically, with multiple perspectives, explored man–woman relations. While Rabindranath began by modelling his novels on Bankimchandra's historical fiction (*Bouthakuranir Hat* [1883] and *Rajarshi* [1887]), the genre he really developed and made into his own was the second kind. In novels such as *Chokher Bali* (1903) (translated as Binodini) and *Jogajog* (1929), he gave to the domestic novel a much greater sense of interiority and psychological depth. Moreover, he blended the domestic plot with the novel of ideas. The love plots were integrated with incessant debate over public political and social issues between the protagonists. This form is represented by *Gora* and *Ghare Baire*.[22] The complex intermixing of issues that this genre produces is what this volume attempts to untangle and develop.

The Home and the World was published in 1919, a year after the World War. It had been serialised in *The Modern Review* from December 1918 as *At Home and Outside*. The translation has often been criticised for its overblown style and its excisions. Its faults—despite the 'Publishers Note' which declares that the author had revised the translation—have been laid at the door of Surendranath Tagore, the translator. Recent research however shows that Rabindranath had done a large part of the translation himself.[23] While this knowledge does not remove the problems of overrhetoricised language, seen in the light of this discovery it indicates less a problem of distortion than of finding the correct register. As Buddhadeb Basu points out, although chalitbhasha is used in *Ghare Baire,* the style is rhetorically excessive in comparison to *Chaturanga,* a novel written at about the same time in sadhubhasha.[24] The excisions are sometimes more difficult to understand. Some may have to do with dropping localised references in order to cater to a more general readership, although this meant dropping certain resonant details. Some excisions may have to do with simplification (such as the dropping of one of the sisters-in-law). A more problematic subtraction is the elaboration of Chandranathbabu, which takes off from the end of part four of the fifth chapter entitled 'Nikhilesh's Story' and carries on for nearly two more pages in *Ghare Baire.*[25] Whatever the motivation may have been for editing Chandranathbabu's presence, a consequence is to reduce the force of ideal types in *The Home and the World.* Another kind of revision is that of rearrangement. Tapobrata Ghosh, in his article in this volume, shows how the English translation tries to make the novel more plot oriented. Despite these differences however, there is no doubt that *The Home and the World* is a very intelligent transposition that captures most of the nuances of the original novel. The proximity of the two novels is shown in the way most contributors to this volume have used *Ghare Baire* as a background resource to the study of *The Home and the World,* sometimes using them interchangeably, and in some cases, actually employing *Ghare Baire* itself as the basic text.

II

i

The history of colonial India is not merely the story of how colonialism exercised power. It is equally the history of attempts by the colonised to acquire power. There were of course many kinds of avenues and projects by which they could combat the sense of powerlessness under colonialism. *The Home and the World* critically elaborates one such avenue, specifically that of gaining control over self and nation by changing one's attitudes, convictions, habits, relationships, in short, one's subjectivity. This idea was crucial to Hindu nationalism which was based on the belief that if Hindus could be persuaded to look upon the nation as an object of religious devotion, then it would inspire them to change their collective subjectivity, empower themselves and thereby recover the power and glory believed to be an intrinsic part of Hindu culture and history.

The Home and the World's exploration of the implications of Hindu nationalism is set within a narrative of the nation that departs from comparable stories which visualise national identity as fixed and existing from time immemorial. Instead, it shows different conceptions of the nation battling each other to produce its shape. *The Home and the World* represents the nation as an entity that is created rather than inherited. Further, the different ideas of nationalism are tied in *The Home and the World* to contrasting conceptions of the ideal national subject and its social relationships. *The Home and the World* is self-reflexively concerned about the crises that afflict the creation of new national subjectivities and intersubjectivities, and this is what makes it a story about modernity.

The Home and the World possesses a double movement. At its primary level it involves a debate between intensely ideational protagonists about the individual, society and nation. Tanika Sarkar is right when she observes that these debates do not change their participants.[26] While the debates may not aim at a consensus (which would dispose participants to changing their views), they allow the protagonists to define and elaborate their ideas by pitting them against the views of others. These characters are venturing into a new world and their only maps are ideas about what they desire their selves and world to become.

The other movement in the novel is generated by the plot. Interestingly, the elaboration of ideas is concentrated in the first part of the novel. The plot here is extremely rudimentary, basically introducing Sandip to the 'home'. But in time the plot takes the story outside the boundaries of the bhadralok home and makes it collide with the social worlds of the poor and marginal. This point of collision is a turning point in the novel. The bhadralok world's encounter with Panchu and Mirjan changes the course of the swadeshi movement and destroys the uneasy equilibrium in the relationships between lover, wife and husband, leading to the apocalyptic conclusion. Above all, the events unfold the implications—and test the worth—of the ideas that are so incessantly debated in the novel. Producing an opposition between imagination and reality and then privileging one over the other is a process that is a crucial strand of the Anglo-American novel and its critical understanding. In *The Home and the World*, however, different conceptions or imaginaries of the nation are shown to mould life equally. But they mould it differently. The differences are crucial, for they relate to questions of identity, relationship and the possibilities of human survival itself.

ii

Although *The Home and the World*'s structure (that gives primary importance to the Bimala–Nikhilesh relationship) and narrative strategy (which associates Sandip with theft and villainy) tends to marginalise Sandip, his character is central to *The Home and the World*'s critique of the Hindu nationalist subject. Together with Bimala, Sandip represents a new personality type of this period. They live a life that they feel is simultaneously a divine drama. Elevating the nation to the level of a god also means that nationalist activity becomes divine work and the nationalist subject, an active divine agent. *The Home and the World* mounts a sustained critique of this notion through Sandip's dilemmas and its resolutions.

Sandip enacts recurrent crises. On the one hand his devotional nationalism is clearly grounded in the politics of desire. He believes his divine power comes from the force of his desire expressed in his mantra of '*I want, I want, I want*' (p. 53). And yet the very idea of religious nationalism is based on a sense of insufficiency and limitation. The fact that Sandip believes that nationalism cannot do without the crutch of religion, that it needs the support of an image which will embody the nation and inspire people through its presence, indicates that he does not believe that the nation can, by itself, provide a sufficient source of inspiration and energy. Indeed, the assumption of a lack is not only something that characterises his understanding of nationalism in general, but also corresponds to a sense of insufficiency about his own self and its desires. This is evident in his relationship with Bimala.

If Sandip has to believe in his powers of divine inspiration, he has to prove it to himself by wielding a 'masterful passion' over women. In his scheme of values, Sandip gives supreme importance to women for they give 'birth to reality'; in other words, they produce the very grounds of reality. For Sandip, the erotic is a way of mastering women and through them, life. Indeed, the erotic is seen as the test of reality. Sandip deftly puts a book on sex next to Bimala's seat, and when Nikhilesh enters, Sandip engages him in a discussion, arguing that sex is the measure of reality. For Sandip sexuality is 'real' not because it represents the 'hard facts' of life alone. The erotic is also a test of his powers of desire. By attracting women, Sandip proves to himself that as a man he possesses the force and intensity of desire with which he can master reality and make the nation.

The Home and the World reveals that the politics of desire is brittle and violent because it cannot come to terms with its feelings of lack and limitation. Typically Sandip confronts his sense of insufficiency by two kinds of evasion—either through abjectness or by violence. With Bimala he is servile. The reason for this is interesting. According to the original *Ghare Baire* Sandip has many lovers but it is only Bimala who inspires him and confirms him in his belief that he is extraordinary. This is because Bimala's nationalist enthusiasm affirms to him that the nation desires him, he who is the master of all desires. Since Bimala's nationalistic adoration of him is simultaneously erotic, she confirms for him his possession of the power of manliness, which he believes to be fundamentally important for nationalism. Bimala's devotion gives to him a sense of self-completion because it merges the erotic with the nationalist. But ironically, this also means that his sense of self-completion is completely dependent on her. Not surprisingly, his desire for Bimala becomes a craving, expressed in analogies of intoxication. He has to constantly seek her out, stalk her, worship her into coming back to him and reaffirm his belief in his newly forged identity.

But Sandip's sense of his own vulnerability is also dangerously violent. Being conscious of his susceptibilities does not make him more self-aware. It merely leads him to insist on his desired identity, for instance, the apprehension that he could be 'tender and merciful' makes him even more anxious to cut off the leg of the live goat in the presence of his followers. Sandip confronts his aporias through force and violence. In *The Home and the World*, the Hindu nationalist subject produces two complementary forms of authoritarian relationships, of servility and violence, in order to overcome an insuperable condition in which its belief that it possesses the divine power of desire keeps crumbling against its sense of deficiency.

The brittle underside of Sandip's self-assurance collides against the world of Panchu and Mirjan and is provoked into a crisis. The two of them challenge the self-absorptive nature of Sandip's nationalism by raising the problems of those who do not belong to the middle class. They articulate the problems of livelihood and social difference. By implication, Panchu and Mirjan underline something that is overlooked because it is taken for granted: Sandip and the student activists are free to create imaginaries of nationalist self-empowerment because they do not have to work. Sandip lives on Nikhilesh's patronage and the students are holidaying. Finding no answer to the problems raised by Panchu and Mirjan, Sandip seeks to remove their sense of powerlessness by gifting them the same kind of empowerment that he has acquired. He converts Bimala from a private object of nation worship to a mass devotional image. The people, he assumes, will join him in the belief that the sheer force of the desire of '*I want*' will be able to inspire them to complete the divine project of making the nation.

The burden of the plot set into motion by Panchu and Mirjan is, of course, to show how Sandip's social fantasy disintegrates. The unity of the transcendental and the everyday begins to look like a contradiction. At the personal level his need to acquire money in order to pursue a stick-and-carrot policy with the petty traders and peasants leads him to get Bimala to steal money from her sister-in-law, and in so doing, he unwittingly severs her from his influence completely. At the public level it produces riots that rip apart the idea of the unitary nation which Sandip worships. But Sandip does not give up and in contrast to Nikhilesh, Sandip's failure begins another phase of his political career. He will now travel with his message and a portable image of the national goddess. By completing the process of turning Bimala into an image, Sandip achieves a higher level of divine self-sufficiency. He realises for himself an ambition he had outlined as: 'Ignorant men worship gods. I, Sandip, shall create them' (p. 166). His new goddess will be free of Bimala's human unpredictability and will be solely within his powers of control. But this achievement too remains precarious. The image cannot be detached from memory; the fact that it is moulded in Bimala's image is a trope for the stubbornness with which the history of loss, violence and division will remain embedded in devotional nationalism. Sandip's nationalist subjectivity can never free itself from the aporias that dot his trail and by the same token, cannot remove the stain of violence that is the last guarantee of his nationalism.

As Sprinker's essay in this volume points out, Sandip is no simple villain. Like Raskolnikov in Dostoevsky's *Crime and Punishment*, he wishes to reinvent himself. Interestingly both are figures inspired by the superman idea in their attempts to create new moralities and identities, although Raskolnikov is introspective and Sandip more ambitious. While Sandip becomes socially conservative because of the logic of his ideas, Bimala begins as a 'modern conservative' who desires the improbable fantasy of making her deeply cherished traditional values a vehicle of her modern desires. In an obvious sense Bimala is like Shorshey, the abandoned child-wife protagonist of a story published in this period called *Tapaswini*; Shorshey is determined to will her absent husband into an imagined existence by simply believing that utter devotion to her husband will fetch its own reward. Bimala is like Shorshey in that both believe in fantasies that are generated by traditional values. Paradoxically, Bimala is also like the very dissimilar Mrinal of *Streer Patra* (a story also set in the swadeshi period) who experiences domesticity as inimical to women and rejects it.[27] Both Bimala and Mrinal choose the trajectory of their lives. However, if Mrinal's rejection of domesticity seems the obvious radical outcome of women gaining the power of self-articulation, Bimala's character is founded on the possibility that the capacity for choice in women may not necessarily lead to a radical critique of traditional social beliefs.

Bimala may idealise domesticity but she is not domesticated. She looks up to her mother for embodying the ideal of wifely devotion, of *pativrata*, but at the same time makes it clear that she wants to be a larger-than-life version of her. Inspired by her reading (an attribute of the modern nineteenth-century woman) of romances, Bimala visualises a public role for her domestic virtues. She wishes to be a model of domestic devotion in contrast to more ordinary women who would hope to follow one. In other words, Bimala converts devotionalism from an act of self-negation to one of self-assertion for it allows her the possibility of becoming a conservative icon. Interestingly, she evaluates her mother's devotion not for its actual presence in the latter's affections but as a series of visible rituals which she finds is 'beauty itself' (p. 10). Bimala's preoccupation with public images makes her reprocess the belief in devotion as an aesthetic spectacle.

Sandip's devotional nationalism delivers her from a dilemma. Bimala was already a nationalist but had difficulties in articulating it for it conflicted with Nikhilesh's plan to serve the poor of the country. Serving the poor would compromise Bimala's life's desire to be a model and inspire people from the distance that the *andarmahal* provided her. Sandip's nationalism allows her to become a nationalist icon through the traditional role of an andarmahal lady. Sandip offers her a dynamic social form to realise her childhood fantasies without the burden of relating to social inferiors.

And yet the very autonomy of Bimala's desire grounds it in a vulnerability that is deeper than Sandip's. Her ambition to inspire the nation without transgressing the boundaries of her home means that she has to make Sandip into a relay of her nationalist inspiration: it can only be through him that she can 'inspire' the movement. Sandip's synedochal status makes Bimala dependent on him for her allegorical life as wife and nationalist icon. And this dependence is greater than Sandip's since, unlike him, she cannot recuperate her losses in the world of mass political action. It is this unequal relationship of interdependence that dramatises her disability as a woman when she is made to steal from her household. As a member of the upper class, she is the inspiring subject of the movement; as a woman she is simply its object of mobilisation, in precise terms, an instrument for empowering its male leadership.

The Home and the World devises an intriguing conclusion for Bimala. She becomes a person traversed by different possibilities, none of which are free from vulnerabilities. At the most obvious level her story is one of a 'return' to Nikhilesh as she falls at his feet. This is actually not quite a 'return' to the earlier times for she now falls at his feet without the desire for acquiring a public reputation. Her remarks on womanhood reveal a new acceptance of the limited sphere of activity and self-expression for womanhood: if they keep to their 'banks' they give nourishment; if they want more 'then we destroy with all that we are'

(p. 59). And yet this return also goes with—impossibly perhaps—the possibility that she may inhabit a more congenial and less husband-centric domestic sphere. The after-effects of the theft raise the possibility of a relationship of solidarity with her sister-in-law who experiences womanhood as an experience of deprivation and who steps in to shield her. And there is Amulya, with whom she forms a relationship of guardianly care—and through whom she intervenes in the practical workings of the swadeshi movement one single time, creating a rift in its leadership.

And yet the separate parts of this possible life are shown as threatened, if they are not repudiated altogether. The very act of the 'return' is shot through with ambiguity. Nikhilesh reflects ironically the second time Bimala falls at his feet, 'Was I the god of her worship that I should have any qualms?' (p. 274). Is this then another fantasy that Bimala is enacting? Can Nikhilesh ever relate to it as if it were not one? The precariousness of domestic self-fulfilment is, of course, underlined by Nikhilesh's uncertain fate in the end. The vulnerabilities of the other possibilities are equally clear. Amulya dies while Bimala's sister-in-law holds her responsible for destroying the only relationship of affection in her life. The only other thing the text lets us know is that Bimala is the sole person to write in the present; it is as if only she, unable to come to terms with her present post-swadeshi life, were condemned to replaying the memory of that tragic, exhilarating and fractured time.

Bimala's undecided state within the world of her domesticity may have been one of the outcomes of Rabindranath's mounting critique of conjugality and the household. In *Streer Patra, Aparachita* (where the girl refuses to marry) and in more complicated ways in *Haimanti, Payla Nambar*, and *Shesher Ratri*, Rabindranath shows these institutions as founded on either gender oppression and discrimination or on fantasies about the person who is the object of love and devotion. The paradox of a woman who chooses domesticity to express herself in public may have, therefore, created an impasse in Rabindranath between the importance of female self-expression and choice on the one hand and the scepticism about domesticity on the other hand. But Bimala's predicament as we have seen, is created not just by the general opposition between domesticity and the importance of public self-articulation, but in specific terms, by her attempts to resolve this split through devotional nationalism. The possibility of figuring the female self as a public, national spectacle even when confined within the home and her class prejudices, raises a general question to which even the question of gender is subject. Can a person relate to herself without taking into account the needs and aspirations of others, especially those very dissimilar to the self? More generally should the exhilarating unities of identity or the complications of relationships make up our modern collective self? The representation of Nikhilesh's life is an attempt to explore these questions.

Nikhilesh is widely regarded as an ideal type. Actually if there is an ideal type in *The Home and the World*, it is not Nikhilesh but Chandranathbabu. He belongs to an older, more stable ethos, which combines an unswerving loyalty to justice with effective social intervention. Indeed, his presence serves to emphasise Nikhilesh's incertitudes. Nikhilesh is actually closer to Sandip, for both of them inhabit a similar modern condition which cannot take its norms for granted. Like Sandip's, Nikhilesh's nationalism is also based on an imaginary which fails; in *Ghare Baire* it is even reported that to the peasants, Nikhilesh became an object of ridicule. And significantly, both men visualise the romantic participation of the woman, Bimala, as a crucial element of nationalism.

However, while the structure of their nationalist imaginaries is similar, the difference in content is more decisive and leads to a transformation of this framework in Nikhilesh. If the nation for Sandip is just a bounded territory that he can fill up with the largeness of his desires, Nikhilesh's imaginary of the nation is based on the everyday nature of its people and their interrelationships. Correspondingly, while Sandip seeks to transport Bimala with him into a transcendental condition that makes questions of choice and equality irrelevant, for Nikhilesh these preoccupations are crucial to his relationship with her.

While questions of choice and mutuality provide the groundwork for the emergence of Nikhilesh's new self, what actually begins the process is the nature of Nikhilesh's suffering. As Tanika Sarkar points out, Nikhilesh undergoes the feminine condition of *viraha*.[28] By relinquishing his authority as a male, Nikhilesh experiences what a woman feels, gaining a capability to free himself from the fixity of social identity. But there is also another element to his suffering. Nikhilesh seeks to understand his suffering by looking at himself through Bimala's eyes. He sees himself as a boring pedant; but that is not important. The point is that Nikhilesh tries to locate his self in relationship to the other's view of it. He does not look to a mirror to find himself, but seeks out the other's gaze. Nikhilesh looks for the exchanges of intersubjectivity as the basis of his new self: a subjectivity that retains a sense of interiority and individual distinctiveness, but experiences it through its relationship with other people.

This process strengthens with Panchu's entry. The sudden appearance of Panchu in the dark night of Nikhilesh's suffering makes him distance himself from Bimala and acknowledge the reality that she could never be a part of his nationalist projects, being too anchored in upper-class assumptions. Panchu's introduction breaks Nikhilesh's romantic coupling of the 'home' with the 'nation' forever. At the same time, however, this disenchantment with Bimala does not lead him to reject her. On the contrary, it produces a critical distance by which he not only recognises her difference from him, but also realises his own 'tyranny' in imposing his ideals on her.

Nikhilesh's discovery of Panchu parallels the eruption of the peasant condition into Rabindranath's consciousness when he was writing *Ghare Baire*. Both events are marked by a sense of joy after a phase of disappointment. For Rabindranath the opportunity to think about the peasantry came as a relief after a series of severe setbacks in running his school at Santiniketan, while it frees Nikhilesh from his obsessive relationship with Bimala. Both also suffer from a sense of distance from the peasantry. Rabindranath is stimulated by the encounter to a much greater degree of introspection about his own commitments, rather than to curiosity about the peasants themselves. Nikhilesh sees (and the text tends to collaborate with his vision here) Panchu and Mirjan dominantly as oppressed by landlords and swadeshi activists alike. But there is one significant way in which Nikhilesh departs from Rabindranath's own vision of this period and this lies in his recognition of Panchu's ethical freedom. Indeed it is Panchu's ethical sense in unexpectedly returning the loan that Nikhilesh had forgotten, which alerts the latter to his condition. More negatively, Panchu's ethical freedom is confirmed through his adherence to brahmanical customs of purity and pollution. He overspends on his wife's funeral and then proceeds to look down upon Chandranathbabu for violating caste taboos: Chandranathbabu had stayed at Panchu's house and saved him by getting his fraudulent aunt to leave. If Panchu is oppressed, he is also complicit in the perpetuation of his oppression.

In contrast to Sandip's suppression of the problem of recognising the other, Nikhilesh's intersubjectivity makes him acknowledge the dissimilarity of Panchu's condition and search for specific knowledge about it. However, despite his important recognition, Nikhilesh is unable to find an adequate form of relationship that can flow from this knowledge. For, between recognition and adequate knowledge falls the shadow of class divides.

While Nikhilesh may seek knowledge, even mutuality with Panchu, the latter is unwilling to reciprocate. Indeed the limits of Nikhilesh's knowledge are constantly underlined. If Panchu surprises him by remembering his debt, he also disappoints Nikhilesh by resenting the fact that he has to return the loan which helped him recover from the losses inflicted by the swadeshi activists. Panchu's annoyance is logical from his viewpoint, according to which, at stake in the movement are not issues of principle; it simply involves a faction fight of landlords between Kundu/Chakravarty and Nikhilesh. In his mind, swadeshi activists burned his goods because he was allied to Nikhilesh and it was only fair that Nikhilesh should recompense him for taking part in his battles. Interestingly, the possibility of bridging the class divide is not raised by the text. Nikhilesh does not—cannot, given the overt sympathies of the text itself—raise questions about his class position since these would also involve a critique of paternalist benevolence to which Rabindranath was too firmly anchored. Nor does he possess the temporary social mobility that allows Chandranathbabu to live in Panchu's world and intervene in it, for landlords are condemned to maintaining a social distance.

'Panchu' can perhaps be seen as a synecdoche for a larger problem of relating to the socially subordinated, a quandary which hedges in Nikhilesh's intersubjectivity and makes his vision of an alternative nationalism a potentially tragic one. All areas of Nikhilesh's life suffer from the same fate. With Bimala, he is left to ironically accept the fact that he is not the object of her desire. In the context of communal mobilisation, Nikhilesh feels confident enough to talk only to his Hindu tenants, which accounts for his underestimation of its dangers and makes him delay banishing Sandip. As I have suggested, the text itself cannot go beyond Nikhilesh in discovering other conditions in which knowledge can be gained. Consequently, the suspension between life and death that marks Nikhilesh's condition in the end becomes a trope through which the text meditates on the irony of intersubjectivity; its allure of hopefulness in the search for knowledge and connection; its inability to acquire adequate knowledge to create relationships of mutuality.

III

The immediate inspiration for this collection of essays was the introduction of the new syllabus in the English Department of Delhi University, which was a landmark process since it involved college teachers in a big way for the first time and introduced a range of literary texts in translation. The aim of this collection stemmed from a general need (in English) to read Rabindranath's texts through some of the current debates in contemporary Indian scholarship such as those relating to modernity, nationalism, gender, caste as well as address questions of love, self-formation and novelistic form that are thrown up by the novel.[29] I may add that all the essays—with the exception of the essay by Sprinker (included here both for its importance and relative inaccessibility) have been written for this volume.

Tanika Sarkar's 'Many Faces of Love: Country, Woman, and God in *The Home and the World*' is a wide-ranging essay which argues that the modernity of *The Home and the World* lies in its complication of historically established conventions of representing love, gender and the country as well as in its attempts to provide alternative forms of representing these themes. Sarkar elaborates the complexity of Bimala: a traditional heroine of Hindu revivalism who is also a modern, independent-minded woman fashioned by the newly available ability to write; an autonomous being but who can represent herself only as a collage of conventional images of womanhood. Sarkar goes on to show how Bimala's representation emerges from a contradiction in the way the nation was embodied as a woman and concludes by looking at the larger implications of the relationship between Nikhilesh and Sandip for nationalism.

Supriya Chaudhuri's 'A Sentimental Education: Love and Marriage in *The Home and the World*' reads *Ghare Baire* as a story about the creation of the self and its relationships and not about the swadeshi movement as is generally argued. Bimala's attempts to create a self are repeatedly self-defeating. For instance, she wishes to be like her mother and lose herself in devotion in a world where wifely devotion has no value. Chaudhuri argues that Bimala's desire to be one with herself makes her undergo a number of experiences and identities without ever achieving a unified state. Towards the end of her essay, Chaudhuri contends that the novel shows a general state of uncertainty which describes the state of modern civilisation rather than something which can be said to have a specific cause. She sees the absence of any reference to children in the novel as a pointer to this intention. This state of incertitude also informs the condition of Nikhilesh whose mission of bringing his wife into the world is undercut by—among other things—revealing the distinction between the home and the world as one of mental categories rather than physical spaces.

Tapobrata Ghosh's 'The Form of *The Home and the World*' criticises E.M. Forster's dismissal of *The Home and the World* as a *roman a trois* by showing that the English translation obscures the real concern of the novel, which is to show the triumph of conjugal love. He also argues that the translation privileges the plot at the expense of the autobiographical form. Shohini Ghosh's 'Passionate Involvements: Love and Politics in Satyajit Ray's *Ghare Baire*' returns us to the question of love and politics through Satyajit Ray's film adaptation. Ghosh vigorously defends the film by arguing that through its pattern of cuts, musical score and exchange between dialogue and gesture, it successfully intertwines the political and the personal. Ghosh points to the film's creative interpretation of the novel in its depiction of the Nikhilesh—Bimala—Sandip relationships as well as in its imposition of widowhood on Bimala. Ghosh concludes with a consideration of female spectatorship and the question of Nikhilesh's gendering.

It is a matter of good fortune for this volume to be able to include an edited version of the late Michael Sprinker's 'Homeboys: Nationalism, Colonialism and Gender in Rabindranath Tagore's *The Home and the World*'. Coming from a background of explorations in ideology and history as well as Indian and canonical European literatures, Sprinker's essay takes us to a consideration of nationalism and historical context. Sprinker observes that the importance of the home—world divide does not lie in its literal reality, but in its dramatisation of an ideological conflict between Bimala who believes that political necessities should override ethical duties and Nikhilesh who thinks ethical considerations to be absolutely important. Sprinker goes on to elaborate the aporias that afflict Nikhilesh. For instance, he believes in freedom, yet also wishes to confer it. On the other hand, Sprinker argues that Bimala's return to domesticity after her involvement with nationalism, serves to reveal the fissures within a nationalism which cooks up an impossible mixture of two images of women: as anti-colonial icon and as pillar of the family and tradition. In the second part of his essay, Sprinker asks why it was not possible for Rabindranath to visualise anything other than a tragic ending to the novel and explains it by Rabindranath's inability to bring together tradition with anti-colonialism.

Malini Bhattacharya's '*Gora* and *The Home and the World*: The Long Quest for Modernity' looks at the ways in which the two novels embody a modernity that springs from anti-colonial struggles. The modernity of *Gora* is straightforwardly anti-colonial and produces a radical universalism that involves solidarity with syncretic cultures and makes possible the emergence of publicly active women protagonists. In contrast *The Home and the World* is ambiguous, belittling Sandip's open confrontation of colonialism and privileging Nikhilesh's questioning. Yet, despite itself, the story also unfolds the historical possibilities of anti-colonial struggle.

Taking issue with evaluating the modern past by looking at it simply in terms of the degree to which it resisted or fell prey to colonialism, Sumit Sarkar's '*Ghare Baire* in its times' evaluates Rabindranath's critique of nationalism by recognising its justness, but by also pointing out—through citing other histories—its insufficient, indeed, reductive understanding of complex social processes involving the conflict between sharecroppers and landlords. In the second part of the essay, Sarkar elaborates the contrasting definitions of masculinity in *The Home and the World*, arguing that Nikhilesh represents the most radical possibilities, and limits, of male reformism.

In '*Anandamath* and *The Home and the World*', Jasodhara Bagchi tells us how Bankimchandra and Rabindranath reshape the ideas of positivism. Bankimchandra radically transforms key elements of this ideology that relate to the figure of the woman, of the spiritual elite, and the representation of social reality. Bagchi suggests that *The Home and the World* critiques *Anandamath* by locating its action in the world of domestic psychology, thereby reducing the stature and impact of the women characters. Further, *Anandamath*'s transformative vision is replaced by a more stable norm in *The Home and the World*'s Nikhilesh.

Finally, Jayanti Chattopadhyay's '*Ghare Baire* and its Readings' offers an evaluation of the critical responses to *The Home and the World*. Chattopadhyay looks at the assumptions of both the orthodox Hindu detractors of *The Home and the World* as well as the stands of its defenders. Chattopadhyay also points to the subsequent history of *The Home and the World*'s criticism which has sought to appropriate it for the purposes of literary rebellion. She concludes by posing a paradoxical problem present in critical readings of gender and politics in *The Home and the World*.

This collection has sought to generate its insights by trying to perch itself between two kinds of disciplinary boundaries. For one, this volume has sought to draw on the work of those engaged in Bengali literary studies. While statistically there are only two contributors who belong to departments of Bengali literature, there is nevertheless a general acquaintance with, and more often, grounding in, cultural bilingualism that informs the work of the contributors. Second, the collection also proceeds from the assumption that the relationship between the disciplines of history and literature is intimate, but varied and possibilistic. Some instances: Supriya Chaudhuri handles history as a backdrop of micro details that leave their tracks on the text in unexpected ways; Tanika Sarkar looks at the historically different conventions and conditions that are remoulded by the text; Sprinker and Bhattacharya identify the historically specific ideologies that go into the making of the text while Sumit Sarkar tries to look at the text through a revised notion of historical 'source' and so on. Looking at disciplinary boundaries as zones of transaction will, one hopes, help in the process, already under way, of making different disciplines unfamiliar to themselves, disturbing their borders, but without surrendering the explanatory rigour of past knowledges that has developed through the maintenance of boundaries.

Endnotes

1. *The Golden Book of Tagore: A Homage to Rabindranath Tagore from India and the World in Celebration of his Seventieth Birthday*, ed. Ramananda Chatterjee (Calcutta: The Golden Book of Tagore Committee, 1931, rpt. 1990), p. 12.
2. It is reported that when he went to Germany in 1921, his talks were

attended by stampedes as people rushed to get into the auditorium. Alex Aronson, 'Tagore through Western Eyes', *Rabindranath Tagore: A Celebration of his Life and Work* (Oxford: Rabindranath Tagore Festival Committee and the Museum of Modern Art, 1986).

3. Cited in Prasanta Pal, *Rabijibani, Saptam Khanda [Vol. VII], 1321–1326, 1914–1920* (Calcutta: Ananda Publishers Private Limited, 1997), p. 3 (my translation). I have drawn on Pal's magnificent research for most of the material on Rabindranath's life, especially in the second section of this part of the introduction.

4. I am grateful to Sumit Sarkar for this observation.

5. Cited in Niharranjan Ray, *An Artist in Life: A Commentary on the Life and Works of Rabindranath Tagore* (Trivandrum: University of Kerala, 1967), p. 32.

6. Sir [sic] Rabindranath Tagore, *Reminiscences* (London; Macmillan & Company Limited, 1921), p. 7.

7. Krishna Kripalani, *Tagore: A Life* (New Delhi: National Book Trust, 1961, rpt. 1986), pp. 23–4.

8. Rabindranath was greatly shocked that Japan, an eastern nation, which he had presumed to be beyond the desire for aggression, should attack China, a neighbouring country of the east. For him, this demonstrated that Japan and the east had fallen prey to the charms of nationalism.

9. The outbreak of the Boer War inspired him to write a poem in 1899 that condemned the greed of nations, while in 1901 he wrote a reply to Renan's article on nationalism where he argued that nationalism was not the outgrowth of social relationships but was something created by the state. Ray Monk, 'Tagore on Nationalism', *Rabindranath Tagore: A Celebration . . .*, op.cit., p. 26.

10. Nationalist activity was often inflected by Hindu revivalism, such as the Hindu Melas in which Rabindranath participated. These were fairs that were periodically held to host works of native industry and discourses on various aspects of Indian life.

11. Cited in Sumit Sarkar, *Swadeshi Movement in Bengal, 1903–1908* (New Delhi: People's Publishing House, 1973), p. 81. I have drawn on this book (specially pp. 53–85) for the details of Rabindranath's participation in the swadeshi movement.

12. Cited in Pal, *Rabindrajibani . . .*, op.cit., p. 7.

13. Cited in Kripalani, *Tagore . . .*, op.cit., p. 153.

14. Cited in Pal, *Rabindrajibani . . .*, op.cit., p. 110.

15. Ibid., p. 128.

16. Buddhadeb Basu, *Rabindranath: Kathasahitya* (Calcutta: New Age Publishers Limited, 1362 [1955]), p. 1.

17. See Tapobrata Ghosh, 'The Artistic Form of *The Home and the World*' in this volume for the differences between these two novels. It may also be mentioned that Rabindranath was also influenced by the form of Robert Browning's *The Ring and the Book*.

18. See Jayanti Chattopadhyay, '*Ghare Baire* and its Readings' in this volume for a short introduction to the Kallol–Rabindranath relationship.

19. He first used it in 'Yuroper Diary' in 1890.

20. See Supriya Chaudhuri, 'A Sentimental Education: Love and Marriage in *The Home and the World*', in this volume.

21. See Sumit Sarkar, '*Ghare Baire* in its Times', in this volume for a more elaborate argument on the importance of these short stories. I am grateful to him for drawing my attention to their significance.

22. It is interesting to note that a writer in Malayalam, the daughter of a reformer, wrote her first work after reading a Malayalam translation of *Ghare Baire*. She says that the novel described her own world very well. *Cast Me Out if You Will: Stories and Memoir by Lalithambika Antarjanam*, tr. Gita Krishnakutty (Calcutta: Stree, 1998).

23. Pal, *Rabindrajibani*, op.cit., p. 354.

24. *Kathasahitya*, op.cit., p. 120.

25. See Rabindranath Tagore, *Ghare Baire* (Calcutta: Visvabharati, 1994), pp. 92–3.

26. See Tanika Sarkar, 'Many Faces of Love: Country, Woman, and God in *The Home and The World*' in this volume.

27. See Sumit Sarkar, '*Ghare Baire* . . .', for a more elaborate analysis of *Streer Patra*.

28. 'Many Faces . . .'. See also Shohini Ghosh's 'Passionate Involvements . . .' in this collection, on the feminisation of Nikhilesh in the context of female viewership.

29. Three recent works in English, which have offered new kinds of insights have been Ashis Nandy, *The Illegitimacy of Nationalism* (Delhi: Oxford University Press, 1994), Shirsendhu Chakravarti, 'In Search of an Elusive Freedom: History, Class and Gender in Tagore's *Ghare Baire*', *Many Indias Many Literatures: New Critical Essays*, ed. Sharmishtha Panja (Delhi: Worldview Publications, 1999), and Chapter 3 of Sangeeta Ray, *En-Gendering India: Woman and Nation in Colonial and Postcolonial Narratives* (Durham etc.: Duke University Press, 2000).

Many Faces of Love: Country, Woman, and God in *The Home and the World*

TANIKA SARKAR

No other work of Rabindranath has attracted quite the same sort of vituperative criticism as *Ghare Baire*. Nationalists of an extremist variety saw in it a compromise with imperialism, and Lukacs endorsed this in his analysis, even though he got the anti-colonial politics within India woefully mixed up.[1] The Bengali orthodoxy thought the depiction of adulterous love in *Ghare Baire* was morally corrupting. E.M. Forster, on the other hand, found the novel a mere boarding-house romance—too safe and tame.[2] Feminists tend to see Bimala as a typically 'made' feminine figure, split between men who construct her subjectivity. It is clear, therefore, that criticism came from a wide cross-section and its terms were various and contradictory. The only thing critics seemed to agree on was that the novel disturbed them, made them uncomfortable.

While working on political nationalism in Bengal, I had found *Ghare Baire* a politically compromised text; the feminist interpretation too made complete sense to me for a long time. More recently, however, I reread the novel for its critique of extremist nationalism. This time, not only did its perspective on nationalism carry enormous new significance, the other 'problem' with the novel—which I could earlier dismiss as simple signs of a patriarchal–feudal disorder—now showed itself to be a difficult and serious negotiation with highly fractured times. I bring my changing responses into the discussion only because I feel that this may be a fairly typical trajectory for a number of readers.

II

Sexual love—especially in its conjugal dimensions—has been a powerful trope for thinking about the nation in conflicted and variegated ways since the nineteenth century. Multiple versions and resolutions of this theme occur in almost all of Rabindranath's major novels too. In *Noukadubi*, for instance, he imagined an accidental switching of wives to see if the pull of the sacramental marriage tie would prove stronger than the habit of living together or the attraction that is formed outside the marriage tie. In *Chokher Bali* and *Chaturanga*, Tagore explored triangles resulting from emotional partnerships outside marriage. In *Jogajog*, he tried to explore if a sacramental marriage tie could overcome profound mutual incompatibility. It was in *Gora* that the themes of religious nationalism and of love forbidden by society—here because the lovers are from two different communities—brought love and nation into close and conflicted interface for the first time.[3] To liberal nationalists, the conjugal connection, as it existed among contemporary Hindus, seemed fundamentally coercive. On the other hand, contemporary Hindu nationalists claimed that they were capable of a more virtuous form of nation-making than what the repressive, colonial state offered, primarily because Hindu families embodied a more loving form of domesticity than Western family norms. Late-nineteenth-century revivalists, moreover, defended Hindu marriage as the country's last, infinitely precious and fragile site of autonomy, which would survive Western cultural onslaughts only with the unswerving commitment of the Hindu wife. To her belonged the special burden as well as the extraordinary privilege of protecting the nucleus of Hindu nationhood, Hindu men having already surrendered themselves to an alien system of meaning.[4]

In the retrospective opening of *The Home and the World* Bimala seems to evoke her mother's tradition-bound aesthetic of Hindu womanhood to suggest such a privilege: mode of being that she too had inherited from her mother. That mode, with its fusing of love and worship, stitched the woman securely with an ancestral tradition, a shared female world, a feminine form that was recognised universally as beautiful. The inheritance, however, is squandered by Nikhilesh and his experiments with liberal-reformist visions of the equal and companionate wife. This dangerous freedom is catastrophic in its consequences; it disrupts moral and social orders fatally and destroys Bimala's feminine selfhood by presenting her with difficult choices that she cannot handle. Bimala thus concludes her final narrative with the conviction that the new modernity is incompatible with Hindu female selfhood. Her contention that the stature of the Hindu wife is equal in real terms through a paradoxical act of submission and adoration is also an argument that Hindu cultural nationalists had regularly used during the debates on marriage reform in the late nineteenth century:

My husband used to say that man and wife are equal in love because of their equal claim on each other . . . but my heart said that devotion never stands in the way of equality . . . My beloved, it was worthy of you that you never expected worship from me. But if you had accepted it, you would have done me a real service . . . (p. 20)[5]

Bimala's opening—and concluding—narrative of lost female innocence and tradition however is soon overlaid and problematised by an unfolding of a far more complicated sensibility that arises out of a new and different history. That history can be identified with some of the formal properties of the novel itself. The woman here speaks herself, alongside the two men who talk about her. She therefore represents herself, and also represents the two male protagonists as much as they represent her. The self-representing woman is not only a newcomer in Rabindranath's writing, she is a startling new character on the Bengali literary and social landscape. From the late nineteenth century on, Bengali women's writings had begun to appear in significant numbers. They spoke of experiences of pain and held out visions of intellectual autonomy that were quite beyond the imagining of the most daring of reformers.[6]

In *The Home and the World*, Nikhilesh's sister-in-law disrupts his nostalgic reveries of a shared childhood by underlining the very different and bleak memories she had of it. If Nikhilesh had deliberately cast out the image of the Hindu wife from Bimala's mind, the sister-in-law reminds him afresh that there had been little in it worth preserving.

'No, brother dear,' she replied with a sigh, 'I would not live my life again— not as a woman! Let what I have had to bear end with this one birth. I could not bear it over again.' (*The Home and the World*, p. 190)

(This widowed sister-in-law, beautiful and alluring though she was in her youth, had been entirely neglected by a philandering husband. Bimala resents the deep affection that Nikhilesh bears towards her, for she cannot help suspecting that it has grown out of sexual attraction. Incidentally, Rabindranath's own relations with his sister-in-law Kadambari were rumoured to be somewhat romantic. Kadambari, it was said, committed suicide because of her husband's growing indifference towards her.)

Women's writings, then, proved an unprecedented new capability, one that patriarchy had strenuously denied women of possessing. This was the presence of a critical mind, an intelligence, an authorial function of their own, all that had so far been male preserves, all that constituted the fundamental gender divide. Their writings were a sign as well as a site of the dismantling of the basic opposition between the sexes, the transcending of the primal 'lack' that constructs sexual difference. It was this new presence of women's writing in the public sphere that enabled Tagore to develop a fresh expressive form at this time. With the short story *Streer Patra* in 1914,[7] he began to use the persona of a female narrator or writer who writes her own life in first person within his narrative. This is not, however, an entirely new departure in Bengali literature. Medieval Vaisnav lyrics of sacred love had frequently borrowed the words of Radha; and among nineteenth-century novelists, Bankimchandra had often used this device. It is, nonetheless, new in the prose writings of Rabindranath himself. The woman's words literally begin to intrude into a sphere in which, in Tagore's earlier work, only men spoke: for her, or about her.

It was not simply the device of the woman-as-author that enabled this new turn. From the beginning of the century, women had begun to register their presence in mass anti-colonial movements—beginning of course with the anti-partition swadeshi upsurge which provides the temporal–political horizon for *The Home and the World*.[8] Women's organisations appeared, demanding suffrage, welfare, and reform in marriage laws. As self-determination came to be accepted as a general good by nationalists of all sorts, and as women signified their political capability within nationalism,[9] sexual and conjugal relationships and traditions were faced with even more troubling possibilities. Rabindranath himself remained deeply ambivalent about women's political volubility and daring—in *Ghare Baire* as well as in a much later novel, *Char Adhyaya*.

III

The Home and the World is set in the backdrop of highly fractured times. It explores breaks in sexual and political traditions through certain astonishing new departures in its form and in its conceptualisation of love and nationhood. In this section, I will briefly indicate the departures, and will further argue that the changes in both were shaped by a particular understanding of the condition of modernity.

The novel is the first one that Rabindranath wrote in a colloquial syntax. It is composed as a series of interwoven soliloquies by three figures who sometimes narrate through flashbacks, and sometimes report on the ongoing flow of events. Sandip and Bimala act as two poles that coalesce and come apart at different times and which frame Nikhilesh, lonely and distinctive at all times.

The novel is split onto several temporal planes which spiral dizzyingly towards the last violent denouement. At the same time, the monologues are framed as introspective musings, providing points of stillness and depth within a narrative that is more crowded with dramatic and surprising turns of events and with violent happenings, than is usual for Rabindranath's novels.

Each separate sub-narrative, designed as a soliloquy (in *Ghare Baire* they are called 'Atmakatha' or autobiography), contains the words of others and the arguments of others, refigured and re-animated by the narrative requirements of each sub-narrative. Rabindranath thus provides a heteroglossia which is neither static nor based on fixed essentialisations. Perspectives are constantly changing and processuality is emphasised. At the same time, the monologic form and even the reported dialogues do not allow for a real dialogic process of self-transformation. Change follows turns of events, and changed perspectives rather than being fully articulated in dialogues, are reported in the monologues. Characters keep their secrets from each other. The monologic form prevails over the constant conversations, arguments. It reflects the fundamental, constitutive loneliness and mutual isolation of the three individuals, each locked into worlds of very different needs and perceptions.

The choice of an experimental and difficult form recapitulates, I think, the difficulties of the modern condition. In the nineteenth century, a busy and active public sphere discussed conjugality and domesticity from a variety of perspectives and vantage points. There was a consequent problematisation of almost all aspects of prespective orders. Yet, the ensuing instabilities did not ultimately lead to stable resolutions, just as debates in the novel do not yield acceptable alternative modes of being or of loving. Husband, wife and lover seek new self-images and forms, but cannot wear their new identities with comfort or confidence. The political domain remains equally mystified. Constant exchanges of opinion do not open up channels of rational and honest communication that are genuinely free. Conversations in the novel mask intentions, arguments rationalise hidden motives. Human relations are open to interlocution, but they remain difficult, painful. Mutual recognition is blocked.

In the realm of departures in concepts of politics and love, there are, I think, three interwoven thrust areas. There is a newly emergent nationalism that is torn between the choices of constructive swadeshi, extremism and revolutionary terrorism.[10] Superimposed upon the political choices are emotional ones: between forms of femininity and masculinity, modes of love and conjugality. Finally, the two realms fuse into a refigured political choice that in turn chooses ways of loving in a commingling of eroticised nationalism and personal autonomy.

Almost all of Rabindranath's major novels explore the possibilities or impossibilities of conjugal love by devising a range of predicaments and diverse contexts against which it is placed and tested. He also elaborated a critical reading of the system of Hindu marriage in a lengthy polemical exchange with Chandranath Basu.[11] Equally, nationalism— both political and cultural—was a pervasive concern in his fictional and discursive writings, registering frequent turns and sharp breaks in stances.[12] In both respects, then, *The Home and the World* constitutes a link in a long and continuous chain of exploration. At the same time, it is also an expressive and conceptual watershed in several crucial ways.

In the first place, Rabindranath's own involvement with nationalism reached new heights and depths with the movement against the partition of Bengal in 1905–8, a mass movement of a radically new order. Rabindranath fashioned the cultural and ritual icons of the movement, he gave it innovative thrusts as it moved onto the streets of Calcutta, he was a major exponent of 'constructive swadeshi', of rural development, mass contact and national education schemes.[13] His Chandranathbabu was possibly based on the figure of Aswini Kumar Datta of Barisal whose rural bases and upliftment schemes he admired and preferred as opposed to the agitational extremism of Aurobindo Ghose and Bepin Chandra Pal. He gradually emerged as a strong critic of the extremists, their violent rhetoric and its encouragement of terrorism among very young people as well as its distance from the needs of the rural masses. He was especially disturbed by the alienation its cultural and political symbolism caused among Muslims. The extremists' programme of boycotting British cloth resulted in great hardship to rural petty traders and peasants, most of them Muslims and low-caste Hindus. Another point of distance lay in his commitment to a universalist vision of undifferentiated moral concepts of justice and truth which could not be divided into nationalistic particularities and interests. Even though, at several points in the past, he had come very close to a hard cultural nationalism himself, Rabindranath now removed himself from a celebration of a closed culture. He now considered culture an inclusive and open value system, though discriminating about ethical stances, which needs to grow through continuous encompassment of new values, not through processes of ethnic cleansing.

Such ideas earned him the reputation of timid moderation, of being a staid good-works person, of cultural surrender. They also marginalised him within the movement, and the expulsion was all the more painful because he remained alive to its vibrancy and power. *The Home and the World* conveys the energies of a radically new awakening from fear and bondage, from passivity and a sense of inferiority. It evokes a sense of momentous new beginnings, almost as frightening as exciting in their heady possibilities. It is significant that though he distanced himself from the nationalist mainstream at mid-point, he came out with an exhaustive and systemic critique—almost an existential refusal of its politics of nation-worship—only in 1915. Perhaps he could not express that kind of a critique until the wound of the partition of Bengal was healed by its rescinding in 1911–12.

Rabindranath thus remained tied to the movement that he was denouncing. In the novel this self-division is ostensibly expressed through the duality between Nikhilesh and Sandip. The duality, however, is too simply polarised to convey the self-division adequately, for Nikhilesh is entirely uninfluenced by the movement and Sandip's extremism rarely consists of more than rhetorical flourishes and conspiracies involving coercion and looting. It is by splitting the figure of the extremist patriot between Sandip and Amulya that an element of heroic commitment is retained. Idealism—crude, unthinking, but vivid and real—is displaced onto the figure of Amulya, the revolutionary terrorist who is manipulated by the older leader, but who, nonetheless, reserves a surplus of genuine patriotism.

The representation of extremism would have seemed unfair had Rabindranath not fleshed out its attractions through Bimala's words. It is significant that this should be so, because the country did occupy a traditionally female space in its nationalist as well as imperialist envisionings—as glorious Mother or as the land of effeminate Indians. Its state of bondage, its imposed burden of silence and endurance in the face of exploitation, seemed to confirm its feminine positionality. Its arousal, therefore, could be most accurately echoed through the awakening of possibilities in the modern Indian woman. The politics of national self-determination and anti-colonialism and the politics of the woman's self-determination are simultaneous. Bimala was not confusing issues and tropes when she conjoined the two and sought in the awakening of the enslaved country an analogue to her own self-assertion:

One night I . . . slipped out of my room on to the open terrace. Beyond our garden and walls are fields of ripening rice. Through the gaps of the village groves to the North glimpses of the river are seen. The whole scene slept in the darkness like the vague embryo of some future creation.

In that future I saw my country, a woman like myself, standing expectant. She has been drawn forth from her home . . . by the sudden call of some Unknown . . . I know well how her very soul responds . . . how her breast rises and falls . . . She is no mother. There is no call of her children in their hunger, . . . no household work to be done . . . So she hies to her tryst, for this is the land of the Vaisnava poets. She has left home, forgotten domestic duties; she has nothing but an unfathomable yearning which hurries her on. . . . (p. 93)

The possibility is a mere snatched glimpse as yet: the ripening corn and river—clear metaphors of sexuality—seen through breaks in walls and groves. Nor is the passage a celebratory one, for Rabindranath found in the choice between being the mother and the beloved, between nurture and sexuality, a disturbing trajectory for nationalism, which discards the welfare of people for a politics of passions and destruction. It is nonetheless an acknowledgement of the power and the glory of a wakening sense of autonomy, which is charged with eroticism.

But Bimala's character indicates another startling function for the sexual metaphor. Nationalism, in our country, is powerfully cast into the mould of Mother-worship and no one has ever suggested an alternative or deviant imaginary. Yet, the novel suggests discarding the posture of obedience and subjection which is far more resonant with the image of the woman who claims and flaunts her sexuality and independence over domestic discipline. Nationalist energies—given this reading—could have far more of a sexual charge than allowed by the tropes of filial duty which mask their self-representation.

In even more explicit words, Sandip pulls lover and motherland together, and Country and Bimala become one. The emotion that animates both, and the emotion that they evoke, are clearly erotic. As Sandip establishes equivalence between Country and Bimala, the patriot becomes lover, evicting the son. 'My watchword has changed since you have come across my vision,' he tells Bimala. 'It is no longer Hail Mother but Hail Beloved . . . The mother protects, the mistress leads to destruction . . .' (p. 177). The novel is about a politics whose slogan is 'Bande Mataram,' a salutation to the Mother. The story has, however, not a single actual mother. When Bimala comes to experience a maternal tenderness for Amulya, she renounces the politics of passion. This transgressive eroticising of the nationalistic impulse was perhaps the most disturbing aspect of the novel for contemporary Bengalis.

The inaugural narrative in the novel is also a recapitulation whose lyrical cadences heighten the violent—at times melodramatic—dislocation of the conclusion. The conclusion is indeed cataclysmic in its violence, conflict and death in which individual and national destinies, emotional and political losses, not only point in the same direction, they also are mutually causative. Yet the enormous and catastrophic happenings are played out as well as introduced almost entirely within the narrow constricted spaces of a home. The weight of events and emotions of so dramatic a nature creates a tension that is suffocating, particularly in its spatial claustrophobia: for the parlour and the inner quarters of women do not simply constrict Bimala, but also the two male protagonists most of the time. Both men complain from time to time, of the paralysis of movement and activity. Both experience the caging of personality that women have habitually to face in domestic incarceration. The tension is steadfastly sustained because while the sexual pull between Bimala and Sandip is strongly articulated, there is no consummation till the end. The narrative is thus overcharged by the unreleased sexual tension. Again, while in all of Rabindranath's novels, the action gradually narrows down to a few central characters, here the range is throughout exceptionally small and knotted. Outside the triangulated or trifurcated protagonists, there are only four others of any significance: Amulya, the young disciple of Sandip, the sister-in-law, Nikhilesh's old teacher Chandranathbabu, and Panchu, the low-caste tenant.

The Home and the World is the first major Bengali work of fiction where the *man* suffers from *viraha*: sexual disregard from a beloved, the wife, the woman. It is, moreover, viraha that is born not out of separation but proximity, unillumined by love or need. There was no available literary prototype for Nikhilesh, nor would he have a place, as the husband betrayed, within conventional notions of masculinity. His love for Bimala therefore comes close to stereotypes of male infatuation or male weakness. On the other hand, Sandip, almost archetypally the virile and ruthless lover bent on conquest, becomes hesitant and tender—a state that he perplexedly describes as an uncharacteristic weakness in himself—when he falls in love with Bimala. He begins to consider her needs and interests, even when Bimala desperately prepares to forget them herself; he draws back when he is certain of his success. Stereotypes associated with masculinity and male love are deliberately inverted and muddied.

The adulterous woman was a well-known figure in Vaisnav literature and in earlier Bengali novels. But the novel, in its own times, earned calumny not only for its depiction of guilty love; the shock for readers was heightened because the woman herself talks at length—and sometimes with brutal clarity and explicitness—about the precisely sexual aspects of it. Again, in Vaisnav lyrics, Radha does describe physical symptoms of longing. Bimala, however, describes the pull of sexual passion even when it has detached itself from love, when Sandip has begun to repel her as a human being: his physicality still proves irresistible.

The nature of observations on love and desire is therefore exceptionally complex. The theme is enlarged into observations on freedom of choice and the morality of this choice. That morality is carefully distinguished from the conventional domestic morality of monogamous love or of female physical fidelity. The one thing that Nikhilesh does not allow himself to question in Bimala is the freedom of her sexual choice. Her disregard and rejection are a source of immense suffering for him, but it is still not unjust, for, he says, she never chose him: he had been imposed on her through the act of marriage. His sister-in-law, moreover, is a constant reminder of the pervasive male privilege of unlimited sexual options. He himself may not exercise them but their very availability is nonetheless real. What is perhaps even more of a surprise is that Bimala is racked with guilt and self-loathing not when she falls in love with Sandip, but when she discovers his moral shallowness and political dishonesty. On the other hand, Nikhilesh feels partially liberated from his obsessive love for Bimala when he realises that her social values are very different: she takes her privileges for granted and she has no compassion for those that her class exploits (p. 89). The realm of moral choice for both is drawn away from prescriptive norms about conjugal monogamy. Love too acquires larger, non-conventional horizons, based on intellectual and political affinities, emotional honesty and capacity for mutual nurture. It is life-affirmative rather than destructive.

IV

It is Bimala who initiates the action that animates the plot, even though it is easy to depict her as a 'made' creature, the product of conflicted male designings. She follows these designs up to a point, and then, in an abrupt move of rejection, she opens up a different trajectory for all the male protagonists: Nikhil, Amulya, Sandip. She fixes her gaze on Sandip when he is brought inside for a lecture, she invites him for a meal, and she decides to break convention by visiting him in the parlour. Her gaze, her will, her desire are demanding, activating, propelling. 'I do not know how it happened, but I found I had impatiently pushed away the screen from before me and had fixed my gaze upon him . . . Only once, I noticed, his eyes, like stars, . . . flashed full in my face . . .' (p. 31).

She is not acting under blind passions beyond her control. She already has political views that are opposed to Nikhil's, and she has already

made him act on them—in sending off Miss Gilby, for instance
(p. 28). She has scant sympathy for his swadeshi projects and responds
to the extremists' call for the destruction of foreign cloth. Her political
subjectivity confirms Sandip's extremism, it is not created by him. She
is impatient with fine-tuned arguments about justice and virtue; she
prefers a politics of exclusions, agitations, demonstrative violence, symbolic
action, great rhetorical aggrandisement (p. 38). Both are superbly
indifferent to the fate of the poor and the Muslim; for both of them
nationalism is an idea without a single social referent. The differences
in ethical stances, therefore, are not irrevocably gendered, for her choices
parallel Sandip's. Nikhilesh sadly acknowledges that her values are
attuned to Sandip's. They are not, however, made by Sandip.

But, finally, Bimala rejects Sandip and his politics. The sexual pull,
powerful though it remains, does not prevent her rejection of Sandip
as a person, once Bimala's values and politics begin to veer away from
Sandip's. Her new-found maternal love for Amulya teaches her the value
of nurture, of caring and building, of saving and healing, of valuing
goodness and innocence (p. 172). Even though she herself sees it as
quintessential female nature reasserting itself, her initial history, as well
as Nikhil's own espousal of such values gives the lie to a conceptualisation
of essentially gendered moralities. The evolution of Bimala's political
history is thus very largely autonomous.

In a strange irony, both Nikhil and Sandip think at different times
that they are creating their perfect partner, a creature of their desires.
Bimala often expresses herself in terms that are typical of feminine
vulnerability, helplessness, weakness, and culpability. Yet she decides
always on courses of action that strain against and overturn plans of
men far stronger than she is. She pulls the narrative out of joint, she
opens up violent trajectories.

Bimala possesses sexual and political will and autonomy, but she
cannot imagine a form or identity that can adequately hold and express
them. She moves between bodies that are dressed by the desires of her
men: the bare neck and the piled up hair that Nikhil adores (p. 98) and
the partly bared bosom, the deep red colours and sinuous silks that
enthrall Sandip (p. 33). When she moves away from both, she can only
imagine herself back in the past, mimicking the gestures of her mother,
almost returning to inhabit her body (p. 17).

Why is there an absence of stable form that is not just a travesty of the old? The turn-of-the-century modern woman acquired split representations: either lampooned as a mimic Victorian lady or a shrewish folk-devil, or as the preternaturally solemn, puritanical, sexless creature of reformist homes, while the transcendent icon at all times is always that of a luminous, gracious mother-figure. Her autonomy therefore had no adequate image from which it could be reflected back to her as a coherent fullness. Her autonomous self appeared to her as a series of dislocations. Perhaps Rabindranath did not develop an alternative embodiment for the modern woman because he saw her as always faced with impossible choices, with a difficult freedom.

V

The significant relationship in the novel is not between Sandip and Bimala, for the quality of their love has all the tropes of adulterous passions familiar from the Bengali literature of Vaisnav and popular romances. What is significantly new is the refiguring of the conjugal relationship that Nikhilesh attempts. It remains unrealisable because Bimala can only return to the old forms of loving her husband, a love that must exalt itself as worship. Nikhilesh's notion of companionate marriage, on the other hand, is strained beyond endurance to acknowledge and admit Bimala's adultery, rejection, duplicity, and, finally, her incompatibility. He finds that the coarseness of character that he sees in Sandip, exists in Bimala too, and is part of her ingrained disposition, not the result of Sandip's influence.

Both Sandip and Bimala see love as something that requires a reification of the object of love, an investment of hyperbole, of metaphoric, symbolic and aesthetic excess that mystifies the real, the ordinary, the everyday. They are kings and queens to each other; they are messengers of a great future, prophets of a new faith. Embodiments of the Nietzschean Superman principle, each regards the other as the source of wild Dionysian ecstasy, unaccountable to ordinary morality, and seeking self-realisation through a mastering over other wills. Love, moreover, is a source of power for both—for each over the other, and, for both together, over all others. And the power is essentially one of destruction, which in their world is a value in itself. Unless love is capable of violent damage and destruction, unless it can kill moral sense, it is not love. 'O Traveller in the path of destruction!' murmurs Bimala in front of Sandip, 'O my king, my god! Ah, the awful power of devastation . . .,' while he, in turn, tells her: 'O love, my love! . . . there is no reality in the world save this one real love of mine . . . My devotion to you has made my cruel . . . me worship of you has lit the raging flame of destruction within me . . .' (pp. 116–17, p. 124, p. 39).

And this is how they both love the country. They see her as a reified Mother, detached from the land and the people who are subordinated to her. She is a divine icon, her command supreme over life and death, beyond good and evil, surpassing justice and morality. The only form of her worship is death, the courting of it and the inflicting of it.

Nikhilesh has different ways of loving. He loves Bimala even when she is no longer the self-created partner, or when the doll's house lies shattered. He does not regret the innocence of the uncomplicated past the way Bimala does, for that was based on a lie. He admits his love has had to survive incompatibility, but is reassured that he no longer lives on deluded images. He loves Bimala, for hers had been the form in which he had experienced love the only time in his life.

The country, again, does not need to be a resplendent icon for him to love her. His is a land of very poor, ignorant, humiliated people such as Panchu. Like King Lear who attains his full humanity when he shares a stormy night with homeless people, and just as Lear forgets his own pain when he realises that he had thought too little of theirs, Nikhilesh too comes to understand the fate of Panchu when he himself inhabits an extremity of pain and loss. He sees, moreover, the face of his beloved country in that peasant's face. This is not even the overidealised peasant wisdom that nationalist populism sentimentalises, but the peasant rendered craven and foolish by endless poverty, cruelty, lies. He sees the peasant whom the British exploit and whom the new nationalist leadership manipulates and overburdens just as cynically (pp. 100–9, 104). That is, after all, the crux of the matter, the heart of the difference between the two: Nikhilesh cannot forget Panchu, Sandip cannot allow himself to remember Panchu. Nikhilesh's country, moreover, is equally the land of Muslims, which, again, the upper-caste Hindu nationalist leader will not accept: 'If the idea of a United India is true,' objects Nikhil, 'Mussulmans are a necessary part of it.' 'Quite so', says Sandip, 'But we must know their place and keep them there . . .' (p. 120).

The inclusion of the peasant within the sparse cast of central characters is a rare and immensely significant move. It is for the first time in Rabindranath's fiction that the peasant is endowed with so much space and narrative function. What remains deeply problematic, however, is that it is Nikhilesh who realises Panchu's significance rather than Panchu himself. He is the object of social engineering or of political manipulation; the novel denies him a political subjectivity of his own. The absence is a deliberate choice and not a failure of imagination. Rabindranath had already encountered several massive peasant uprisings in his lifetime, including one on the Tagore estates in Pabna in 1873.

VI

The two friends, Sandip and Nikhilesh, with their totally opposed ways of loving the woman and the country, form the most significant relationship within the novel. They talk mostly to each other, each loves the same woman, the same nation. This is a relationship based on arguments and differences where one cannot do without the other (pp. 83–4).

The source and site of the argument can be captured through two songs. Sandip leads the 'Bande Mataram Party', whose motto is Bankimchandra Chattopadhyay's hymn to the motherland. The hymn is sung in the novel *Anandamath*, on the eve of a battle between Hindu ascetics and an eighteenth-century Muslim Nawab who is backed by British forces. Sanyasis pledge themselves to demolishing mosques and constructing temples in their place.[14]

The song begins with an evocation of the land—green, peaceful, nurturing, bounteous. 'Heavy with crops and shining with water, cooled by the spring winds/green with vegetation . . . whose nights smile in the silver moonlight/. . . whose laughter is bright, whose words are sweet/ Mother who gives us happiness, who blesses us . . .' Mother is plenty, she is pleasure. Then the land becomes the goddess—fully armed, vindictive, death-dealing. She is crowned as the Supreme Deity within the Hindu pantheon. 'All the myriad arms bear sharp weapons . . . all temples worship your image . . .' (translation mine). The words initially are elongated, lush, flowing deep sounds. They then become harsh, jagged, slashing like the swipes of a fatal sword.

The nation, in its imagining, is at war, is War itself. It can compel worship only in this incarnation. It can be realised through death, vengeance, and violent expulsion of what is foreign. The nation is no longer a land that nourishes the people. It is entirely separated from both land and people, and is elevated over both. It cares nothing for their welfare, their livelihood, and their survival. It commands their death in war just as much as it commands the death of its enemies. It requires endless human sacrifice.

And, of course, the nation is a Hindu goddess and the enemy that is about to be killed is a Muslim army.

Is there any other way of loving the country?

In 1913, during his exile from nationalism, Rabindranath wrote 'Jana gana mana,' a song for the nation in which a very different form of patriotic love is imagined. The land is dedicated to a God above all nations, presiding equally over all of them. In the same more, the nation is separated from God. God is universal justice, goodness and morality, qualities to which the nation must aspire. It cannot engulf these values and then claim to have transcended their significance in the interests of her own particular demands. It cannot claim divinity.

Moreover, the synecdotal operation of 'Bande Mataram' is undone; the country is evoked as an entity made up of many peoples, many landscapes, many histories and cultures, including the latest deposit of the Western one. It is not a sacred substance, one and indivisible and beyond history. The nation is not the melding of diversities. It is a space of dispersion of identities, a field where differences are displayed.

'Punjaba-Sindhu-Gujarata-Maratha-Drabira-Utkala-Banga . : .
Vindhya-Himachala-Jamuna-Ganga . . .
Hindu-Bouddha-Sikha-Jaina-Parasika-Musalmana-Khrishtani . . .
The East meets the West and unite in love . . .'[15]

In the song, pluralities harmonise. In the novel, however, they are contentious, contradictory. There is an inexorable, necessary conflict between Panchu the peasant and Harish Kundu, the exploitative land-lord; between Nikhilesh and Sandip.

As soon as the song was published, a slander campaign began. The God of the song was a British emperor, it was claimed. Later, when the Congress decided to adopt it as the national anthem there was an outcry, demanding that it be replaced with 'Bande Mataram'. Nation as war, as Hindu goddess, as a singular, monolithic, sacred substance, had become the authoritative version. Any different form of imagining had to be thwarted as anti-national. To this day, the RSS maintains that 'Bande Mataram' is the authentic anthem. Sadhvi Rithambhara's audio-cassette which urged the killing of Muslims in the early 1990s referred to Rabindranath's song as a form of betrayal.

Asked to clear himself of the charge of loyalism to a British emperor in the song, Rabindranath had replied; 'I should only insult myself if I care to answer those who consider me capable of such unbounded stupidity as to sing in praise of George the Fourth or George the Fifth as the Eternal Charioteer leading the pilgrims on their journey through the countless ages of the timeless history of mankind . . .'.[16]

The slander, nonetheless, stuck. The novel and the song offer us a transgressive nation. In the cause of the nation, the Muslim must not be made to accept burdens because a Hindu landed leadership commands it in the name of a Hindu goddess. The nation cannot be elevated above poverty and ignorance, for it is poor and ignorant, and this must be acknowledged as its true face till both are removed. The nation is not above universal laws of morality and justice, it has to conform to them. The nation cannot humiliate the Miss Gilbys, nor impose the burning of cheap foreign cloth that the peasant buys and sells just because it is foreign. Foreign rule should go because it offends universal ideas of morality, not because the nation is above morality.

Husband and wife argue thus in the novel:

'I do not care about fine distinctions,' I [Bimala] broke out. '. . . I am only human. I am covetous. I would have good things for my country. If I am obliged, I would snatch them and filch them. I have anger. I would be angry for my country's sake . . . I would smite and slay to avenge her insults . . . I would . . . call her Mother, Goddess, Durga—for whom I would redden the earth with sacrificial offerings. I am human, not divine.'

Sandip Babu leapt to his feet with uplifted arms and shouted, 'Hurrah.' The next moment be corrected himself and cried, 'Bande Mataram.'

A shadow of pain passed over the face of my husband. He said to me in a very gentle voice: 'Neither am I divine, I am human. And therefore I dare not permit the evil which is in me to be exaggerated into an image of my country—never, never [p. 38].'

Endnotes

1. Georg Lukacs, *Reviews and Articles for Die Rote Fahne*, trans. Peter Palmer (London: 1983), pp. 9–11.

2. E.M. Forster, *Abinger Harvest* (London: 1983), pp. 365–7.

3. See *Rabindra Rachanabali*, vols 3, 7, 9, 6 (Calcutta: Vishvabharati edition, 1940, 1941, 1941, 1940 respectively). There are translations into English as well.

4. I have developed these connections between nineteenth-century Hindu nationalism and Hindu domesticity in my *Hindu Wife, Hindu Nation: Community, Religion and Cultural Nationalism* (Delhi: Permanent Black, 2001).

5. All citations are from Rabindranath Tagore, *The Home and the World*, trans. Surendranath Tagore. (New Delhi: Penguin Books India, 1985) (first published London: Macmillan, 1919).

6. See, for instance, Rosalind O'Hanlon, *A Comparison between Women and Men: Tarabai Shinde and the Critique of Gender Relations in Colonial India* (Madras: Oxford University Press, 1994). Also my *Words to Win: Amar Jiban, A Modern Autobiography* (Delhi, Kali for Women, 1999).

7. See *Galpaguchha, Rabindra Rachanabali*, op. cit., vol. 23. See also my 'Mrinal: Anya Itihasher Sakshar', *Desh*, 5 August 2000.

8. See Sumit Sarkar, *The Swadeshi Movement in Bengal, 1903–1908*, Delhi: Peoples' Publishing House, 1973.

9. See Geraldine Forbes, *Women in Modern India*, in *New Cambridge History of India* (Cambridge: Cambridge University Press, 1996), passim.

10. For a classification of the varieties of swadeshi politics, see Sumit Sarkar, *The Swadeshi Movement in Bengal*, op. cit.

11. 'Hinduvivaha', 1887, *Rabindra Rachanabali*, vol. XIII.

12. See Sumit Sarkar, *Swadeshi Movement*, op. cit.

13. Ibid.

14. *Anandamath, Bankim Rachanabali*, vol. 1, ed. J.C. Bagal (Calcutta: 1953).

15. *Sanchaita*, Vishvabharati Publications, Calcutta, 1931, pp. 696–7.

16. Cited in Ashis Nandy, *The Illegitimacy of Nationalism* (Delhi: Oxford University Press, 1994), p. 87.

A Sentimental Education: Love and Marriage in *The Home and the World*

SUPRIYA CHAUDHURI

One lesson we may take from a reading of Theodore Zeldin's *An Intimate History of Humanity* is that there are styles of feeling, as of other aspects of civilised behaviour. However deeply rooted in emotion and instinct, the forms of human attachment are accessible to understanding only as social phenomena, naturalised within a known register of expression. When, for complicated reasons to do with the history of mental life in its irreducibly material involvements, a change in style or even a radical break with past forms becomes necessary, we may witness also the birth of new techniques of representation, whether in the usages of daily life or in the mimetic structures of literature and art.

Rabindranath Tagore's novel *Ghare Baire* (*The Home and the World*), first published serially in 1915, seems to mark precisely such a shift in the modes of feeling available to the educated Bengali gentry of the early twentieth century. In their personal lives, and especially within the domestic space marked out by the bond of marriage, the novel's central figures struggle to come to terms with the experience of love. For them, at their individual juncture of social history, this experience comes as an engagement with new ways of feeling and expressing emotion, of understanding the nature of intimacy or companionship, of recognising and controlling desire. These are centrally related, as we shall see in our reading of the novel, to the formation of the self as a responsive social entity. *The Home and the World* is much less a novel

about nationalism or swadeshi politics than it is an examination of the
social construction of personal life. The three narratives that constitute
the novel's text offer us, not alternative readings of the same situation,
but alternative possibilities of extricating a form of selfhood from a
violent and disruptive social encounter. In choosing this strategy of
representation, Rabindranath, the male author of all three narratives,
attempts to come to terms as much with the discursive and tonal shifts
affecting the formation of personal identity at a time of crisis, as with
new categorisations of feeling and desire.

The novel opens in a mode of address: rhetorically, in the figure of
apostrophe, directed by Bimala to her absent mother. For Bimala, her
mother represents what she had thought to be the ideal of womanliness;
she identifies in her the kind of love she would herself want to embody
in her married life. This ideal consists in complete devotion to one's
husband, unquestioning self-surrender to the rituals of the *andarmahal*,
conjugal duty seen as an act of faith, even of piety: from such custom
and ceremony, Bimala feels, are innocence and beauty born. In its
cultural and historical specificity, this is the ideal of Hindu womanhood
set out in the *Manusmriti*, represented here by the figure of the veiled
Hindu wife with vermilion in her hair, serving her husband a plate of
fruit or fanning him at mealtimes. The image serves as an iconic marker
of values Bimala associates with the past, with a way of life that appears
to her perfectly integrated, whole, filled with dignity and grace. For
the woman in whose being these values are personified, love is identical
with devotion and self-submission: a self-submission which in the
traditional form is a source of power. The spiritual strength ascribed
to the chaste and devoted wife is premised upon her full internalisation
of the values of Hindu patriarchy, in such a way that her own abnegation
can draw to her the power of the system as a whole.

Yet, as Bimala obscurely recognises, far from being a resource for
Bimala's own self-construction, the idealised image of her mother which
she sets at one limit of her personal narrative is both threatening and
inaccessible. Moreover, the power of its fictional projection of a fulfilled
conjugal life must be set against the domestic realities of the family
which Bimala enters as a bride, a family whose sons have traditionally
despised their chaste and devoted wives and pursued other women.
Against the symbolic force of the vermilion in the parting of Bimala's

mother's hair (mentioned in the very first line of the novel) are ranged the figures of the widows in Nikhilesh's family, his grandmother and his two sisters-in-law. We cannot fail to see that these possibilities all belong to the same order of existence. The wife's devotion and purity are taken as a constant: whether the husband is faithful or debauched, receptive to domestic care or neglectful and self-destructive (like Nikhilesh's brothers) is the merest trick of fortune. The auspicious signs read in Bimala's palm by the family astrologer are enough to decide her marriage. What she is said to have inherited from her mother is as much luck as character—the virtue of the faithful Sati, the good fortune attendant upon the goddess Lakshmi. That both her virtue and her fortune— the reputation of fidelity and the life of her husband—should be in doubt at the end of the novel is an intended irony.

Bimala wants to be like her mother, and in her early married life she thinks that she can *feel* in the same way, by expressing love in acts of worship: a conversion natural, so she writes, to a woman's heart. In her, however, these acts appear to be related more to the care of the self than to the recognition of the other, to an egoism as blind as it is naive. Emphatically she denies the desire to earn merit or to impress Nikhilesh; yet in the romantic idealisations of her early relationship with a husband who has both disappointed and baffled her, she is wholly absorbed in the fashioning of a self she can recognise. Indeed, it is because she does not understand or recognise Nikhilesh that she is so caught up in the specular dynamics of her own process of self-making. From the critical vantage point of her narrative re-examination of this past self, Bimala sees her attitudes as impossibly poetic and unreal, although, as she says, they would then have seemed to her the merest prose of life. The narrative draws attention to a shift in modes of feeling that has accompanied social change: a shift that Bimala records in her own life as a passage from the naive to the sentimental.

My education has made me acquainted with the present age in its own language, and so what I write seems, even to me, to be like poetry. If I had not engaged with the present, my past feelings would have been to me the simplest prose. I would have known in my heart that just as the fact of being born a woman was not my invention, so too the dissolution of love in worship was perfectly natural—it would be unnecessary to imagine, even for a moment, that there might be some extraordinary poetic beauty in such a feeling.

But in the passage from adolescence to the mid-point of my youth, I have entered another age. What was as easy as breathing is now being recommended to us as an aesthetic exercise. The thinking men of this age are loud in their praises of the unique poetry of the wife's devotion to her husband, the widow's ascetic restraint. From this it is clear how great a distance has developed, in this aspect of our lives, between truth and beauty. Is it possible, now, to recover truth on the excuse of beauty alone? (p. 143)[1]

Bimala marks this shift as having occurred between her own adolescence and her present youth. Earlier, she felt naturally; now (as Schiller would put it, writing of poetic styles[2]) she feels a sentimental longing for the natural. For us as readers of Bimala's narrative, however, it is impossible to miss the pathos of this self-deception. The past self which Bimala imagines to have been perfectly at home in its naive worship seems to us already at odds with its cultural belatedness; a romantic construction forced into the service of disappointed egotism. Bimala is aware from the beginning that her husband neither wants nor needs her worship; that he wants something from her that it would endanger her (or her notion of self) to give. Nikhilesh wants what he understands as love, and in a sense the emotions he places at the heart of a modern companionate marriage are as much a project of his own ego as Bimala's longing for the protective cocoon of ritual devotion is of hers. For Bimala, her husband's love is a threat; for Nikhilesh, Bimala's devotion is a burden. The novel begins in a tone of desperate nostalgia for a way of life, a way of feeling, that Bimala knows to be already past, or always just out of reach. Yet, to the end of the novel, she wants to recover these habits of feeling. Addressing her husband, in tones of irrevocable modernity, as 'beloved', she speaks of the oppressiveness of his love, and says that he would have been better advised to accept her worship:

Beloved, it befitted you that you did not want my worship, but it would have been better for you to have taken it. In your love you have adorned me, educated me, given me what I asked for, given me what I have not asked for—I have seen no respite in your love, but I have noted that you have sighed secretly at mine. You have loved my body as though it were a heaven-born flower, you have loved my nature as though it were your good fortune. This filled me with pride; it made me think that it was for my own wealth that you had come to my door. Then I thought myself a queen and demanded honour;

my demands only grew, they could never be satisfied. Can the thought that I have the power to subdue a man be the source of a woman's happiness, or of her good? Her salvation lies in letting this pride be swept away on the current of worship. (p. 145)

Is it only with hindsight, in the knowledge of the perilous consequences of Nikhilesh's 'freeing' love, that Bimala says this? If so, she is doubly deceived. At one level her narrative seeks to represent her emotional history chronologically, as a movement from the simplicity of conjugal devotion (*bhakti*), through the emotional turbulence and false pride instilled by modern ideas of love, to the realisation that the true salvation of a woman lies in the re-conversion of love to a purer, deeper devotion. Towards the end of the novel, when she resists her husband's attempt to embrace her and bows her head at his feet, she asks him not to deny her the privilege of worshipping him. Nikhilesh acquiesces, not because he accepts her worship, but because, as he says, he realises that it is not he, but something beyond him, that is being honoured. There is a great deal in the novel to support this reading of Bimala's sentimental education as one that Rabindranath himself intended. Nevertheless, it is equally possible to mark in her narrative the signs of a discontent that precedes and determines what she learns from Nikhilesh's emancipatory project. To the extent that Bimala is constituted by this discontent, by a certain restlessness that afflicts her social and emotional being, she cannot simply be seen as the exemplary subject of a progress from tradition to modernity. Her suffering is more radical and absolute; her discontent a condition, as in Freud's classic formulation, of civilisation as we know it, not a product of Nikhilesh's exposure of her to unprecedented social dangers. Nor can it be redressed by her arrival, through reason and freedom, at a truer valuation of conjugal life and a renewed dedication of love in bhakti. The open ending of the novel leaves many such issues in doubt.

The 'advice to women' texts of the nineteenth century, a signal example being an article purporting to be a mother's advice to her married daughter published in the *Bamabodhini Patrika* of May–June 1893, would certainly have enjoined upon Bimala the ideals she seeks to emulate: self-sacrifice, faithfulness, devotion. At the same time, from the middle of the nineteenth century onwards, some enlightened men, like Rabindranath's elder brother Satyendranath Tagore or his cousin,

Prasanna Kumar Tagore's son Jnanendramohan, undertook the task of educating their wives for the responsibilities of companionate marriage. These examples might serve as the immediate context for the treatment both of Bimala's unreformed sensibility and of Nikhilesh's emancipatory programme in *The Home and the World*. Yet history does not consist of these instances alone, and to cite them as the only available background for this novel would be a distortion. The year before *The Home and the World* commenced serial publication, Rabindranath had published his long short story *Streer Patra* (*The Wife's Letter*), a much clearer, far less equivocal espousal of a woman's point of view in marriage. The polemical thrust of this work, which Rabindranath later took pride in recalling as the first to take the woman's part, sets it apart from other stories about women written around this time, as well as from the dialogic form deliberately chosen for *The Home and the World*. Mrinal, the heroine of *Streer Patra*, undertakes the task of her own emancipation aided only by her intelligence and by the tragic awakening that comes to her through the death of the hapless Bindu. (Most readers have noted a contemporary parallel in the widely reported suicide of a young girl called Snehalata, declaredly to spare her father the burden of providing her dowry.) Everything in Mrinal's narrative is touched by her anger, as by her contempt for the social laws that bind her to a family she clearly despises. She scarcely ever mentions her husband individually, and certainly the story grants him no personal space. Conjugal love forms no part of the domestic relations she describes; any reference to bhakti is ironic. Here, as in several other short stories and later in the savage exposure of domestic infelicity in Rabindranath's novel *Jogajog* (1929), conjugal life is never romanticised, whatever the ideological imperatives controlling the institution of marriage as a whole. The reality of contemporary experience is likely in any case to have presented a far bleaker picture.[3]

By contrast, Bimala's insistence on viewing marriage through an ideal image of the virtuous and devoted wife seems fraught with danger. What her narrative presents as a simple naturalisation of the ideology of Hindu womanhood is, we realise, neither inevitable nor universal. Rather, it is the product of her discontent, of her desire for a lost unity or integrity of being which she associates with the past, with her mother's life, with traditional modes of feeling projected as a refuge from the terrible emotional responsibilities Nikhilesh's love would impose upon her. To the extent that Bimala's emotional history, within the novel, is predicated upon this sense of lack, it may be read as a history of desire; but a desire returning upon the self, not (despite all appearances) directed towards husband or lover. Bimala wants intensely what she fears she will never have, a state of completeness or rest in her own being which she confuses now with her mother's image, now with her husband's love, now with material possessions, now with a lover's flattery. That this desire should remain unsatisfied is, Rabindranath implies, an inescapable condition of her modernity.

If Bimala, on this reading, is herself the subject of her narrative quest, it is appropriate that the novel as a whole should concern her emancipation or, more accurately, the project of her social and psychological awakening. She is the novel's centre in more ways than one, drawing to herself both private emotions and social aspirations, inhabiting the domestic space which is to become a site of contestation, constituting herself as an insoluble moral problem in her combination of innocence and egotism. Of the three voices that make up the complex narrative structure of *The Home and the World*, hers is the most compelling, most sincere and most deluded. Even in the eyes of the two men who tell her story, both egoists with ends of their own to accomplish, she is a subject of extraordinary interest, a project in whom they have invested more than they can afford to lose. What binds these three characters together is love. It is not, in each case, the same emotion; but in each case it is a mode of feeling that can only be understood in the context of altered social conditions and relationships, as a product of change itself.

Assuming the historical time of the novel, on the evidence of Sandip's swadeshi campaign for the boycott of British goods, to be the first decade of the twentieth century, Bimala's emergence from the andarmahal, her passage from *ghar* to *bahir*, the inner quarters to the outer world, is not really a novel proposition. Rabindranath's sister-in-law Jnanadanandini, the wife of his elder brother Satyendranath, the first Indian to enter the Civil Service, had been taken out of purdah by her husband in the 1860s. Her emergence from their Jorasanko home to ride in a carriage and to attend a party in the Governor's House attracted considerable public attention. A relation by marriage belonging to the Pathuriaghata family, Prasanna Kumar Tagore, met her at the Governor's party and was so overcome by mortification that he left abruptly. Not only did Jnanadanandini show the way for others in her own family and among progressive Brahmos to bring their women-folk into society, she also initiated new modes of dress appropriate for women who were to be seen in public. In *The Home and the World*, Nikhilesh pampers his wife with these fashionable articles of clothing almost as a matter of course: 'colourful jackets, saris, chemises, petti-coats' (p. 146). For Jnanadanandini, the question of clothing was a serious practical matter, an acceptable result being achieved only through considerable trial and error, when she was required to accompany her husband to Bombay or to take part in a social engagement. In Bimala's case clothes are signs of Nikhilesh's reforming love, initially a source of both satisfaction and embarrassment to her, while they are ironically and enviously viewed by her sisters-in-law. They indicate the process of her modernisation and her loss of emotional innocence in compli-cated and ambiguous ways, as when she puts on a jacket which she knows has a special association for Sandip (p. 203), or when Nikhilesh is overcome with love and regret as he looks at the slippers she first wore with embarrassed reluctance (p. 220).

Despite the advances made by liberal Brahmo and even some Hindu households in urban settings, society remained fairly conservative. This was above all the case with traditional Hindu aristocratic families living on their country estates, especially if they had large numbers of Muslim tenants. Given this context, Nikhilesh's decision to take his wife out of the inner quarters of the house needs to be carefully understood. Simply in physical terms, Bimala is required to journey out of the women's quarters to the outer rooms of their house, in particular to a sitting-room which, though withdrawn to some extent, may be visited by men not related to her family. Its location is, however, intermediate: at one point Sandip is refused entry to this room by an officious servant posted by Bimala's middle sister-in-law, the Mejorani. Apart from Nikhilesh's old teacher and Sandip's disciple Amulya, there are no visitors to this room except Sandip himself. Without Sandip's presence, Bimala's daily excursions would be purely a matter of form; for, as we note, she goes nowhere else, visits no tenants, surveys no social conditions, meets no British officials. Nikhilesh wants Bimala to accompany him to

Calcutta, where he might have introduced her in society; but, in a typically self-protective and possessive reaction, Bimala refuses to go on the ground that her sisters-in-law would make free with their property in their absence.

What then is the 'world' which Bimala enters in consequence of Nikhilesh's emancipatory project? One problem that we are likely to encounter in reading this novel concerns the physical location of the bahir, as opposed to the ghar, which is relatively fixed and known. In one sense Bimala never leaves the ghar, or home, at all. The bahir which she encounters is a disruptive entrant into this home; it is not the world as such. What is established fairly early in the novel is that the only purpose of Bimala's daily visits to the outer sitting-room is to meet Sandip. She meets him with her husband's consent, even his connivance. Sandip tries to give their meetings the colour of an engagement with the wider social and political world of nationalist struggle, but Bimala is never really deceived by this charade. She knows that Sandip is attracted to her, and she is also, despite herself, excited by his interest in her, by the audacity of his courtship of his friend's wife, by the persuasiveness of his rhetoric. She is herself, as the context makes clear, a sexually attractive woman drawn by Sandip's animal magnetism even as she despises the meanness of his mind and the transparency of his deceptions.

Why, we may ask ourselves, is Nikhilesh content to bring his wife 'out' in this incomplete and unsatisfactory way? At the start of the novel Bimala speaks of her husband's belief that a true companionate marriage should consist in equal rights and duties for both partners. Her own education has equipped her to understand her husband's insistence on freedom and his desire that she should emerge from the *antahpur* to engage in the affairs of the world. She is also overwhelmingly conscious of his love for her, a love that values her at a rate she is unwilling to accept, and which requires from her a response she is unwilling to give on Nikhilesh's terms. The opening pages of the novel convey the multiple pressures of Bimala's existence in the seclusion of the antahpur, bound by the petty resentments and restricted satisfactions of domesticity. In accordance with custom, she is denied the opportunity to meet her husband during the day, and must be content with various tasks of household management (not particularly onerous for a rich landowner's wife who is not the sole mistress of her extended household) and trivial quarrels with her sisters-in-law. Repeatedly, she attempts to draw her husband into these matters, but he refuses to discuss them with her; yet he is, compared with his peers, untypically devoted to his wife, actively concerned in matters of her education and in providing her with mental companionship. There is a parallel here with Rabindranath himself, in the exceptional series of letters he wrote to his wife Mrinalini when she had complained to him of troubles at home in the extended family at Jorasanko, urging her to remain calm, to overcome discontent, and to cherish their own love above everything else.

We can see Nikhilesh, here, making his own distinction between degrees of innerness, between the narrow concerns of everyday domesticity and the private relationship he has with Bimala. In rejecting the one, he seeks to nourish the other by bringing it 'outside', into the light and air of the world:

I said to Bimal one day, you must come outside. Bimal was within my house— she was a household Bimal, made by the trivial, set rules of a small place. Was the love that I regularly got from her gathered from a deep source within her heart, or was it like the daily ration of tap water provided by the municipality's pump?

Am I covetous? Was my desire far in excess of what I had received? No, I am not covetous—I am a lover. For this reason I did not want something that had been kept locked up in an iron safe; I wanted that which cannot be got unless it lets itself be caught. I did not wish to decorate my room with flowers cut out of the pages of scripture; I wished with all my heart to see Bimal, fully-blossomed in understanding, strength and love, in the midst of the world.

I did not, at the time, realise that if one truly wishes to see a human being in wholeness and freedom, then one must abandon the hope of retaining a definite claim upon her. Why did I fail to realise this? Was it in the pride of a husband's unchanging hold upon his wife? No, that was not so. It was because I placed my trust completely upon love. (pp. 169–70)

Nikhilesh's love, by definition a personal and private emotion, leads him to draw Bimala into an outer world where she can be most fully herself, freed from the conventions and restrictions of narrow domesticity. In his desire thus to 'free' his wife into what he regards as a fuller humanness, in his liberal ideology as well as his emotional idealism, Nikhilesh is not unlike his nineteenth-century predecessors who had similarly urged the impossibility of achieving a complete emotional relationship with a wife who knew nothing of the world. By a paradox, however, the opposition of ghar and bahir crucial to his project is undermined by the terms in which it is realised.

The most signal achievement of Bimala's emancipation is the freedom she is given to meet other men, particularly her husband's friend Sandip. Bimala says specifically that her husband had repeatedly expressed the wish to introduce her to his friends, but she had always refused. Only after hearing Sandip speak (from behind the seclusion of a screen) does she consent to meet him. That 'coming outside' should carry so strong an implication of being displayed to other men should not surprise us. Even in Bimala's account of Sandip's entry into their courtyard, borne along by a crowd of saffron-clad followers, to deliver an impassioned speech urging the adoption of swadeshi principles, two acts are emphasised: seeing and being seen. We see the incident through Bimala's eyes as, fascinated and overwhelmed, she witnesses Sandip bringing the current of nationalism to their barren parochial enclosure like a river in flood. The cries of 'Bande Mataram' accompanying his entry, the ochre flood of revolutionaries that fills their courtyard like the first rains quickening a dry river-bed, the thrilling rhetoric of his speech, overwhelm her more critical earlier reaction to his photograph. The womenfolk listen to Sandip's speech from behind a wicker screen, but at some point Bimala's impatience can no longer be contained, and she pushes it aside to look at Sandip. No one else in the assembly sees her; but Sandip's gaze falls upon her for an instant, and the fire of his eloquence is rekindled:

Was I, then, the daughter-in-law of a noble family? At that moment I was the sole representative of all the women of Bengal—and he was the hero of Bengal. Just as the light of the sun in the sky had fallen upon his forehead, so too must it be washed and consecrated by the hearts of Bengal's women. How otherwise could the auspiciousness of his battle-march be complete? (p. 158)

This is an extraordinary moment. Bimala glimpses through this passage of glances what she imagines to be the face of a newly awakened country, and the gaze of that new world rests upon her, caught, in an instant of transgressive eagerness, upon the boundary of inner and outer, looking out from behind her screen. Or so she would like to believe:

for already, in that exchange of glances which Bimala's narrative presents as a critical moment of recognition, another transaction has taken place. That transaction is as crucial to the act of 'coming out' as the larger possibility of political action may be to its motivation. The bahir is constituted not only by society and politics in a general sense but, specifically and physically, by the gaze of the other. This is the first time Bimala knows herself to have been seen by another man; and the development of the novel from this point records not only her identification of herself with nation and cause, but her hunger for the full reciprocity of that gaze. A whole world of difference lies between Bimala's response to this moment and the instinctive gesture, described by Rassundari Debi in her autobiography, with which she retreated to her room to avoid being seen by her husband's horse.[4]

Rabindranath's sister-in-law Jnanadanandini narrates an incident in her early married relationship with her husband Satyendranath which may be of interest here. Prior to Jnanadanandini's actual emergence from the antahpur, her husband's friend Manomohan Ghose wanted to see her. Satyendranath was willing, but the only means he could find of arranging a meeting was to bring his friend secretly not only into his bedroom at night, but into the private space of the bed, within the mosquito net. He then lay down, leaving his tongue-tied wife to converse with the stranger. No conversation ensued, and after a while Manomohan was escorted out of the room and the house by his friend, both presumably satisfied that a point had been made.[5] This remarkable incident, not a source for anything in this novel, nevertheless indicates one specific focus of emancipation: the entry of outer into inner, as much as the emergence of inner into outer. The symbolic act through which an enlightened husband makes public proof of his determination to liberate his wife from the restrictions of the women's quarters is by allowing his male friends to *see* her. For Nikhilesh in *The Home and the World*, it is after all as important that he should permit Sandip to enter his house, take up residence indefinitely, visit the drawing room and meet his wife, as that he should allow his wife to come out to receive him. As the novel progresses, it is Sandip's presence that becomes increasingly intolerable to those who love Nikhilesh, such as his sister-in-law and his old teacher; on one occasion at least, his way into the sitting-room is barred. (In a parallel instance Bimala's sister-in-law concocts a minor domestic *fracas* in order to prevent her from meeting Sandip; but this is a diversion, not a barrier.) By contrast, the process of taking Bimala out of the women's quarters attracts relatively little censure, and there is no effort to reverse its direction.

If it is difficult in physical terms to demarcate the limits of inner and outer, socially and psychologically too, their boundaries are shifting and inexact. 'Bahir' remains an oppositional category, yet its location is imprecise. It cannot simply be translated as 'the world', though for Nikhilesh Bimala's emergence does carry the implication of entering into the world at large. It is closer to 'the outside' as opposed to 'the inside', a mental category rather than a physical place. Where it signifies the external world of action, conflict and contemplation as against the restricted interiority of the home, it can be seen positively, as a space of freedom and moral responsibility. Equally, it may become a place of licence and immorality, threatening the security of the home, as it does when, in its confusion of nationalist self-glorification and sexual desire, it invades the 'interiority' of Bimala's heart.

Bimala's desire to remain 'at home' on their country estates rather than travel with her husband to Calcutta is paralleled by her initial reluctance to emerge from the andarmahal. It places her, especially in her obscurantist self-image, in resistance to the winds of change that are sweeping through Bengal. Nikhilesh's progressive ideology marks her out as a subject of transformation, a transformation that he wishes to achieve through the agency of love. This love which Nikhilesh feels for his wife is distinct from any other emotion in the novel, a complex of sentiment, romantic idealism, erotic attachment (achingly present in the treatment of the period when their marital relationship is under the greatest strain and he is no longer sharing her bedroom) and intellectual hope. It is an emotion that appears to us peculiarly modern in its preoccupation with the autonomy of the individual, as in its effort simultaneously to universalise the realm of the personal.

Ideologically, thus, Nikhilesh's love is committed to a model of openness and freedom. Nikhilesh invests all the resources of his heart in allowing Bimala a 'free' space within marriage where the world can see her. For him this is a test of his love as of hers, a proof that this love is no fugitive or cloistered virtue but ready to take on all the dangers of the world. He will therefore put up with Sandip's presence to a point where his closest friends think him either foolhardy or weak. As we have already noted, what is most perturbing about the episode is the extent to which Nikhilesh's planned emancipation of his wife becomes limited by her confusion of the world with Sandip. When he tells Bimala that she must come 'out' because, although she may not need the outer world, the outer world may need her, he projects an image of fulfilled human worth which must be placed at odds with Sandip's conversion of Bimala to a nationalist icon. Yet Bimala never reaches the world which needs her in the way Nikhilesh had envisaged; she is overtaken midway by the demands placed upon her by Sandip, who identifies her with an image of resurgent Bengali womanhood inspiring its revolutionary youth. This image, Bimala indicates in the critical re-examination of the episode which she provides in her narrative, is not only false but corrupt: as much a product of her own vanity and her eagerness to be deluded as of Sandip's half-specious, half-seductive rhetoric. Nevertheless, it remains important, culturally and psychologically, to note the universalising thrust of Nikhilesh's love, a love which, while it clings to a single object of desire, seeks to project this object into the world it inhabits. It may be argued that in his romantic idealisation of a 'fully-blossomed' Bimala in the midst of the universe, Nikhilesh is as guilty of confusing Bimala with the values of his own liberal humanism as Sandip is in identifying her with the resurgent Hindu nation. It is in this respect that his emancipatory project is ultimately a project of his own ego; that the love which seeks to translate Bimala from ghar to bahir is inattentive to Bimala's own desires and aspirations. Modern, sympathetic, liberal, painfully anxious to grant the woman her right to education, choice and freedom, Nikhilesh's love is in the last analysis uncomfortably paternalistic and self-absorbed.

Yet this love is also, historically, the first form of human attachment to set a very high value on emotional privacy, upon the interiorisation of the values of intimate life. By contrast with an earlier form of marriage where the wife's ritual devotion and the husband's indifference are equally available for public scrutiny (as in the images of conjugal life Bimala represents through her mother and her account of her husband's family), Nikhilesh's feelings for his wife, conveyed through his own narrative, cannot be understood by anyone else in his household, perhaps not even by Bimala. The other woman who loves him, his sister-in-law, shares with him a relation of considerable emotional inwardness, but its tenor is nostalgic and restrained. His friend Sandip, to whom he is bound by a psychological dependence which seems almost as deep as that which ties him to his wife, betrays him as a matter of habit. Nikhilesh's loneliness is immense and incalculable. In part this is the loneliness of the transition to modern forms of thought and behaviour. If Nikhilesh seeks companionship in Bimala, he must change her; but he is mistaken in thinking that change can be controlled, or that two human beings will change at the same time in the same way. Even within the space of this novel, so carefully situated at a recorded juncture of Bengali social history, time is personal; mental events cannot be synchronised.

Everything in Nikhilesh's narrative is touched by his loneliness, by his sense of distance from his fellows. But he is most solitary in his love, an emotion touched equally by prescience as by obtuseness, and treated by Rabindranath as a mark of his difference. Contemporary history will provide other instances of men like Nikhilesh, deeply and romantically attached to their wives, undertaking the task of their education and emancipation; but what Rabindranath projects in this fictional character is not simply a study of mentality. Fiction provides, rather, the opportunity to seize upon the most private and irreducible elements of attachment, as in the remarkable scene where Nikhilesh enters the bedroom he has now abandoned and is visited by an inexpressible tenderness at the traces of Bimala's physical presence: her comb, hairpins, slippers.

At a moment of deep unhappiness, Nikhilesh asserts the need for a new kind of exteriority: he must try to see himself and Bimala from 'the outside', not from the inner perspective of his own ideals and desires:

Today I must look at Bimal, as at myself, wholly from the outside. So long I have invested Bimal with ideals I set a high value on for myself. It was not that the Bimal I knew in my domestic life matched that mental image at every point, yet still I worshipped her through it. This was not a virtue in me— rather, it was a great vice. . . . Bimal is what she is. Why should she become perfect for my sake? (pp. 196–7)

Whom does Bimala love? The conventional answer to this question would be that she loves her husband, though for a time she is attracted to the magnetic but unprincipled Sandip. The ideological weight of the novel as a whole, and certainly the thrust of her own narrative, would support such a reading. The story would then appear to us an exemplary moral fable, a kind of *bildungsroman* in which Bimala's sentimental education takes her through unforeseen dangers to a re-affirmation of the worth of conjugal love, though this is achieved only through crisis and its future left uncertain.

Fictional truths are plural: in a sense this is as valid a reading as any. But it is this novel's strength that it opens itself to a more sceptical and ironic view of its characters than they can take of themselves. Technically this is achieved by the splitting of the narrative into three, and through the contrasting subjectivities of the speakers, each almost wholly self-absorbed. Discursively, each of the narrators inhabits a set of realities which seem to take absolute precedence over all others. In fact this is the way in which truth works in the world, where we cannot see except with our own eyes. By contrast fiction is unnatural: it presents us with more truths than one. Our understanding of Bimala in *The Home and the World* depends crucially on this unreality. Because we see her both as she sees herself and as she can never see herself, she is for us a character divided between desire and fulfilment.

From this external perspective, the characters of this novel are defined also by another kind of lack, one that is never allowed to disturb the tenor of the fictional discourse as it stands. There are no children in *The Home and the World*; the youngest character is the idealistic student Amulya. It is worth a moment's pause to reflect on the nature of this absence, and on the fact that no one in the novel mentions it. Bimala's sisters-in-law appear to be childless; Bimala herself, after eleven years of marriage, is still narrowly focused upon the intimate ties that bind her to husband or lover. Beyond these relationships, the domestic space she inhabits seems to hold no more than trivial problems of household management and the tidying of her bedroom. How should we read the silence of this text on a matter that no treatment of Indian married life in the early twentieth century could realistically ignore? It is true that Nikhilesh's family seems dogged by misfortune, and to some extent his freedom of action in the novel depends on his position as the sole male heir to a considerable estate. Nevertheless, children never figure even within the space of personal desires and hopes. Their absence is not *noticed*, not even by Bimala or by Nikhilesh. One could read this as a representational choice on the part of the author: concentrating on the classic emotional triangle, Rabindranath dispenses with anything that might be considered extraneous to the emotional and moral intensity of the situation. Or we could speculate on the physical relationship of Bimala and Nikhilesh: what is the true source of Bimala's discontent, why does Nikhilesh permit his friend to seduce his wife?

But much more important than the absence itself, as we quickly recognise, is the failure of the text to acknowledge it as such. Bimala's unhappiness is left without objective *cause* (to use an unsatisfactory term); it is unlocalised in the fiction, spreading like an aura over the whole space of her marriage and her household. Her desire is always in excess of any object that she can set for it, however she may strive to fill her horizon with individual or nation. In this respect we may see in her, as in Nikhilesh, the 'unhappy consciousness' Hegel set at the beginning of any modern age. Bimala's desire is directed towards objects outside herself: her mother, her husband, material possessions, the nation, Sandip. But what she projects onto these objects is herself: she wants to become something that they constitute or represent. This too is a kind of love: a love that, impelled by lack, seeks to identify itself with the object of its desire. For Bimala her love is a feeling that can make her what she is not: a virtuous and devoted wife like her mother, the sole recipient of her husband's bounty instead of being forced to share it with others, the protective goddess of a reborn nation, the sexually conscious woman in control of the favours she grants.

When the novel opens, Bimala's narrative perspective places these stages of her emotional history in the past: even later, when all three of the speakers seem to be focusing on the immediate present, Bimala's tone is retrospective. By contrast with Nikhilesh and Sandip, Bimala seems most consistently to be *looking back* at events that have already occurred. She is therefore intensely conscious of her mistakes, most of all in the crucial episode of her infatuation with the image of herself that Sandip projects. As she realises, this infatuation depends upon a confusion which is both willed and involuntary. She recognises Sandip's rhetoric, which makes her a personification of the spirit of the nation, to be flawed from its inception, tainted by self-interest and sexual desire; yet she wants as much to be part of this nationalist struggle as to become a woman who is desired by men. Even before she meets Sandip, she seeks identity with a movement whose political justification she cannot yet analyse: she tells her husband to burn her foreign clothes and to dismiss her companion Miss Gilby. Rabindranath's sympathies in this encounter are clearly, as his essays on nationalism indicate, with the inflexibly 'liberal' Nikhilesh. Here too Nikhilesh defends an idea of the 'world' as opposed to the narrowness and obscurantism of the swadeshi model of history, just as Rabindranath, in the English essay on Nationalism in India, had reproved the excesses of nationalist historiography:

For all our miseries and shortcomings, we hold responsible the historical surprises that burst upon us from outside. This is the reason why we think that our one task is to build a political miracle of freedom upon the quicksand of social slavery.[6]

The Home and the World is usually read as Rabindranath's most sustained critique of contemporary nationalist politics, especially the swadeshi ideology disseminated all over Bengal in the early decades of the twentieth century by men like Bepin Chandra Pal and Aswini Kumar Datta. His disagreement with Bepin Chandra Pal, who had already attacked *Streer Patra*, was open and acknowledged. If the cynical, amoral and corrupt Sandip is not actually a representation of a recognisable contemporary figure, he is certainly a savage indictment of the self-deluded and self-seeking revolutionary. In the conflict of principles, Nikhilesh is gifted with so overwhelming an ethical advantage that the political argument of the novel is scarcely an argument at all. By contrast, the conflict of emotional and sexual interests is complex and profound. Sandip is as necessary to Bimala's sentimental education as he is to her husband's adult acknowledgement of the nature of sexual jealousy. Bimala recognises in Sandip, above all, the temptation of power. It is a power associated on the one hand with the intoxications of armed revolutionary struggle—the opportunities for coercion of the weak, for harassment of the strong; on the other hand, it is the power of the sexually mature woman in control of her destiny. In the end both these forms of power are destructive, as Bimala sees; further, they are in a sense illusory, because they fail to recognise the political and social conditions which limit their operation.

What is likely to cause us most difficulty in the novel is its representation of Sandip as the classic seducer. In many respects Sandip is an embarrassment. He makes a scandal of the political plot, which is forced to identify militant nationalism with lack of moral and sexual scruple; he embarrasses feminist readings which are compelled to note the implication that women brought out of the andarmahal are likely to be unfaithful to their husbands. If we are finally reluctant to believe that these are the overt lessons Rabindranath seeks to convey in this novel, this is because of the way in which the relationship between Bimala and Nikhilesh is represented. The love that binds them in an absence of mutual understanding, their intimate yearning for companionship, in a sense *produces* Sandip as the catalyst who will take these two egoists to disaster and—possibly—recuperation. The scandal that Sandip constitutes in the home as in the world, the bad faith that he brings to both, is in his own narrative linked to yet another identity formation: that of the amoral opportunist, seeking to exploit people and causes for his own advantage. As a newly modern man, Sandip is himself unembarrassed by the vices he marks in his own character. The unity of his being is based on his readiness to be true to that nature. What he wants, as Bimala sees, is power, whether political or sexual.

In *The Nation and Its Fragments*, Partha Chatterjee suggests that the distinction between inner and outer is important to early nationalist discourse. It divides the world of the colonised into two realms, the material and the spiritual. 'The material is the domain of the "outside", of the economy and of statecraft, of science and technology . . . the spiritual, on the other hand, is an "inner" domain bearing the "essential" marks of cultural identity.' Over time, this inner world of 'language or religion or the elements of personal and family life' was increasingly made the vehicle of colonial difference, its familial, personal and spiritual aspects actively guarded against the touch of the coloniser. In the outer domain of the state, however, nationalism sought to erase the marks of cultural difference in order to share, and ultimately to take over, the 'modern regime of power'.[7]

Bimala's relationship with Sandip is based on a confusion of inner with outer, a confusion that is present in his corrupt version of a nationalist ideology. The model of Hindu womanhood with which she seeks to identify herself belongs to the inner realm of cultural practice; in projecting it, as a source of spiritual power, into the outer world of political struggle, she risks its corruption and distortion. In the very act of committing herself to the ideology of the nation, she admits other motives and interests, interests that will eventually transform her as they are bound to transform, in time, the whole of the 'inner' world. It is for this reason that Bimala's history is exemplary in a way that Nikhilesh's is not. Her sentimental education leads her from a traditional model of womanhood to a state of radical incompleteness where the models she seeks have disintegrated, leaving her in the confusion and uncertainty which Rabindranath sees as characteristic of modernity. Even without the physical fact of adultery, her marital relationship with Nikhilesh has progressed from innocence to experience. Bimala's sexual and moral awakening is integral to her new sensibility, a sensibility which, at the end of the novel, is left open to the future.

Endnotes

1. All citations of *The Home and the World* are from the text of *Ghare Baire* in *Rabindra Rachanabali* vol. 8 (Calcutta: Visvabharati, 1941), in my translation. Page references are to this Bengali edition.

2. On the contrast of naive and sentimental modes of feeling, see Friedrich Schiller, 'On Naive and Sentimental Poetry' (1795–6), trans. J.A. Elias, in H.B. Nisbet, ed., *German Aesthetic and Literary Criticism: Winckelmann, Lessing, Hamann, Herder, Schiller and Goethe* (Cambridge: Cambridge University Press, 1985), pp. 180–232. This contrast may also appear as a contrast of the natural and the artificial, an opposition that can be resolved only through the agency of an enlightened culture: 'our culture, by means of reason and freedom, should lead us back to nature.' (p. 181)

3. Much recent social history has focused on the condition of women in nineteenth- and early-twentieth-century Bengal. The history of conjugal relations is relatively underworked, though important texts exist in the form of the autobiographies of nineteenth-century men and women, as well as 'advice for women' books setting out their conjugal duties (such as Joykrishna Mitra's *Ramanir Kartavya*, which first appeared as a series of articles in the *Bamabodhini Patrika* in 1881, or Ishan Chandra Basu's *Nari Niti*, 1884). On marriage, see Ronald B. Inden, *Marriage and Rank in Bengali Culture* (New Delhi, 1976) and on conjugal relations, see Sambuddha Chakrabarti, 'Changing Notions of Conjugal Relations in Nineteenth Century Bengal', in Rajat Kanta Ray, ed., *Mind, Body and Society: Life and Mentality in Colonial Bengal* (Calcutta: Oxford University

Press, 1995), pp. 297–330, and Tapan Raychaudhuri, 'Love in a Colonial Climate', in his *Perceptions, Emotions, Sensibilities: Essays on India's Colonial and Post-Colonial Experiences* (New Delhi: Oxford University Press, 1999), pp. 65–95. On life in the andarmahal, see Sambuddha Chakrabarti, *Andare Antare: Unish Shatake Bangali Bhadramahila* (Calcutta: Stree, 1995).

4. See Srimati Rassundari, *Amar Jiban*, p. 33 in N. Jana et al., eds., *Atmakatha*, vol. 1 (Calcutta: Ananya Prakashan, 1981).

5. The incident is related by Jnanadanandini herself in Indira Debi Chaudhurani, ed. *Puratani* (Calcutta: Indian Associated Publishing Company, 1957). Jnanadanandini's reminiscences, *Smritikatha*, were reprinted in *Ekshan*, vol. 19 (1990), pp. 14–15.

6. 'Nationalism in India', in Sisir Kumar Das, ed., *The English Writings of Rabindranath Tagore*, vol. 2 (New Delhi: Sahitya Akademi, 1996), p. 462.

7. Partha Chatterjee, *The Nation and Its Fragments: Colonial and Postcolonial Histories* (1993; rpt. Delhi: Oxford University Press, 1994), pp. 6, 26.

The Form of *The Home and the World**

TAPOBRATA GHOSH

It is necessary to state at the beginning of this discussion that *Ghare Baire* (1916) and its English translation, *The Home and the World* (1919), are not exactly the same text. Although the translation of the original was done by Rabindranath's nephew Surendranath Tagore and published after corrections were made by Rabindranath himself, nevertheless it is dangerous for the two texts to be regarded as equivalent. The nature of this danger can be demonstrated through a single example. In the first paragraph of *The Home and the World*, recalling her mother's 'vermilion mark' and the 'sari . . . with its wide red border', Bimala writes, 'they came at the start of my life's journey, like the first streak of dawn, giving me golden provision to carry me on my way.'[1] In the first paragraph of *Ghare Baire* on the other hand, there are four queries contained in Bimala's reminiscences which are absent in the English translation: 'After that? Did the black clouds rush in on my path like dacoits? Did they not leave a single spark of that light that sustained me? Yet can the chaste gift of the dawn at the beginning of my life be ever obliterated, even if obscured by distress?'[2]

In the *kakuvakrokti alankar* (*exotesis*), the answer is implicit in the question, which is signalled by a change in tone. The last question of *Ghare Baire* contains the vital answer to all four queries. What is that answer? The gift of her mother's memory can never be destroyed, even

*Translated from the Bengali by Sunanda Das.

if it is temporarily covered by gloom. Satyajit Ray based his script of *Ghare Baire* on *The Home and the World* and deleted one of the two sisters-in-law (the husband's brothers' wives) of Bimala; did he miss the significance of the four questions posed in the first paragraph of *Ghare Baire*? These questions contain clear and irrefutable evidence that Bimala's marriage had not ended. Did Satyajit Ray condemn Bimala to widowhood in the last scene because he overlooked the implication of these four questions?

II

The Home and the World is presented through the first person narratives of three individuals. Many Bengali critics mention the influence of Bankimchandra Chattopadhyay's *Rajani* (1877) on the form of *Ghare Baire*. It is only natural that the first person narratives of Bimala, Nikhilesh and Sandip should remind the reader of the corresponding stories of Rajani, Shachindra, Amarnath and others. But one must also be aware of the differences between the two novels. Bimala, Nikhilesh and Sandip write about themselves, but it is not possible for the illiterate and blind flower seller Rajani to write about herself; she has only *told* her story and that too, not fully. After proceeding for a bit, Rajani confesses, '. . . I do not feel like narrating this incessantly troubled life. Someone else will relate it.'[3] Taking his cue from this, Shachindra says, 'I have been given this responsibility—I have to write up this part of Rajani's life. I will write it.'[4] In other words, Shachindra is not going to write about himself at all; he will be writing about a portion of Rajani's life using the pronoun 'I'. Moreover, in the section entitled 'About Everyone',[5] when everybody is shown to be writing or talking about Rajani, the main features of the autobiographical form, that is, the indivisible identity of the subject and its self-absorption, are lost in the proliferation of the several 'I's. When the personal pronoun does not refer to the speaker but to someone else, then outwardness becomes more important than introspection, and once this happens, a crucial element of the autobiographical form becomes a casualty. In fact, if we leave aside the depiction of Amarnath, the first solitary figure in the Bengali novel, then the autobiographical nature of *Rajani* can be said to be manufactured and not created. It is precisely on this count

that the form of *The Home and the World* is more successful than that
of *Rajani*. It must be emphasised that the three protagonists of *The
Home and the World* are spontaneously and of their own volition involved
in continual introspection and self-analysis. It is not impossible to
conceive of Rajani as a product of the omniscient first person narrator.
It is difficult to imagine Bimala, Nikhilesh and Sandip separated from
their personal pronouns.

III

Is *The Home and the World* a novel of triangular love? A *roman a trois*?
At least E.M. Forster thought so. In 1919, while writing a review of this
novel, Forster posed the question, 'Having triumphed in *Chitra* or
Gitanjali why should he [Rabindranath] indite a "*roman a trois*" with all
the hackneyed situations from which novelists are trying to emancipate
themselves in the West?'[6] It is not relevant here to go into the historical
reasons for Forster's contempt and mockery of Rabindranath, but his
categorisation of *The Home and the World* as a *roman a trois* proves that
he could not enter the world of the novel.

The Home and the World is not at all a novel of triangular love—the
main concern of the novel is Nikhilesh's unique and daring experiment
with conjugal relations. The prolific use of the phrase 'conjugality' in
Indian culture has given to it such a degree of acceptability that it is
often forgotten that conjugality and love are not the same thing. The
main difference between these two relations is that there is no scope for
individual choice in conjugal relations when elders arrange the relationship, whereas individual choice forms the basis of love. Recalling
the nine years of his married life with Bimala, Nikhilesh asks himself,
'Did the love which I received from her, I asked myself, come from the
deep spring of her heart, or was it merely like the daily provision of pipe
water pumped up by the municipal steam-engine of society?' (*The Home
and the World*, p. 43). It is for this reason that Nikhilesh wishes to
extract Bimala from the narrow domestic world and meet her in the
wide open world—only then, he imagines, will their marital union
realise its truth in a union of love. When Bimala asks why their union
within the walls of their home is not a true one, Nikhilesh replies, 'Here
you are wrapped up in me. You know neither what you have, nor what

you want. . . . If we meet, and recognise each other, in the real world, then only will our love be true' (*The Home and the World*, p. 12). But given the freedom to choose, is there any guarantee that a wife will choose her husband as her lover? Why did Nikhilesh not think of this eventuality? Nikhilesh asks himself this and replies, 'Was it because of the husband's pride of possession over his wife? No. It was because I placed the fullest trust upon love' (*The Home and the World*, p. 43). That the answer given by Nikhilesh is not mere self-deception engineered to protect himself is evident from his behaviour. As landlord and master of the house, Nikhilesh could have turned out Sandip by force—the Sandip who was entrapping Bimala day by day, living in Nikhilesh's zamindari outhouse—and returned Bimala to the confines of the home. He would thereby have protected his rights as a husband; but he would have failed miserably as a lover. Nikhilesh's ultimate aim is to prove himself as Bimala's lover in the world outside even if he remains her husband in the home. This is the point of his experiment. Will Nikhilesh fail before the commencement of the experiment? By no means: 'If Bimala should say that she is not mine, what care I where my society wife may be?' (*The Home and the World*, p. 85). So curtailing all his social authority, Nikhilesh waits in silent anguish for Bimala to free herself from her infatuation. He reveals his unique manhood through his power to wait. It is through his ability to wait that Nikhilesh proves his credentials as an examiner of his own abilities. He knows that, 'The passage from the narrow to the larger world is stormy' (*The Home and the World*, p. 49). Sandip too has appeared like a storm in the middle of that passage from the home to the world, but then, the zamindari outhouse is not the immense world outside! So they proceed to Calcutta—Bimala's initiation will take place in that centre of modern international awareness generated by the Bengali cultural renaissance; it is here that Bimala and Nikhilesh's married life will transform itself into a free union of love. But before departing, he has one more task to complete. Nikhilesh can fulfil his duties as a zamindar only when he has been able to control the Hindu–Muslim riot which Sandip had started and then run away from like a coward. Nikhilesh is injured during his attempt to stop the riot. But does he die?

In order to allay a doubt, I had earlier taken the help of an image from the introductory paragraph of the novel; now I will take the help of another image that occurs towards the end of the novel. Nikhilesh rides away in the sunset to control the riot, and Bimala writes, 'I can see every different shade of that sunset even today. Two masses of clouds on either side of the sinking orb made it look like a great bird with fiery-feathered wings outspread. It seemed to me that this fateful day was taking its flight to cross the ocean of night' (*The Home and the World*, pp. 330–1). Stretching its blazing wings on either side, the great sun bird flies to cross the ocean of night. If we look at the two images together, then we are left in no doubt that the vermilion mark of marriage, the red-bordered sari, will reappear with the promise of a new bright dawn in Bimala's life like the red sun which crosses the ocean of night: 'It may be masked by disaster, but can it ever be destroyed' (*Ghare Baire*, p. 407), Bimala observes in *Ghare Baire*. We have to discard the observations of the critic who characterises this novel as a *roman a trois*, however great a theoretician he may be of Western narratives, in order to enter its world and witness the story of the triumph of conjugal love over everything, even death.

IV

That Rabindranath's *The Home and the World* is a novel about the restoration of conjugal relations is expressed by its structure. Let us look at the way that *Ghare Baire*, the original Bengali novel, is structured by three separate autobiographical strands:

1. Bimala–Nikhilesh–Sandip
2. Bimala–Sandip–Nikhilesh
3. Bimala–Sandip–Nikhilesh
4. Bimala–Nikhilesh–Sandip
5. Nikhilesh–Bimala–Nikhilesh
6. Bimala–Nikhilesh–Bimala

First, Sandip appears by the side of Bimala and Nikhilesh's shared life; in the second and third parts, Sandip appears in the middle and separates Bimala and Nikhilesh. In the fourth part Bimala and Nikhilesh are again positioned alongside each other and relegate Sandip to the background. Sandip is totally absent in the fifth and sixth parts: in the fifth, Bimala is in the centre and Nikhilesh on both sides. And in the sixth, Nikhilesh is in the centre and Bimala appears on both sides of him. It is only in the second and third parts that, in keeping with the accepted conventions of *roman a trois,* Sandip comes between husband and wife. But can a mere two sections out of a total of six be taken as a definitive indicator of triangular love? The last two sections, in particular, reaffirm the theme of conjugal love in *The Home and the World* by repeatedly placing Bimala with Nikhilesh and Nikhilesh with Bimala, a pattern which indicates a mutuality between them, expressed through the exchange of positions between centre and circumference. In other words, the unity of the home and the world is also affirmed.

It is to be noted that what are 'autobiographies' of *Ghare Baire* have been called 'stories' in *The Home and the World.* The story of each character is continually subdivided by numbered sections; but, on the other hand, one or more stories of one or more characters, go to form a chapter. Along with the division into sections, *The Home and the World* has been reorganised into a total of twelve chapters. In the Bengali, Bimala, Nikhilesh and Sandip do not divide their uninterrupted life-stories *into chapters* and since none of them write their autobiographies in the knowledge of the others, it is not possible for them to have any role in dividing up their respective autobiographies *into different parts.* In other words, the three characters of *Ghare Baire* are given full control over their own autobiographies. But in the English version, the power of the characters to write their own autobiographies is limited by the intervention of the masterful author. Besides, if one looks a little deeper, it will be apparent that the chapterisation of the English version is planned according to the new developments in the plot. For instance, the second chapter begins with Sandip's appearance in Nikhilesh's household during swadeshi. The sixth chapter starts with the report of Harish Kundu's torture of Panchu. The ninth is introduced by Bimala's theft, while the twelfth commences with the news of Bimala's and Nikhilesh's imminent departure for Calcutta. Of course, when the autobiographies were turned into 'stories' in *The Home and the World,* one could make out that the plot had become more important than the characters. But it is doubtful if the restructuring of *Ghare Baire* into an event-based plot in *The Home and the World* has marked an improvement on the character-centred story of the original. Despite this, it has to be noted that chapters eight to twelve of *The Home and the World*, that is, the last five chapters, do not contain Sandip's stories. The last two parts of *Ghare Baire* were those of Nikhilesh–Bimala– Nikhilesh and Bimala–Nikhilesh–Bimala; the last five movements of *The Home and the World* are:

8. Nikhilesh–Bimala
9. Bimala
10. Nikhilesh–Bimala
11. Bimala
12. Nikhilesh–Bimala

In this patterning of conjugal relations by a 2-1-2-1-2 arrangement, Forster's third character does not get a chance to intrude.

V

Is this novel integrally related to the swadeshi period? Or does the swadeshi simply provide an incidental and fortuitous backdrop to the action? In terms of structural analysis, the question could be posed in the following manner: has the intrinsic nature of the relationship between this novel and its historical setting been conclusively proved? Sumit Sarkar has divided the swadeshi leadership into four categories according to their *modus operandi*: moderates, extremists, terrorists and constructive swadeshi.[7] From a general look the narrative subject of *The Home and the World* may appear to be the conflict between Nikhilesh's constructive swadeshi and Sandip's extremism (although Sandip's ruthless attempt to compel unwilling and helpless people to boycott foreign goods indicates a combination of extremism and terrorism).

But when investigated in greater depth, the story reveals that neither Nikhilesh's constructive swadeshi nor Sandip's terrorist boycott activity is causally related to the swadeshi period. In other words, it cannot be definitely stated that Nikhilesh turned to constructive swadeshi or Sandip to terrorism from the inception of the swadeshi movement. Bimala writes that, 'From the time my husband had been a college student he had been trying to get the things required by our people produced in our country. . . . After a while he came to the conclusion that our attempts at reviving our industries were not succeeding for want of a bank of our own . . . and then he actually started a small bank' (*The*

Home and the World, p. 44). One can see that Nikhilesh took to constructive work much before the onset of the swadeshi period and tried to make his country self-sufficient. If one side of Nikhilesh's nature is directed to the building of his country, the other is committed to the establishment of true conjugal relations. The attitude that propels Nikhilesh to empower his own country is the same that drives him to discard the feudal pride of a householder and acquire real conjugality in the world outside. Nikhilesh's attitude can in no way be a direct result of the swadeshi period.

If we consider Sandip's extremism in the backdrop of the swadeshi period, then it will become apparent that his choice of terrorism was inherent in his pre-swadeshi nature. His drive towards creating terror was evident even when Sandip was with the Congress. Without going into too much detail, it is sufficient to state that the pleasure of oppression by creating terror can gratify both sexual and authoritarian impulses. That 'the shock of fear' increases 'desire' in women (*Ghare Baire*, p. 445) is one of Sandip's assumptions from his previous experiences. He writes in *Ghare Baire* that, 'I have seen many such. The widow Kusum surrendered to me, trembling in fear. And it seemed as if that Anglo-Indian girl near our hostel would tear me to pieces when she got angry with me. I remember that day very well when she drove me out of her room shouting, "Go, go"—and as soon as I crossed the threshold, she came running to me and falling at my feet, beat her head against the floor, cried copiously and fainted' (*Ghare Baire*, pp. 445–6). In *The Home and the World*, this portion from the *Ghare Baire* narrative is left out. And so the connection between his drive to create political terror during swadeshi and his desire to inflict sexual terror in his pre-swadeshi life, is left somewhat vague here. Needless to say, there is no intrinsic connection between Sandip's mentality and the swadeshi movement.

Just as it is natural for Sandip to find joy in terrorising others, it is pleasurable for Bimala to be terrorised by men. Of this tendency in Bimala which reflects her feudal mindset, Nikhilesh observes, 'She loves to find in men the turbulent, the angry, the unjust. Her respect must have its element of fear' (*The Home and the World*, p. 44). Even before swadeshi, Nikhilesh had sought to extract Bimala from her feudal world and set her free in the world outside; but she had steadfastly refused to follow his direction. Nikhilesh writes, 'I had hoped that when Bimala found herself free in the outer world she would be rescued from her infatuation with tyranny. But now I feel sure that this infatuation is deep down in her nature' (*The Home and the World*, p. 44).

In other words, the characters of *The Home and the World* do not simply derive their inherent nature from the swadeshi movement. However, Bimala's character is skilfully made to correspond to the idea of Bengal, while the natural attitudes and tendencies of Nikhilesh (constructive swadeshi) and Sandip (terroristic boycott) parallel the two main tendencies of swadeshi. Bimala writes, 'The thing that was agitating me within was merely a variation of the stormy passion outside, which swept the country from one end to the other' (*The Home and the World*, p. 135). Sandip is inferior to Nikhilesh in all respects, yet Bimala's inherent enjoyment of fear attracts her to his turbulent spirit. When Sandip's devious jealousy and cowardice is revealed, not only is Bimala freed of her infatuation for Sandip, but also emancipated from her deep-rooted feudal obsessions. Sandip injects the poison of discontent among Hindus and Muslims in Nikhilesh's zamindari; Nikhilesh needs to remove that communal toxin before taking Bimala to Calcutta where, through the spread of capitalism, a new man–woman relationship is emerging.

The swadeshi movement is present neither at the beginning nor at the end of the novel. Only in the middle are its psychological problems internalised with extreme finesse. It should now be quite clear why, in spite of the presence of two men and a woman, this novel cannot be termed a conventional *roman a trois*. Can a novel of triangular relationships be based on a plot that seeks to prove the complementary nature of the main couple, where the arrival and exit of the third protagonist is really an instrument to highlight this complementarity?

VI

I have stated that the division of the chapters according to the necessities of the plot is not appropriate, since the original *Ghare Baire* focused on character. The technique of viewing the same event through the perspective of two characters has been repeatedly deployed. If the novel was based mainly on events, then this repeated use of the multiple perspective would have been considered a reiterated mistake. But the main point of the novel is to show how the same event, when seen through the eyes of different characters, is transformed into multiple events.

Some examples of these are:

1. When Nikhilesh refuses to stop the inflow of foreign goods into the weekly zamindari market, Sandip's boycott movement comes up against a barrier. Infatuated by Sandip's praises, Bimala, in her pride, sits down to do up her hair to seduce Nikhilesh into enforcing Sandip's boycott: 'brushing it up from the neck and piling it in a knot over my head' (*The Home and the World*, p. 144). This hairstyle had been very dear to Nikhilesh, who had said once, 'I feel it to be a torch, holding aloft the black flame of your hair.' Bimala writes, 'But what was it that happened? Never in all these nine years have I seen such a far-away, distraught look in his eyes—like the desert sky—with no merciful moisture of its own, no colour reflected, even, from what it looked upon' (*The Home and the World*, p. 213).

How does the same incident appear to Nikhilesh? 'Till that moment I had never viewed Bimala's adornment as a thing apart from herself. But today the elaborate manner in which she had done up her hair, in the English fashion, made it appear a mere decoration. That which before had the mystery of her personality about it, and was priceless to me, was now out to sell itself cheap' (*The Home and the World*, p. 164). Nikhilesh feels that his marital nest has been destroyed and that he has been freed tragically from that 'broken cage of a bedroom' (*The Home and the World*, p. 164).

2. The 'cruel load of Bimala's misery' (*The Home and the World*, p. 206) becomes clear to Nikhilesh the moment he sees her rise up noiselessly from 'the grass below the chrysanthemum decked steps in the garden' (*Ghare Baire*, p. 500) and depart when he suddenly reaches the spot:

'Bimala,' said I, 'Why should I seek to keep you fast in this closed cage of mine? Do I not know that thus you can not but pine and droop? . . . 'So,' I concluded, 'I tell you, truly, Bimala, you are free. Whatever I may or may not have been to you, I refuse to be your fetters.' (*The Home and the World*, p. 207)

Bimala reacts differently to the same incident: '. . . the other day in the garden, how easy my husband found it to tell me that he set me free! But can freedom—empty freedom—be given and taken so easily as well?' (*The Home and the World*, pp. 213–14).

3. Bimala steals six thousand rupees from Nikhilesh's safe and gives it to Sandip. She sends Amulya to Calcutta to sell her ornaments and raise the cash with which to replace what she had stolen. But Amulya does not return on time and Bimala is faced with the possibility of being publicly proven a thief the very next day. In the middle of the night when Nikhilesh wakes up on hearing the sounds of Bimala crying, he thinks, 'We give these sufferings names, bad or good, according to the classifications of the books, but this agony which is welling up from a torn heart, pouring into the fathomless dark, has it any name?' (*The Home and the World*, p. 265). At that time, Nikhilesh is not aware of the real cause for Bimala's tears. He simply tells himself, 'Who am I to judge her?' (*The Home and the World*, p. 266). At that moment Nikhilesh touches Bimala's head to console her and she breaks down crying and presses his feet to her breast.

The same event is repeated in Bimala's writing where Nikhilesh's consolation is transformed into a beautiful gesture full of mercy and blessing: 'I received his blessing. Now I shall be able to take up the penalty of public humiliation which will be mine tomorrow, and offer it, in all sincerity, at the feet of my God' (*The Home and the World*, p. 301).

VII

Two Recurring Images: Fire and Water

Fire

The word 'Sandip' means that which is manifestly bright and burning. Bimala writes, 'I was reminded of the day on which I first heard him speak, when I could not be sure whether he was a person, or just *a living flame*' (*The Home and the World*, p. 100). Later, '. . . he shook like *a quivering tongue of fire*' (*The Home and the World*, p. 100) 'whose youth flared so vigorously in a *hundred points of flame*' (*The Home and the World*, p. 91).

And on the day when Sandip first sees Bimala, she becomes a figure of flame lit by the fire of his eyes: 'It seemed to me that the *gold border* of her sari was her own *inner fire flaming out and twining round her*' (*The Home and the World*, p. 58). Sandip writes that Bimala '*burnt* her wings in the *blaze* of the full strength of my unhesitating manliness' (*The Home and the World*, p. 118).

The swadeshi movement which illuminates Bimala's life through Sandip is also coloured red, like the fire: 'My sight and my mind, my hopes and desires, became *red* with the passion of this new age' (*The Home and the World*, p. 17). When Sandip first meets Bimala, her hair is done up in a plait 'by a cunningly intertwined *red* silk ribbon' (*The Home and the World*, p. 28). Sandip writes, 'The little *red* ribbon which peeps through the luxuriant masses of her hair, with its flush of secret longing, it is the *lolling tongue of the red stormy cloud*' (*The Home and the World*, p. 68).

While reciting the enchanting mantra of *deshlakshmi* to Bimala, Sandip says, '. . . the blazing summer heat, which makes the whole sky lie gasping like a red-tongued lion in the desert, is nothing but your *cruel radiance*' (*The Home and the World*, p. 190).

Sandip explains to Bimala that she has been able to spread fire in a boy like Amulya! 'Amulya is a boy no longer, *the wick of his life is all blaze!*' (*The Home and the World*, 144). Similarly, Bimala will light up all the lamps in the country: 'What *a grand carnival of a Dewali* we shall have in the country!' (*The Home and the World*, p. 144).

Condemning the unrestrained nature of fire, Nikhilesh writes, 'Man has so fanned the *flames* of the loves of the men and women, as to make it overpass its rightful domain and now, even in the name of humanity itself, he can not bring it back under control!' (*The Home and the World*, p. 124). Is Bimala unaware of this? Forecasting the ashes of complete destruction left by this terrible bonfire, Bimala writes, 'The immovable world shall sway under our feet, *fire* shall flash from our eyes, a storm shall roar in our ears, what is or is not in front shall become equally dim. And then with tottering footsteps we shall plunge to our death; in a moment *all fire will be extinguished, the ashes will be scattered,* and nothing will remain behind' (*The Home and the World*, p. 222).

At the end, Bimala writes, '*I have passed through fire. What was inflammable has been burnt to ashes; what is left is deathless.* I have dedicated myself to the feet of him, who has received all my sin into the depths of his own pain' (*The Home and the World*, pp. 325–6)

Water

Sandip writes, 'Women find in my features, my manner, my gait, my speech, a masterful passion' (*The Home and the World*, p. 55). What is the character of this passion? Sandip describes it: 'It roars and rolls on, *like a flood*, with the cry: "I want, I want, I want"' (*The Home and the World*, p. 55). According to Sandip, 'That terrible word "I want" has taken flesh in woman, and therefore men, who are cowards, try with all their might to keep back this *primeval flood* with their earthen dykes. . . . Now it is *calm and deep like a lake*, but *gradually its pressure will increase*, the dykes will give way, *and the force which has so long been dumb will rush forward* with the roar: "I want!"' (*The Home and the World*, p. 107).

Bimala writes, 'So long I had been *like a small river* at the border of a village, my rhythm and my language were different from what they are now' (*The Home and the World*, pp. 58–9). Why does she change? 'When, *like a river*, we women keep to our banks, we give nourishment with all that we have, when we *overflow* them we will destroy all that we are' (*The Home and the World*, p. 62). Whirlpools are created from time to time in the middle of this destructive overflowing of the banks. Bimala writes, 'My days and nights were passing in a *whirl, like an eddy* with myself in the centre. No gap was left for hesitation or delicacy to enter' (*The Home and the World*, p. 57).

One day the ever-rising pride of the ocean tide had bloated Bimala with its foam: 'My banks gave way and the *great drum beats of the sea waves echoed in my mad current* . . . Whence came foaming into me this *surging flood of glory?*' (*The Home and the World*, p. 59). And finally the pull of the eddy controls her bloated and foamy pride, and leads her towards the vast sea: 'Now is the time to set sail towards that *great confluence*, where the *river of love meets the sea of worship*. In that pure blue all the weight of its muddiness sinks and disappears' (*The Home and the World*, p. 325).

After all, the meaning of the word 'Bimala' is where 'muddiness sinks and disappears'.

VIII

Time

According to the government resolution, the decision to partition Bengal was taken on 19 July 1905, that is, in the month of Shravan (July). As Sandip first appears with his young, saffron-clad followers at the temple pavilion of Nikhilesh's estate, Bimala thinks to herself that this was like 'a silt-reddened freshet into a dry river-bed at the first burst of rains!' (*The Home and the World*, p. 23).

Amulya was to return with the money from selling off Bimala's ornaments on the third day of *Magh* (*The Home and the World*, p. 296). And on the next day, that is, on the fourth of Magh, the arrangements for Bimala and Nikhilesh's departure for Calcutta are made; the novel ends on this day.

The time-span of the novel spreads from Shravan to Magh and within it, Sharat (autumn) finds the most important place, followed by Hemanta (late autumn) (*The Home and the World*, p. 204). Describing the marriage of Shiva and Parvati that takes place in the seventh canto of his *Kumarasambhava*, Kalidas writes, 'When, after her ritual bath, Parvati wore the dresses appropriate for going to her husband, then she looked as beautiful as the earth when it was decked with the white *kash* flower which blooms after the rains'[8]: *prafullakāṣha basudeva reje.*[9] This wonderful image of conjugality in autumn impressed Rabindranath so much, that he placed the days of his own married bliss in his *Jiban-smriti* in the autumn season.[10] Conjugality fructifies in late autumn. Rabindranath says, 'When the crop ripens in late autumn, nothing is left of its restlessness'; 'The late autumn raises its quiet success to gather the blessings of the world.'[11]

Out of the nine years of Nikhilesh and Bimala's married life, for seven autumns they had visited 'the broads of Samalda' by boat (*The Home and the World*, p. 122). Nikhilesh writes, 'I used to tell Bimala that a song must come back to its refrain over and over again. The original refrain of every song is in Nature, where the rain-laden wind passes over the rippling stream, where the green earth, drawing its shadow-veil over its face, keeps its ear close to the speaking water. . . . And therefore we two must come back to Nature, at least once a year, to tune our love anew to the first pure note of the meeting of hearts' (*The Home and the World*, pp. 122–3). In *Ghare Baire*, the first note of the meeting of hearts was said to have taken place in the 'union of Shiva and Parvati in the lotus groves of Lake Manas in Kailash' (*Ghare Baire*, p. 468).

In the year of the events in the novel, they are not able to return to that river, the refrain of their conjugal melody. Nikhilesh writes that 'in this symphony of Autumn I remain voiceless!' (*The Home and the World*, p. 121).

In a late autumn dusk before the turmoil in his life, Nikhilesh thinks contentedly 'while the day is bright and the world in the pursuit of its numberless tasks crowds around, then it seems as if my life wants nothing else. But when the colours of the sky fade away and the blinds are drawn down over the windows of heaven, then my heart tells me that evening falls just for the purpose of shutting out the world, to mark the time when the darkness must be filled with the One' (*The Home and the World*, pp. 204–5).

This year when the full moon of late autumn rises, and the desolate Nikhilesh thinks of the night: '. . . She had come a-tiptoe from behind, and clasped the darkness over the eyes, smiling mischievously' (*The Home and the World*, p. 206); on that night, Nikhilesh had told Bimala that he was freeing her from their conjugal nest.

It has been mentioned that *The Home and the World* ends in an afternoon of *Magh* (mid-winter)—the day the sun bird spread its fiery-feathered wings and flew across the ocean of night. The winter nights are long, but the winter dusk passes very fast. We can only hope that it will not take too long for Bimala's dawn to appear.

Endnotes

1. *The Home and the World* (London: Macmillan, rpt. 1945). All citations to this text are taken from this edition. All citations from *Ghare Baire* are taken from *Rabindra Rachanabali*, vol. IX, Birth Anniversary edition, Government of West Bengal.

2. *Ghare Baire*, p. 407. All citations from *Ghare Baire* and from other Bengali and Sanskrit texts are translated by Sunanda Das.

3. *Rajani, Bankim Rachanabali*, vol. I (Calcutta: Sahitya Sansad, Chaitra 1376 [1970]), p. 503.

4. Ibid., p. 513.

5. Ibid., p. 523.

6. E.M. Forster, *Abinger Harvest* (London: Edward Arnold & Company, rpt. 1936), p. 321.

7. Sumit Sarkar, *The Swadeshi Movement in Bengal, 1903–1908* (Calcutta: People's Publishing House, 1994), p. 33.

8. 'sā maṅgalasnānabiśuddhagātrī gṛhītapatyudgamanīya bastrā/nirvtta-parjanyajalābhiṣekā prafullakāṣavasudeva reje' Kalidas, *Kumarasambha-vam [7/11]*. Jagadish Bhattacharya, in the first volume of his *Kabimanasi* (first Bharavi ed. January 1997, pp. 209–11) was the first to discuss the influence of this *sloka* on Rabindranath.

9. Ibid.

10. *Jibansmriti, Rabindra Rachanabali*, vol. X, Birth Anniversary edition, Government of West Bengal, p. 121.

11. Rabindranath's comment with reference to poem no. 23, *Balaka*, (composed Magh 20, 1321 [1915]), 'Afterword' to *Balaka*, p. 138.

Passionate Involvement:
Love and Politics in Satyajit Ray's *Ghare Baire*

SHOHINI GHOSH

S atyajit Ray wrote his first serious screenplay in 1948 and it was an adaptation of Rabindranath Tagore's *Ghare Baire*. Ray was commissioned to write a screenplay of the novel for a film that was to be directed by his friend Harisadhan Dasgupta. For various reasons the project never materialised. With *Pather Panchali* (The Song of the Little Road) in 1955, Ray started his illustrious career in films. In 1983, when Ray finally made *Ghare Baire* he said that he felt fortunate the film was never made in 1948 as the script that he had written then had been 'superficial, Hollywoodish and certainly not true to the spirit'.

Prior to *Ghare Baire*, Ray had made two feature-length films based on Tagore's fiction. These were *Teen Kanya* (Three Daughters, 1961) and *Charulata* (The Lonely Wife, 1964).[1] In 1961, Ray made a feature-length documentary on Tagore. *Charulata* is perhaps Ray's most acclaimed film and is often compared to *Ghare Baire*. Both films are based on Tagore stories and feature strong female protagonists. In both films, the female protagonists fall in love with men who are not their husbands. However, the two films are stylistically very different having been made at two very different phases in Ray's life and career. Unlike

*I am grateful to P.K. Datta for his deeply insightful comments on my preliminary drafts. I thank my niece Rukmini Bose for watching the film many times over with me. I dedicate this essay to my dear friend Tanika Sarkar whose writings continue to enrich my understanding of Bengal's history and literature.

Charulata, Ghare Baire is a dark and introspective film that is primarily shot indoors. *Ghare Baire* is also conventionally less 'cinematic' than *Charulata* in that it relies less on visuals and more on dialogue. Most of the physical action in *Ghare Baire* happens off-screen or in brief visual sequences. Consequently, the actors are required to express more through nuanced acting and minimal gestures. For this reason, the film uses a large number of close-ups and mid-shots and very rarely features full shots of its characters. The film begins and ends with fire burning against a black backdrop foregrounding the sombre tone of the narrative. Even the music composed by Ray is for the most part heavy and full of foreboding.

Historical Context and the Cinematic Text

Ghare Baire is set around 1905 when Lord Curzon divided the Bengal Presidency into eastern and Western halves as a consequence of the colonial policy of divide and rule. Curzon's policy evoked widespread protests and led to the swadeshi movement. During its early days, Rabindranath Tagore was an enthusiastic advocate of the swadeshi movement. Many of the songs that he composed during this time served to inspire and mobilise the people of Bengal. But as the movement spread, Tagore began to get increasingly disillusioned with it. He was distressed that the movement had begun to valorise violence and become vulnerable to communal impulses. The Hindu–Muslim riots between 1906 and 1907 had made some swadeshi activists self-critical and Tagore was one of them. The communal fallout, in the words of Nicholas Dirks, 'also brought home the contradictions of mass politics and the socioeconomic conditions of colonial India'.[2] The movement exposed the deep chasm between the Hindu elite that initiated the movement and the landless Muslim peasants who survived through the trade of imported goods. Ironically, the patronage of local goods was a luxury that only the rich could afford.

When a disillusioned Tagore began to retreat from the movement, many swadeshi advocates saw it as betrayal. The novel *Ghare Baire* emerged from Tagore's experiences during the swadeshi years. Written and published serially in 1915–16, *Ghare Baire* (translated as *The Home and the World* in 1919) remains a cautionary tale about the dangers of nationalism. The story revolves around Bimala who is caught between her love for her husband Nikhilesh and infatuation for his best friend Sandip. Set against the turbulence created by Lord Curzon's divisive policy and the swadeshi movement, Bimala's personal dilemma is inextricable from the choice that she has to make between opposed political and ideological impulses.

The Home and the World is structured like diary entries from the alternating points of view of the three protagonists. The novel has a total of twelve chapters, each comprising a protagonist's point of view or a combination of viewpoints. Through the various diary entries, Bimala's story appears nine times, Nikhilesh's story eight times and Sandip's only five. It is possible to read *The Home and the World* as primarily Bimala's story as the novel begins and ends with her point of view. Initially Ray had planned to structure the film sequentially around Bimala, Nikhilesh, Sandip and finally the filmmaker's point of view. The final film modifies this initial plan. The film begins with Bimala's point of view then moves to Sandip's point of view, briefly again to Bimala's point of view and then to Nikhilesh's. Finally, the filmmaker's point of view takes over the narrative. Stylistically, Tagore's novel makes for a more complex narrative as the same events are narrated and interpreted differently by the three protagonists. This overlapping narrative style is rejected in the film in favour of a more linear and chronological narrative.

In Ray's film Nikhilesh (played by Victor Bannerjee) is the liberal humanist landowner of Sukhsayor who, unlike the rest of the men in his family, has rejected a life of decadence and dissipation. Nikhilesh's wife Bimala (Swatilekha Chatterjee) is a woman with an independent mind. Lavished by her husband's affections, she is all set to become a 'memsahib' under the tutelage of her English instructor Miss Gilby (Jennifer Kendall). Her independence in her marital home stands in contrast to the life of Bouthan (Gopa Aich), Nikhilesh's widowed sister-in-law. Deeply influenced by Western education, Nikhilesh wants his wife Bimala to defy convention and step out of the inner quarters of the home into the world outside. Behind this egalitarian impulse lies Nikhilesh's desire that his wife should love him not out of compulsion but out of choice after having experienced the world around her. 'If she is "his" in the "home", he wants her to be "his" in the "world" too after she has experienced it.'[3] To this end, he introduces her to his best friend Sandip (Soumitra Chatterjee), a popular swadeshi leader. As Bimala and Sandip become lovers both the home and the world are thrown into crisis. Finally, all three characters are complicit in the cataclysmic consequences that overtake Sukhsayor.

As the film reaches its climax, Bimala and Nikhilesh are reconciled, but briefly. Riots break out in the village and Nikhilesh rides out to try and intervene. The next morning a quiet and sombre cortege wends its way towards the house. The camera pans to hold a distraught and dishevelled Bimala in close-up. In one of the most controversial sequences in the film, Ray uses a series of overlapping dissolves, to strip Bimala of her marital adornments and 'metamorphose' her into a widow. Dressed in the widow's traditional white, with her hair cropped short, Bimala begins to bear an uncanny resemblance to Bouthan. Ray's definitive statement about Nikhilesh's death is a departure from the conclusion of the novel. Tagore's Nikhilesh is seriously wounded but does not die. To this, I will return later.

Passionate Involvement

All cinematic adaptations are the interpretative retelling of not just the story but the narrative strategy itself. Cinematic adaptations of literature are not visual illustrations of the text. The adaptation of the text from one medium to another must be accompanied by a willingness to make an imaginative leap that allows, in the process, a certain transformation of the narrative itself. The worth of many a good cinematic adaptation has been diminished by a literary, often literal, expectation that the film should be 'faithful' to the novel. Ray's *Ghare Baire* too has been subject to scrutiny that has frequently decentred the cinematic impulse. Shormistha Panja's essay on *Ghare Baire* indicts the film for its lack of fidelity to the text and for the interpretative liberties taken. The efficacy of the film is thereby measured through Ray's directorial decisions to either stay with or stray from the novel. The following passage represents the essay's attitudinal thrust:

Significantly, Ponchu is completely omitted by Ray—an omission impossible to account for because Ray usually revels in these cameo roles. Instead, Ray adds a totally unnecessary scene of Nikhil going around on horseback assessing the Hindu–Muslim situation and then addressing the rural gentry of Sukhsayor. Bimala, Sondip and Nikhil change guise and become less nuanced. . . . In fact, the two rather forced kisses between Bimola and Sandip are not there in the novel: they are inserted by Ray artificially to suggest the passion, which Tagore so subtly evokes with a mere touch of the hand.[4]

For the purposes of this essay, I will deal with the characters and situations that Ray has selected and/or created, referring to the text only to underscore certain critical departures.

Ray's adaptation of Tagore's dense and elaborate novel is marked by a sense of great economy. Within meticulously crafted and ornate sets, Ray's deployment of characters, situations and spaces is austere. The script is Ray's invention and few dialogues are lifted entirely from the novel. The controlled and restrained performances of the actors rely on gestures, looks and measured movements as opposed to elaborate dialogue or broad actions. This results in a de-dramatisation of a potentially dramatic story thereby creating a dark and brooding atmosphere in which tragedy seems inevitable.

In the *Encyclopedia of Indian Cinema*, Rajadhyaksha and Willeman contend that in the film *Ghare Baire*, 'Ray played down the novel's political overtones in favour of a straight love triangle, enacted in a meticulously researched period setting.' I will argue that on the contrary, the personal and political stories are integrally linked and that the love story is inextricable from the larger political crisis. While Ray alters the style, treatment and structure of the novel he remains true to Tagore's political and philosophical concerns by maintaining the inextricability of the 'home' and the 'world', political imperatives and personal compulsions. This, to my mind, addresses the central philosophical concerns of the text.

The impossibility of separating the issue of personal and political choices is foregrounded early in the film. Anticipating Sandip's arrival in Sukhsayor, Nikhilesh describes him to Bimala as both an important swadeshi leader and someone who has a 'way with women'.[5] Till Bimala meets Sandip for the first time, she has nothing but reservations about him. 'I have no desire to meet a man,' she says, 'who through a hundred wiles, exploits you for money.' Nikhilesh condescendingly insists that it would be 'instructive' for Bimala to meet him, as Sandip is his complete opposite. To this, Bimala retorts, 'Who told you that I want someone who is your exact opposite?' As she bustles around the room doing her little chores, she adds 'I am happy in my seclusion—I have no desire to be like the great classical heroines.' In the very next sequence Bimala's voice-over says: 'I was completely unprepared for whatever happened next.' At this point, the audience almost expects the unfolding of an event involving Bimala's relationship with Sandip. Instead, the voice-over cuts to a sequence with Miss Gilby. A bandaged and traumatised Miss Gilby recounts how unruly students shouting swadeshi slogans assaulted her. This sequence marks the film's first explicit moment of discomfort with swadeshi politics.

Bimala first sets eyes on Sandip when he arrives to address a meeting in the quadrangle of Nikhilesh's house. Amidst chants of 'Bande Mataram' Sandip arrives sitting on the shoulders of his saffron-clad disciples. In his eloquent and passionate speech he condemns Curzon's policy of 'divide and rule' and pleads for the boycott of imported goods. Towering larger than life over a low-angled camera, he urges people to draw their inspiration from the mantra of 'Bande Mataram' and dedicate themselves to the service of the country. Without resorting to dramatic cuts, the camera keeps moving between the impassioned swadeshi leader and Bimala's enraptured face as she watches him from behind a bamboo screen. As he asks for an end to the oppression and exploitation of his people, the camera gradually moves into a close-up of a transfixed Bimala. In their bedroom that night she comments to Nikhilesh that Sandip is a good speaker and that whatever he said 'seems to make sense'. Nikhilesh patronisingly instructs her to 'tell him that'. She is preoccupied and thoughtful, not just about swadeshi politics, but also about what she should wear when she meets him.

Despite the energy and dynamism that characterises Sandip's first arrival, there are foreboding markers of future discontent within the *mise-en-scene*. Sandip's entry, literally on the shoulders of young activists, carries uncomfortable overtones of self-aggrandisement.[6] The saffron-coloured clothes of the activists and the centrality of 'Bande Mataram' as their rallying cry points to the Hinduisation of swadeshi politics and foreshadows its disastrous consequences. That Muslims are—understandably—unmoved by the slogan is revealed in a later sequence when Sandip addresses traders in the Sukhsayor marketplace.

Tragically, Bimala misreads these signs of future catastrophe. She is attracted to the saffron-clad boys shouting slogans of 'Bande Mataram' and to Sandip's powerful rhetoric. During their first meeting the next day, Sandip will praise Bimala's 'rare quality of women's intuition'. It is ironic that Sandip should praise Bimala's 'intuition' at a time when she is totally abandoned by it. Yet the strength of the sequence lies in its ability to straddle the ambivalence of desirability and discomfort. Ray provides enough evidence to point to the reasons for Bimala's attraction towards Sandip's personality and politics.

The next morning, Bimala, accompanied by Nikhilesh, crosses for the first time the threshold between the inner and outer quarters of their home. Ray underscores the significance of this 'cross-over' in what is perhaps the most lyrical sequence in the film. In poetic slow motion the doors of the *andarmahal* (inner quarters) gradually swing open as Nikhilesh and Bimala step out to start their 'journey' towards the outer quarters. Through a series of differently sized and angulated shots, we see Nikhilesh and Bimala cross the threshold and walk down the stained glass corridor. Bimala's red silk sari, Nikhilesh's richly textured shawl and the colours of the stained glass are shot in soft, diffused light creating a dream-like ambience. Using slow motion in combination with a variety of shot sizes and angles, Ray edits the shots on overlapping action thereby imposing a screen time that is much longer than the real time it takes to cross the corridor. The consequent elongation of time invests this simple action with iconic significance. Interestingly, such a formal device is never used again in the film. Not only is this a transformative event in Bimala's life, it is also a definitive one. The rites of passage are to effect irreversibly the lives of all the players in the story. Moreover, this is the last time that Bimala and Nikhilesh will walk through this corridor together. For the rest of the film both of them will negotiate this corridor on their own.

The space of the parlour is where Bimala has her limited encounters with the world. This is where she interacts with Miss Gilby, Sandip and the other two significant characters in the film, Mastermoshai (Manoj Mitra) and Amulya (Indrapramit Ray). Mastermoshai is Nikhilesh's old teacher and a sharp critic of Sandip's brand of 'destructive swadeshi'. Amulya is a young idealistic revolutionary who forms a deep bond with Bimala. In contrast to the bedroom where most of the Nikhilesh–Bimala interactions are shot, the parlour becomes the liminal space between the home and the world. As Bimala becomes increasingly intimate with Sandip, she begins to visit the parlour more frequently. In contrast, Nikhilesh begins to retreat into the inner quarters.

When Sandip meets Bimala for the first time in the parlour, he reacts by gaping at her ludicrously. He makes no attempt to hide his instant fascination for her. Throughout the sequence he makes sexual advances through political pleas. When Nikhilesh good-humouredly asks Sandip to stop praising Bimala lest the adulation go to her head, he says: 'I am shameless when it comes to winning people over to my side.' Sandip's attraction towards Bimala is an ambivalent blend of the political and the erotic. He tells Bimala that the thought of winning her support excites him because they have never had a woman on their side. 'Of course, I can't say just yet, whether we have her on our side,' he adds cautiously, 'but that I will be delighted if she were to decide to . . .' Sandip spares no effort at winning her to his side. He concludes his efforts with a stirring patriotic song. To Sandip's delight, Bimala is mesmerised by his performance. Nikhilesh, who has also enjoyed the 'admirable song', is quick to point out that his appreciation of the song has nothing to do with his views on swadeshi politics.

This sequence, like most other sequences in the film, is almost entirely invented by Ray and does not exist in the novel. It introduces an intertextual reference about Tagore's own experience with swadeshi politics. Tagore had written this immensely popular song ('Are you so strong as to break the bonds of destiny?') when he was a swadeshi enthusiast in the early days of the movement. The new swadeshi enthusiast Bimala is enthralled by the song. But like Tagore, Bimala's enthusiasm too will be short-lived and will eventually suffer disillusion.

Throughout the sequence, the interaction between Nikhilesh, Bimala and Sandip is marked by constant slips between personal and political choices. The carefully crafted dialogue in this sequence serves also to highlight the inconsistencies of the Hindu middle-class approach to swadeshi politics. The note is struck when Bimala asks Sandip how many spoons of sugar he would like in his tea. 'One of its *videshi* [imported] and two of its *swadeshi* [indigenous],' replies Sandip. Nikhilesh then insists that Sandip eat the sweets that have been served with the tea as Bimala has prepared them herself:

Sandip	:	Then I must have them [putting one in his mouth and settling down in a chair]. . . . I have not been able to get over my weakness for sweets.
Nikhilesh	:	I can see that you have not been able to get over your weakness for foreign cigarettes either.
Sandip	:	[Laughing] I shudder at the thought of local brands . . . have you seen the 'Spectacle' and 'Scales' brand cigarettes . . . Just looking at them repels me.
Bimala	:	Isn't it better to just give them up?
Sandip	:	'Smoking?'
Bimala	:	'Don't you have the willpower?'
Sandip	:	[Surprised, speechless, but also happy]: Okay, when you join our side I will give up smoking.

The personal and political are again inextricable. At the end of the meeting, Sandip leaves Bimala more than just a swadeshi pamphlet. She notices that his lit but unsmoked cigarette continues to turn to ash in the ashtray. Sandip has already begun to do her bidding.

At their second meeting, that is, their first meeting alone, erotic tension becomes integral to political articulations. Bimala arrives in the parlour after Sandip sends for her the next day with a note that reads: 'I hope the rule was not broken for a day.' While waiting for her, he discovers her hairclip on the sofa. Studying it carefully he puts it away in his pocket. When she enters the room and is about to sit on a sofa in front of him, he insists that she sit right next to him. He tells her that he has changed his travel plans and is now planning to work from Sukhsayor. 'I am telling you frankly,' he says, 'I want to stay close to you and work.' In a response that could be read as addressing both personal and political concerns, Bimala says, 'My husband will not take kindly to this.' Equally, ambiguously, Sandip replies, 'I know . . . But I am a very stubborn man.' Sandip, who by now has left his seat on the sofa, moves up close behind Bimala and says, 'May I tell you something?' Bimala is mildly startled. As he leans over and brings his face closer to hers, a confessional moment is anticipated. But instead of making a personal disclosure, he requests a political favour. He asks her to try and persuade Nikhilesh to impose swadeshi in Sukhsayor. At the end of the conversation, just as she is about to leave the room he calls her back. He holds up the hairclip. As she reaches out for it, he puts it back in his pocket with the comment that this is one foreign object that he would like to possess.

The two subsequent sequences between Bimala and Nikhilesh build simultaneously on erotic and political tension. While Nikhilesh has his dinner, Bimala informs him of Sandip's decision to stay back in Sukhsayor and carry out his campaign. Nikhilesh argues that he has no moral right to impose swadeshi in the market in his zamindari as the market belonged not to him but those who traded for a living there. Bimala wonders whether it is possible to practise swadeshi without hurting the interests of the poor. Had that been possible, Nikhilesh tells her, then he would have joined the swadeshi activists. In the following sequence, they continue their conversation in a darkly lit balcony. In a somewhat patronising tone, Nikhilesh asks whether Bimala was pleading Sandip's case. 'It seems to me,' says Nikhil, 'that you are managing the home while he manages the world outside.' Despite his attempts to remain non-judgemental, he snidely asks whether the two of them were going to hold daily meetings, since they had 'teamed up in right earnest to work for the country.' An angry Bimala tells him that he had no business to first drag her out of seclusion and then make nasty insinuations. His attempt to retract does not convince Bimala. It is evident that none of the three protagonists believes that Sandip's work in Sukhsayor is only political in nature.

As the film unfolds, it becomes increasingly evident that Sandip's swadeshi has little to do with lived experience. Swadeshi for Sandip is really an abstract mode of protest symbolised through public spectacles of mass burning and chants of 'Bande Mataram'. Similarly, his worship of the country as 'mother' and 'nurturing woman' is also an abstraction. Bimala herself is deeply attracted to this metonymic connection between herself and the country. In the novel, Bimala writes in her diary, 'I was no longer the lady of the Rajah's house, but the sole representative of Bengal's womanhood. And he was the champion of Bengal. As the sky had shed its light over him, so he must receive the consecration of a woman's benediction.'[7] Nikhilesh rightly tells Bimala that 'I believe that what [the advocates of swadeshi] care for is an abstract image of the country.' In a letter to an English friend in 1921, Tagore wrote: '. . . the anarchy of emptiness never tempts me, even when it is resorted to as a temporary measure. I am frightened at an abstraction, which is ready to ignore living reality.' In the novel, Sandip plays on the metonymy of woman and nation so skilfully that Bimala often confuses the distinction. After a burst of oratory from Sandip, she writes: 'It was not clear to whom Sandip Babu addressed his last appeal. It might have been She whom he worshipped with his 'Bande Mataram'. It might have been the womanhood of his country. Or it might have been its representative, the woman before him' (p. 34).

The cinematic Bimala is inspired by Sandip's dual address but is not subsumed by it. As Cooper notes, Sandip endows her with the 'dual personification' of the powerful 'mother' who preserves and nurtures and the sexual Queen Bee who attracts and entices. Ray's Bimala is attracted to Sandip not only because he sees in her the motherland, but also because he acknowledges her as an individual (Cooper, pp. 90–6). Ray provides enough reason for Bimala to be attracted to Sandip. Nikhilesh is devoted to Bimala but he does not treat her like an equal. In one of the early sequences in the film, Nikhilesh walks into one of Bimala's music lessons with Miss Gilby. Addressing her in English, he asks: 'What did you learn today, Bimala?' and 'Bimala, have you learnt how to pour tea?' Bimala makes no secret of her displeasure and retorts in Bengali, 'What business did you have to come here?' Nikhilesh treats his wife like a ward who needs to be educated, enlightened, dressed and decorated. In one scene, Bimala refers to him as 'Mr Schoolmaster' while Bouthan half-enviously remarks, 'I thought only women played with dolls. I didn't know that even men indulged in this pastime.'

Nikhilesh seems to imagine that Bimala's agency must stem from his initiatives. Therefore, he is taken aback to learn that Bimala has read all about swadeshi in the newspapers. Unlike Sandip who asks her what she *thinks* about swadeshi, Nikhilesh asks her what she *knows* about swadeshi. Sandip treats her not just as an ally but an inspiration. He accurately observes, 'I can see that you have conducted a social revolution all by yourself. . . . You may be Nikhilesh's wife but, you are by no means merely his shadow.' Nikhilesh imagines that by liberating his wife from seclusion he will be able to give her freedom; but Bimala attains true freedom when she is able to make her own choices. Choosing to love a man who is not her husband is her first entirely autonomous decision. Early in the film there is a hint that Bimala is not shackled by the moralities of monogamy. Had she the option of choosing her own husband, says Bimala light-heartedly even before she has met Sandip, she may not have chosen Nikhilesh. In another comment that becomes ironic in retrospect, she tells him, 'I am jealous of Draupadi with all her five husbands.' Coming to terms with this, Nikhilesh confesses in the novel that in trying to find the truth of Bimala's personality he had forgotten he would have to renounce all claims based on conventional morality. Despite his best intention Nikhilesh is not able to treat his wife as an equal.

Unlike Tagore's protagonist, Ray's Bimala does not follow the dictates of swadeshi politics blindly. In the book Nikhilesh writes, 'Bimala has no patience for patience. She loves to find in men the turbulent, the angry, and the unjust. Her respect must have its element of fear. . . . I know Bimala finds it difficult to respect me for this, taking my scruples for feebleness—and she's quite angry with me for not running amuck crying "Bande Mataram"' (p. 42). Tagore's Bimala is sympathetic to the swadeshi movement even before Sandip enters her life. When Miss Gilby is attacked by swadeshi activists Bimala does not share her husband's distress. When Nikhilesh turns Noren, the boy who attacked Miss Gilby, out of the house, Bimala writes: 'There was not a single soul, that day, who could forgive my husband for that act—not even I . . . I had often become anxious at my husband's doing, but never before had I been so ashamed; yet now I had to blush for him . . . I could not but look upon it as a sign of cowardice in my husband' (p. 28). In the film, however, Bimala has information about swadeshi but does not feel committed to its politics. When Miss Gilby is attacked, she sits holding the distraught woman's hand. The voice-over observes that public fury with the British made them harm even harmless people like Miss Gilby.

Bimala's swadeshi politics is neither like Sandip's nor oppositional like Nikhilesh's. In the film, her alter ego is Amulya, the young and idealistic revolutionary. In their final confrontation, Nikhilesh tells Sandip that despite his reservations about the movement there were many swadeshi leaders whom he deeply respected but he had no respect for leaders whose rhetoric did not match their actions. It is evident that both Tagore and Ray respect Amulya because his commitment to politics transcends personal gains. Amulya has no self-interest, nor does his conscience ever abandon him. Moreover, he has the power and insight to challenge opportunism and populism. When Sandip plots to coerce the traders into boycotting foreign goods, Amulya advocates picketing rather than force. Unlike Sandip, Amulya is not ready to flee the moment communal riots break out in Sukhsayor. He makes amends for Sandip's exploitation of Bimala by returning to her both her money and her jewels. Through Bimala's turbulent rites of passage between the home and the world, it is Amulya who becomes her ally. Amulya dies at the end of Tagore's novel but he survives in the film. Having refused to flee with Sandip he stays back to face the consequences of his actions. Like Amulya, Bimala too believes in the politics of persuasion and not of coercion. Somewhat naively she asks Nikhilesh whether it is possible to practise swadeshi without hurting the poor. Later, she tells Sandip. 'I firmly believe that you will not hurt the poor and that you will do only as much is possible through dialogue and negotiation.' Bimala genuinely believes this to be Sandip's politics till she learns better at the end of the film. Sandip knows of Bimala's' aversion to coercion and violence. He is careful not to reveal his strategies to her even though he is open about them with Nikhilesh. Sandip knows too well that, unlike her husband, Bimala would not hesitate to act on her displeasure.

The film moves towards its climax with crises breaking out both within the home and in the 'world' outside. Bimala's sexual involvement with Sandip, along with the financial and moral support that she provides him makes her an accomplice in Sukhsayor's devastation. Her political complicity is integrally bound to her sexual involvement with him. Ray builds this tension in two critical sequences in the film.

Bimala and Sandip's third meeting follows his failure to convince the traders of Sukhsayor to adopt swadeshi. The sequence in which Sandip addresses the traders in the market stands in total contrast to the speech that he made at Nikhilesh's quadrangle where he spoke to an audience that was primarily Hindu, middle class and converted. Ray shoots this sequence through several long shots and intercuts Sandip's speech with reaction shots of resistant and even hostile traders. The captivated audience of the first speech is replaced by traders who continue with their daily work despite Sandip's attempt at fiery oratory. Amulya and a few other saffron-clad boys ineffectually ask people to relinquish foreign goods. As he watches the debacle from his podium, Sandip's voice-over states: 'It is clear that persuasion won't work in Nikhilesh's area. We have to use other means. Any compromise would cripple the movement.' A series of vignettes follow. Traders are attacked; their goods forcibly confiscated and set on fire. Sandip conspires with the manager of Nikhilesh's estate so that the traders' boats are sunk before the goods can even reach the market. Therefore when Sandip meets Bimala next he has been revealed to the audience as not only a failed leader but also a degenerate one.

A brief sequence prior to the meeting shows Bimala ruminating on the futility of not having met Sandip the previous day. Staying away from him did not prevent her from thinking about him. As Bimala sits on the bed embroidering, the camera gradually moves into a close-up of the pamphlet titled 'Our Struggle' lying among her sewing accessories. At this point, Sandip summons Bimala. The subsequent meeting is critical for several reasons.

As always, the two meet in the brightly lit parlour that stands in contrast to the dank, dark makeshift swadeshi 'office' from which Sandip operates. Bimala, resplendent in a black-bordered red sari, is clearly happy to meet Sandip again. With every meeting, she becomes less inhibited and more forthright. The scene begins with Sandip introducing Bimala to Amulya, a young swadeshi activist who comes to seek her blessings having heard that she is their supporter. Bimala is impressed with Amulya's fearless devotion to the cause. Perhaps sensing Bimala's admiration for Amulya, Sandip curtly asks him to leave. Sandip, whose rhetoric and charisma have suffered a blow at Sukhsayor, is feeling unsure and somewhat defeated. In a moment of rare honesty, he admits that his pride as a leader has suffered a blow. 'I worry, Queen Bee,' says Sandip thoughtfully. 'What if this leader disappoints you?' Unlike Sandip who seems riddled with doubts, Bimala is confident and self-possessed. The *mise-en-scene* underscores their contrasting emotional states by having him sit immobile while she walks about humming a song and playfully handling various objects around the room. There is a reversal of roles in this meeting. It is Bimala who is now active and performative while Sandip sits captivated and transfixed. The camera frequently frames the protagonists through large mirrors, making the room seem even larger than it is. Bimala will eventually discover that the 'world' that Sandip presents her is delusional. It is not a window through which she can see the 'world' for herself.

Here, for the first time, Bimala openly states her opposition to her husband's politics and urges Sandip to continue with his campaign in Sukhsayor. It is evident that she mistakenly attributes her husband's political stance to his 'placid' temperament. Bimala seems to attribute Nikhilesh's 'placidity' to a lack of male aggression. Conversely, she mistakes Sandip's aggressive posturing with virile political commitment. In a moment of rare vulnerability, Sandip confess that he is not fearless like his younger colleagues about confronting death and danger. This fleeting comment becomes a precursor of thing to come.

The emotional tenor of the sequence shifts when Sandip refuses to disclose his new political strategies since persuasion has failed in Sukhsayor. Bimala feels insulted by Sandip's inability to confide in her. In rage and humiliation, she attempts to leave the room. Sandip rushes to block her path and clasps her hands in his. 'Is politics, my work, the only thing we must talk about? Is there nothing else between us?' he asks still holding her hand. During this moment of high passion, Bimala and Sandip exchange promises: she to see him that evening and at least once every day and he to take money from her when the need arises. Bimala's growing vulnerability is concurrent with Sandip's rapid recovery of self-confidence. This emotionally charged sequence ends with a telling shot. The camera holds Sandip in close-up as he watches her leave and then slowly turns towards the audience with a smile. For the first time in the sequence, he looks triumphant. His political failure in Sukhsayor has been compensated for.

During their next meeting Bimala's involvement with Sandip and his politics becomes complete and consequently irreversible. Like a musical composition, this meeting is preceded by the same pattern of sequences as the last. A brief sequence of swadeshi activists setting fire to crops to the chant of 'Bande Mataram' is followed by yet another meeting between Sandip and the estate manager. Sandip is informed that he will have to procure more money for bribes and compensations. The meeting ends with the manager advising Sandip to wind up and leave Sukhsayor. 'You may be a leader,' he says, 'but not a very popular one. If you get caught, they are unlikely to treat you like a pampered son-in-law.'

The next morning Sandip and Bimala meet again. The sequence opens with a high-spirited Sandip, playing the piano and singing another popular swadeshi song: 'March on sons of India/The Motherland calls/ March fearlessly and with manly pride/To serve the nation's cause.'[8] The song extols the virtues of virile male aggression that Bimala feels is integral to revolutionary politics. Half-jokingly, she remarks that he should have been a singer and not a revolutionary. Sandip confesses he considered being an actor for the special thrill of being able to captivate many hearts at the same time. 'But of course,' he adds, 'that does not compare with the thrill of having won a woman's heart.' Bimala, who has been moving around the room, picks up his packet of Pompadour cigarettes and looks at the picture of a woman in a flouncy dress printed on the box. 'I believe you have captivated many women's hearts,' she says, 'both foreign and Indian.' Dismissing his past affairs as 'youthful indiscretions' he sings her a flirtatious ditty about the enigmatic nature of women. For the first time, their conversation abandons the political in favour of the overtly personal.

Bimala [in response to the ditty]: Is that the reason why you never married?
Sandip : I did not marry because I did not find the woman after my heart.
Bimala : I waited for a long time for you last night. You didn't come.
Sandip : I got delayed with my work and returned very late.
Bimala : What work?
Sandip : What other work? Swadeshi work. . . . Actually, my work here is
          coming to an end . . . It is important for our campaign to move on.
Bimala : [shocked] You are leaving? . . . What if Queen Bee does not let you
          go?
Sandip : Then no one will be happier than I . . . but Bee, I am not thinking of
          leaving just yet.
Bimala : [breaking down] If I get you the money, you won't go, will you? I
          come out to meet you despite so much criticism . . . and you . . .

Bimala's emotional outburst and Sandip's attempts to console her result in their first kiss. During this meeting, Sandip takes up Bimala's offer and asks her for five thousand rupees.

  Bimala's insistence that Sandip should take money from her deserves some attention. In all their meetings alone, it is Bimala who initiates the talk around giving Sandip money. Bimala possibly feels that by helping to fund the movement she would be making a tangible and material contribution to the struggle. It is also possible, however, that she *intuitively* realises that she alone is not enough to hold Sandip back in Sukhsayor. She begins to suspect that, in fact, he needs more than just love and politics to keep him back. Yet Bimala must be able to justify this act to herself in the name of swadeshi. In a brief but eloquent sequence, Bimala holds a candle before the family safe and quietly whispers 'Bande Mataram'. It is important to note that between her promise and its delivery, her emotions undergo a perceptible shift. Late at night, when she enters the parlour to meet a waiting Sandip, she is subtly changed. This time, she meets his kiss with less ardour. Her movements are studied and cautious.

Bimala's disillusion with Sandip happens through a succession of revelatory moments. When she hands the money over to Sandip, her intuition receives confirmation. She studies him carefully as he exults at the touch of gold: this is her first revelatory moment. Then the film moves swiftly towards its climax as several events converge. Communal riots break out in Sukhsayor. Nikhilesh finally confronts Sandip asking him to leave and another critical revelation results as Bimala learns the truth about Sandip's political activities. Amulya delivers the final confirmation: Sandip was a comfort-loving leader who spent lavishly on himself; as a result he had extracted more money from Bimala than was actually needed. Significantly, Bimala's last meeting alone with Sandip occurs in the same stained-glass corridor through which she had first come to meet him. As Sandip pleads with her to relent, she stands with her back to him. 'The note of discord has been struck,' she tells him. 'My husband used to say that the less one knows you the better one likes you. I think I've got to know you a bit too well.' The camera watches as she crosses the corridor and walks into the inner quarters.

All three protagonists meet for the last time when Sandip walks into their bedroom before fleeing Sukhsayor. This meeting confirms for Bimala everything that she has recently learnt about him. 'This is the age of breaking rules,' he says. 'Your wife came out of seclusion and I have invaded the privacy of your bedroom.' His brazen intrusion into the inner quarters becomes a visual equivalent of his transgressions into Nikhilesh's household. Having failed to impose swadeshi in Sukhsayor and lost Bimala, he has no reason to either pretend or dissemble. 'I am concerned only with action and not the result,' he declares un-apologetically. 'It is Ravana, not Ram who has always been my hero. The straight path is not for me. . . . I am making the proverbial escape . . . after all, I must survive in order to continue with my work.' Having entered their most private space, Sandip is unlikely to leave without revealing the extent of his intimacy with Bimala. He takes out Bimala's hairclip and holds it out for them to see. 'I would like to keep this one item as a memento.'

The events leave Bimala, Nikhilesh and Amulya irrevocably transformed. Sandip is the only character who remains unchanged. Throughout the film, Sandip is shown to inhabit different spaces like the quadrangle, the parlour, the marketplace, the swadeshi hideout and finally Bimala and Nikhilesh's inner quarters. In each space and with each character he appears different. With Bimala he is the committed activist-leader and ardent lover, with Nikhilesh he is obstinate and egregious, with Mastermoshai he is errant and irreverent, with Amulya he is pragmatic and with the estate manager he is shrewd and unscrupulous. While Bimala, Nikhilesh and Amulya evolve with the unfolding events, their self-representation in relation to others or themselves is never in conflict. Sandip stands out by contrast. Impelled and driven by a schizophrenic impulse, he allows different people and spaces to glimpse only fragments of his personality. It is only in the very last sequence that he allows all the fragments of his fractured personality to be reconciled. In the confessional space of the inner quarters Sandip sheds his disguises. To Bimala he confirms the truth about his ruthless politics and to Nikhilesh he admits his sexual transgression. Before making his exit from Sukhsayor and consequently the film, Sandip unmasks himself and erases all contradictions between his actions and rhetoric. The diverse fragments finally add up to create an individual driven by monomaniacal narcissism and greed.

The gap between the lofty rhetoric of swadeshi and its practise is effectively underscored by Ray's imaginative use of the salutation 'Bande Mataram'. At various moments in the film, different characters utter the salutation and invest it with different meanings. The salutation first appears when, accompanied by the musical theme of the film, credits roll out over visuals of burning fire. As the opening credits come to an end, the title music merges with chants of 'Bande Mataram'. We next hear the words when Nikhilesh, in their bedroom, tests Bimala's knowledge about swadeshi. She feels the intoxicating effect of the words for the first time when Sandip ends his speech with the salutation and the crowd joins him. For Bimala, Sandip seems to invest the salutation with a magical quality. He urges her to feel the thrill and excitement of simply uttering the phrase. He tells Bimala that the whole country had woken up to the call and the only person who refused to be stirred by it was her husband. Nikhilesh replies that he finds it hard to be inspired by 'artificial stimulants'. Later in the film, Mastermoshai also refers to 'Bande Mataram' as a 'delusional spell'. As the film progresses, a collectively chanted 'Bande Mataram' accompanies shots of Sukhsayor being set on fire by swadeshi activists. When Bimala stands poised over the family locker to steal money for Sandip, she utters 'Bande Mataram'. In the end, when a disillusioned Amulya parts ways with Sandip they bid farewell with 'Bande Mataram'. 'Hail Motherland' sounds deeply ironic in the context of communal riots and Sandip's opportunistic flight from the scene. As the salutation is exchanged, Sandip is unable to meet Amulya's gaze. Finally, in the last sequence, when Sandip takes leave in the bedroom with 'Bande Mataram' no one reciprocates. Silence greets the salutation as the horrors unleashed by its intoxicating power break over Sukhsayor. Used indiscriminately by the cynical and the deluded, this inspirational battle-cry is reduced to an empty and hollow slogan.

In a departure from Tagore's more ambiguous ending, where Nikhilesh is severely wounded but not dead, Ray depicts Nikhilesh's death through the now controversial series of dissolves whereby Bimala transforms into a widow, a mirror-image of Bouthan. In an essay on women characters in the films of Satyajit Ray, Chidananda Dasgupta writes that while *Ghare Baire* revolves around a woman, it is not a woman-oriented film.[9] On the contrary, Bimala is punished for 'adultery' and has to face widowhood. Shormistha Panja makes the same point when she writes: 'Ray, in fact, punishes Bimola by killing Nikhil off in the Hindu–Muslim riot, and in the last frame, chopping off a frozen Bimola's hair and dressing her in widow's whites.'[10] The writers therefore suggest that by rejecting Tagore's ambiguous ending in favour of a more definitive one, Ray leaves Bimala with nothing more than suffering in the end.

If Bimala were punished for her extramarital relationship with Sandip then her widowhood would indeed be problematic. However, such a reading seems inconsistent with Ray's treatment of the Sandip–Bimala relationship in the film. As I have argued above, the film provides good reason for Bimala to fall in love with Sandip. Moreover, the complex visual field of the *mise-en-scene* underscores Ray's moral and philosophical concerns in the film. The sequence in which Bimala and Sandip kiss for the first time bears testimony to this. The sequence begins with Sandip singing Jyotirindranath Tagore's patriotic song to a smiling Bimala. Daylight washes the interiors of the parlour while the piano and song lends music and colour to the sequence. The *mise-en-scene* is rich with brightness, colour and heady emotions. The relationship is framed as passionate, not problematic.

The climactic sequences, foretelling the impending ruin of Sukhsayor, stand in complete contrast. The *mise-en-scene* becomes heavy and foreboding. Dull pools of light from the night lamps break the shadowy interiors of the house. The preponderance of heavy curtains and ornate furniture creates a sense of psychological confinement. As Mastermoshai looks for a phial of sleeping pills in Nikhilesh's library, melancholia hangs in the air. In this dark atmosphere, Bimala steals money from the family locker. The act is never shown, only suggested. She holds a candle and stands in front of the locker. The sequence ends with her softly chanting 'Bande Mataram'. When she enters the parlour she is wrapped in a heavy shawl that camouflages the stolen gold. Sandip, also covered in a shawl, reaches out to kiss her as she arrives. Her response lacks passion. Unlike the earlier sequences, her movements are reluctant and cautious. As a stray gunshot ruptures the deathly silence outside, we are prepared for a night of revelations leading to inevitable destruction. Impelled by political disclosures in this claustrophobic visual topography, Bimala rejects Sandip. Ray's indictment of Sandip's political actions is underscored not just by Bimala's rejection and Nikhilesh's moral victory but also through a complex layering of visual and aural information. The film's moral imperative is woven into the texture of the narrative.

Ray's pessimistic and unambiguous conclusion expressed through Bimala's widowhood opens itself up for another, and to my mind more plausible, reading. It is possible that having witnessed communal atrocities before and after partition, Ray is even less optimistic than Tagore about the consequences of aggressive nationalism, particularly Hindu nationalism. Between *Pather Panchali* and *Ghare Baire*, Ray also witnessed the atrocities perpetrated during the tyrannical regime of Indira Gandhi's Emergency when civil and democratic rights were ruthlessly violated in the name of 'national interest'. Ray's post-partition and post-Emergency adaptation not only reflects greater pessimism about the rhetoric of nationalism but also proves to be prophetic. In the late-1980s and 1990s, India would witness the rise of the Hindu Right whose communalist discourse would be concealed by the rhetoric of nationalism and patriotic duty.

Consequently, Ray's film is a more contemporary interpretation of Tagore's story. In her essay on Godard's *Le Mepris*, Marsha Kinder writes that every adaptation 'must appeal to a contemporary audience in a different time–space continuum from that of its original'. In this sense it 'explores the relationship between two time periods and cultures, implying that a work accumulates a variety of meanings through the ages and that no adaptation can escape the particular subjective and cultural biases of the artist'.[11] I have argued throughout the essay that Bimala's love for Sandip is inextricable from her investment in swadeshi politics. Similarly, Nikhilesh's sense of loss is both personal and political. Bimala's sexual attraction for Sandip makes Nikhilesh deeply unhappy. However, his sense of *moral* outrage emerges, not from the fact of Bimala and Sandip's relationship but from the unethical political choices that they make.

The moral universe of Tagore and Ray transcends the home and encompasses the world. Bimala's widowhood, therefore, is not a punishment for personal transgressions but a consequence of the destructiveness inherent in the politics of revolutionary terrorism. Still, what could be legitimately seen to be problematic is that Ray should have focused on Bimala's widowhood, instead of Nikhilesh's death, to highlight the destructiveness of swadeshi politics.

Closures and New Openings

The physical spaces of the 'home' and the 'world' are never entirely distinct in *Ghare Baire*. The compulsions of home constantly shape and inflect the politics of the world. Visually, there is very little of the outside world in Ray's film. Most of the outdoor sequences are shot around Sandip. Nikhilesh seldom ventures outdoors and Bimala appears outdoors in only one shot in the beginning where she is sailing in a houseboat with her husband. Yet, the home is 'infiltrated' with the outside world. Here, the world is not just the space outside of the home but the country in relation to the world. In one of the initial sequences,

Nikhilesh identifies every bit of clothing and cosmetic that Bimala possesses as imports from abroad. Bimala is surprised to learn just how much of the seemingly 'swadeshi' materials in the home are actually from countries abroad. Even Bouthan, who as a widow is deprived of all material indulgences, amuses herself by listening to her 'music machine'—the gramophone player. The homes of the Hindu rich continue to be replete with foreign materials even as they are publicly renounced through spectacles of mass burnings.

Nikhilesh articulates Tagore's own politics around swadeshi. Like Nikhilesh, Tagore had made several attempts at setting up swadeshi projects. Also, like Nikhilesh, his swadeshi ventures led only to financial loss. As Ashis Nandy writes, Tagore's politics made a distinction between anti-imperialism and nationalism.[12] This is a distinction that Ray too makes in the film. Like Tagore, Nikhilesh embodies the idea of '*Bharatchinta*' or '*Swadeshichinta*', which literally means 'thinking about or being concerned about one's country'. Nandy points out that both terms convey the idea of patriotism without nationalism and that a conscious effort was made by some Indians to develop a *Bharatchinta* that would 'project a self-definition transcending the geographical barriers in India'. Like Tagore, Nikhil practises anti-imperialistic politics but rejects the idea of nationalism. He can therefore never be part of a campaign that indiscriminately targets people like Miss Gilby. Tagore himself articulated this reservation in a lecture in 1908 when he wrote, 'Some of us are reported to be of the opinion that it is mass animosity against the British that will unify India . . . So this anti-British animus, they say must be our chief weapon . . . If that is true, then once the cause of the animosity is gone, in other words, when the British leave the country, that artificial bond of unity will snap in a moment. Where then, shall we find a second target for animosity? We shall not need to travel far. We shall find it here, in our country, where we shall mangle each other in mutual antagonism, and thirst for each other's blood.'[13]

Ray's film reinforces this presciently accurate observation. His ironic use of Bankim's 'Bande Mataram' not only indicates the futility of aggressive nationalism but also foreshadows the rise of the Hindu Right in contemporary India. Tanika Sarkar points out that this 'potent patriotic slogan' has functioned as a rallying cry for Hindus mobilising against Muslims; for the Sangh Parivar, 'Bande Mataram' is the authentic

national anthem and not Tagore's 'Jana gana mana.'[14] Therefore it is
only fitting that Nikhilesh should be destroyed by the communal mad-
ness invoked by the advocates of 'Bande Mataram'.

Before I conclude my essay I would like to move away from the
intended politics of the film and digress briefly into the fluid and complex domain of identity and processes of spectatorial identification. To
this end, I would like to return briefly to Chidananda Dasgupta's contention that despite being a woman-centred film, *Ghare Baire* fails to
be a woman-oriented film because its central concern remains Nikhilesh's
idealistic pursuit. I will venture to suggest that Nikhilesh's idealistic
pursuit could well be the desiring subject of at least some women in
the audiences. In the context of long-standing cinematic conventions
around gender roles, *Ghare Baire* offers an interesting reversal. Here, it
is Nikhilesh who occupies the diagetic space of the tragic heroine and
not Bimala. He suffers the consequences of 'non-masculinity' and passivity, traits that are normatively associated with women. Time and
again, his 'emasculation' is invoked by Bimala who tells Sandip: '[My
husband] is much too placid. I don't think it is useful for the country to
be so placid.' As a rare male counterpart to the quintessential suffering
wife, Nikhilesh watches helplessly as his wife falls in love with another
man. Acquiescing to destiny, Nikhilesh uncomplainingly endures the
torment of being rejected and waits patiently for his wife to return. In
one brief but significant sequence, he climbs up the stairs to retire for
the night and sees Bimala looking out of the window, waiting for Sandip
to return. He is tortured by the carelessly spilt *sindoor* on Bimala's
dressing table. He feels no loss of 'manly pride' in either his suffering or
his vulnerability and feels no shame or hesitation in discussing his predicament with Bouthan. Unlike Sandip, whose virile masculinity needs
constant nurturing, Nikhil's strength lies in being able to confront his
own fragility in the face of crisis. In the section in the film that begins
with his point of view, he says: 'I believed I had the strength to bear
whatever misfortune had in store for me. I would call up visions of
suffering and steel myself against them. Visions of poverty, imprison-
ment, dishonour, death and even Bimala's death. But one thing I could
never imagine happening. Now I keep asking myself again and again,
have I the strength to bear this?' Most interestingly, while Bimala occupies the parlour, Nikhilesh retreats more and more into the melancholic

interiors of the andarmahal. His face, ravaged by emotional exhaustion and sleeplessness, begins to embody the ruin and devastation overtaking Sukhsayor.

When Bimala finally returns to him, Nikhilesh gently asks, 'You have come back to me, Bimala, haven't you?' His predicament is doubly tragic because he wins his wife only to lose his life. Like the conventional suffering cinematic female protagonist, Nikhilesh's victory is only a moral one and transcends his material existence. The filmmaker celebrates Nikhilesh's moral victory by beginning the film with the end of the story. Against a backdrop of burning fire, Bimala says. 'I have passed through fire. Whatever could burn has been consumed. Whatever remains, cannot perish. I dedicate it all to him who had accepted my failings at the depths of his stricken heart.'

Endnotes

1. *Teen Kanya* is a feature-length triptych of three Tagore stories, *Monihara, Postmaster* and *Samapti. Monihara* is part horror film and part psychological thriller about an avaricious woman. *Postmaster* is a part tragic story about the relationship between a little girl and a village postmaster. *Samapti* is a light-hearted story about a tomboy's rites of passage into womanhood.

2. Nicholas B. Dirks, '*The Home and the World*: The Invention of Modernity in Colonial India', *Revisioning History: Film and the Construction and the New Past*, ed. Robert. A. Rosenstone (Princeton: Princeton University Press, 1995).

3. Darius Cooper, *The Cinema of Satyajit Ray: Between Tradition and Modernity* (Cambridge: Cambridge University Press, 2000).

4. See '"The Elusive Mystery and Fluidity of Life" and what Satyajit Ray Does with it: Ray's Sandipization of Tagore's *Ghore Baire*', in *Many Indias, Many Literatures: New Critical Essays*, ed. Shormistha Panja (Delhi: World View Literary Criticism, 1999) is a good example, pp. 112–13.

5. I have cited the English subtitles of the film, unless stated otherwise.

6. In an interview with *Sananda* (5 May 1988) on her role as Bimala, Swatilekha Chatterjee observes that Bimala's inexperience and lack of exposure to the world prevents her from recognising the scoundrel in Sandip. 'I have seen much of men's villainy,' she says, 'therefore if I had seen a man arrive on the shoulders of others to deliver a speech, I would immediately have been able to make an assessment about him.'

7. Rabindranath Tagore, *The Home and the World*, trans. Surendranath Tagore (London, 1919, rpt. Delhi: Penguin Books, 1985), p. 31. All further references are to this edition.

8. In the film, the song has been translated as 'Onward Sons of India/The Motherland Calls/The Strong, the Brave, the Proud/To Serve the Nation's Cause.' I see this as an inaccurate translation and have therefore translated the words myself in order to highlight its emphasis on 'manly pride'.

9. Chidananda Dasgupta, 'Satyajiter Chobitey Naari', *Sananda* (Anandabazar Publications), 5 May 1988 (pp. 13–17).

10. See *Many Indias, Many Literatures*, p. 114.

11. S. Andrew Horton and Joan Magretta, *Modern European Filmmakers and the Art of Adaptation* (New York: Fredrick Unger Publishing Company, 1981), pp. 110–14.

12. Ashis Nandy, *The Illegitimacy of Nationalism* (Delhi: Oxford University Press, 1994).

13. This excerpt is from a lecture that Rabindranath Tagore delivered on 25 May 1908 entitled '*Path o Patheya*' [Ends and Means]. *Rabindra Rachanabali*, vol. 10, p. 447.

14. Tanika Sarkar, 'Imagining Hindu Rashtra: The Hindu and the Muslim in Bankim Chandra's Writings', *Making India Hindu: Religion, Community and the Politics of Democracy in India*, ed. David Ludden (Delhi: Oxford University Press, 1996).

Homeboys: Nationalism, Colonialism, and Gender in *The Home and the World* *

MICHAEL SPRINKER

There is only one history—the history of man.

Rabindranath Tagore

Like the overwhelming majority of subcontinental authors who have written in one or more of its indigenous languages— even those whose work has been translated into English (Tagore's has been generally available since the 1910s)—Rabindranath has signally failed to achieve the same notoriety as more recent Indian and Pakistani authors who write primarily in English.[1] Among his major writings, if we except the selection in *The Tagore Reader*, only *The Home and the World* remains in print in an inexpensive paperback edition here in the United States or in Britain, and that only sporadically. This contrasts with the general circulation of texts by Salman Rushdie, Anita Desai, Bharati Mukherjee, V.S. Naipaul, Vikram Seth, or Ruth Prawer Jhabvala (the latter not of Indian descent, but since the publication of *Heat and Dust*, one of the 'voices' most prominently licensed in the West to speak authoritatively about India and Indians). Although earlier in the twentieth century Rabindranath was much celebrated around the

*This essay has been somewhat abridged with the help of Aijaz Ahmed for this volume. The original version appeared in *Reading the Shape of the World: Towards an International Cultural Studies*, eds Henry Schwartz and Richard Dienst. *Politics and Culture 4*, 1996.

world, his writings, having once migrated from their homeland, in recent years have been returned there stamped 'unclaimed'.

This is not the place to recount the causes for the decline in Tagore's Western fame, which would require telling a complex story about the rise and fall of the Indian subcontinent as a focus of attention for the Anglophone world, the fortunes of the English language on the sub-continent itself, and the migration of people and texts to the imperial metropole and their uneven assimilation into the dominant cultures in the United States, Canada and Britain. It would appear that history has passed Rabindranath by, that his universal humanism has been more or less swamped in the tidal wave of post-colonial nationalism, while his continuing attachment to the localised subjects of Bengali culture and society strikes Western readers, I imagine, as merely quaint.[2] Rabindranath's novels have particularly suffered in their Western reception for being suffused in the lifeworld of Indian civilisation while not appearing sufficiently exotic to Westerners, who are more inclined to want 'Eastern mysticism' from such figures—and of course they have managed to extract that in abundance, as even a cursory glance at the Tagore bibliography will attest, but not from his novels. In short, reading Tagore's fiction, we are unlikely to get anything like the standard story of massive poverty and ignorance, matched by spiritual transcendence, that has been a staple of Western accounts since Kipling and Forster established the basic coordinates for 'imagining India'. Instead, we are faced with the more mundane problems of everyday life among the Hindu upper castes and classes, set in quite particular historical situations that seem to us remote in time and experience.

Yet it is worth recalling that Rabindranath was deeply immersed in the nationalist struggle during an important period, that his life and his art were firmly imbricated in the historical conditions of colonial India, and that therefore one has a perfect right—indeed, an obligation—to consider him as part of the canon of colonial writing that has become the focus of so much attention here in recent years.[3] If his texts, having migrated to the West, failed to become rooted in the Western imagi-nation, this has less to do with their intrinsic interest than with the fortunes of the ideological programme with which they were identified. It is with the ideology of Tagore's novelistic practice, in particular with his views on Indian nationalism, that I shall be primarily concerned here.

* * *

I begin somewhat obliquely, with an oft-quoted letter from Joseph Conrad to his friend, the socialist R.B. Cunninghame Graham, which offers a convenient point to enter the problematic of colonial history and writing:

There is—let us say—a machine. It evolved (I am severely scientific) out of a chaos of scraps of iron and behold!—it knits. I am horrified at the horrible work and stand appalled. I feel it ought to embroider—but it goes on knitting. You come and say: 'this is all right; it's only a question of the right kind of oil. Let us use this—for instance—celestial oil and the machine will embroider a most beautiful design in purple and gold.' Will it? Alas, no. You cannot by any special lubrication make embroidery with a knitting machine. And the most withering thought is that the infamous thing has made itself; made itself without thought, without conscience, without foresight, without eyes, without heart. It is a tragic accident—and it has happened. You can't even smash it. The last drop of bitterness is in the suspicion that you can't even smash it. In virtue of that truth one and immortal which lurks in the force that made it spring into existence it is what it is—and it is indestructible!

It knits us in and it knits us out. It has knitted time, space, pain, death, corruption, despair and all the illusions—and nothing matters. I'll admit however that to look at the remorseless process is sometimes amusing.[4]

This text has characteristically been interpreted—in the first instance by Conrad himself—as a metaphysic. But it is well to recall the context in which Conrad was writing. He was responding to Graham's pressure to become involved in socialist politics, a mission on Graham's part that in retrospect seems almost risible. Conrad expresses his scepticism in metaphysical terms, but the basis for his doubts is determinately political. These issued, we may surmise, from some quite specific historical experiences: in the first place, the memory of his father's failed revolutionary romanticism, but more proximately his own experiences in the Congo Free State, where the high-minded rhetoric of improvement and civilisation had been revealed to be, as Marlow says of Kurtz in *Heart of Darkness*, 'hollow at the core'.

I am suggesting, then, that we can more profitably construe this passage's stark pessimism as having to do with imperialism. Further, it is possible, although Conrad himself probably did not intend it, to take the image of the cosmic knitting-machine itself to be a figure for the imperial project as a whole, not only during the era of colonialism but into the contemporary period of post-colonial history and writing. For 'the most withering thought' suggested by the legacy of imperialism, particularly for those who have suffered most from its depradations, is not just the memory of what was done in the past, but that 'the infamous thing . . . has happened', and that 'it is indestructible'. I mean by this not that imperialism cannot be overthrown, but that the fact of its having happened cannot easily be erased. This is the situation of anti-colonial writing that I wish to consider in this essay. The text I shall discuss is Rabindranath Tagore's *The Home and the World*,[5] written during the First World War but dealing with the previous decade when, in the wake of the partition of Bengal, the movement for swadeshi or self-development swept across British India and seemed to threaten the political stability of the Raj. My purpose will be to situate this text in the history that produced it, which stretches from the period between 1903 and 1908, when swadeshi was in full swing, through the subsequent decade during which Rabindranath's relationship to the mainstream nationalist movement altered decisively and permanently, and when nationalism itself would begin to assume its better-known guise of Gandhian satyagraha. Without further preamble, then, let us consider this history and Rabindranath's place in it.

By 1915, when *The Home and the World* was first published, Rabindranath Tagore had become a staunch opponent of the Indian nationalist movement. Only two years later, he would denounce nationalism globally in a famous series of lectures, arguing that only a universal humanism could possibly solve the social problems that lay at the heart of his country's misery, or indeed any political problem pitting one group of people against another. While condemning any and all nationalist feeling, Rabindranath comes down especially hard on two instances, as it happens, the very ones then opposing each other in his native land. Of the so-called extremists in the Indian National Congress, he has this to say:

Their ideals were based on Western history. They had no sympathy with the special problems of India. They did not recognize the patent fact that there were causes in our social organization which made the Indian incapable of coping with the alien. What should we do if, for any reason, England was driven away? We should simply be victims for other nations. The same social weaknesses would prevail. The thing we in India have to think of is this—to remove those social customs and ideas which have generated a want of self-respect and a complete dependence on those above us,—a state of affairs which has been brought about entirely by the domination in India of the caste system, and the blind and lazy habit of relying upon the authority of traditions that are incongruous anachronisms in the present age.[6]

The extremists' failure derived from their inappropriately importing Western political ideals into the Indian context; it lay above all in their incapacity to grasp the solidity and perdurance of the caste system, which constituted the fundamental obstacle to any social reformation in India. David Kopf is probably correct to locate Rabindranath's implicit programme for social change at this period—exemplified in the statement made just prior to his condemnation of extremism: 'It was my conviction [during the early years of the Indian National Congress] that what India most needed was constructive work coming from within herself'[7]— in the context of his lifelong association with the Brahmo Samaj, co-founded by the poet's grandfather Sir Dwarkanath Tagore and reformed by his father Debendranath.[8] What is more difficult to account for is the poet's equally fervent espousal of the nationalist cause during the previous decade; little in his previous writing and training could have prepared one for the zeal with which he embraced swadeshi from 1903 until around 1906–7.[9]

One possible clue to the source of this curious and generally atypical moment in Rabindranath's career comes in the poet's characterisation of the nationalism that the British introduced in India:

Before the Nation came to rule over us we had other governments which were foreign, and these, like all governments, had some element of the machine in them. But the difference between them and the government by the Nation is like the difference between the hand loom and the power loom. In the products of the hand loom the magic of man's living fingers finds its expression, and its hum harmonizes with the music of life. But the power loom is relentlessly lifeless and accurate and monotonous in its production.[10]

The analogy here is far from innocent or fortuitous. In his famous tract of 1909, *Hind Swaraj*, Gandhi had condemned British rule in India for having subjected the subcontinent to the dominance of modern industrial civilisation, thereby warping—albeit not irreversibly in Gandhi's view—India's natural development. Rabindranath, while never so determinedly anti-Western as Gandhi, nonetheless participated in this passage—and indeed throughout the lectures on nationalism— in the essence of the Gandhian programme, which rejected modernisation

and cultivated indigenous crafts as an alternative developmental path
for contemporary India.[11] So-called 'constructive swadeshi', of which
Rabindranath was an early advocate and fervent adherent, anticipated
much that was considered novel and distinctive in the Gandhian
programme of social reform and political resistance.[12]

Over many issues Gandhi and Rabindranath would divide—including, famously, the former's interpreting the 1934 Bihar earthquake as
divine retribution for India's failure to reform itself spiritually—but
both joined in seeing the introduction of industrial technology and
the modern state form aligned with it as an unmitigated disaster for the
subcontinent. They also agreed that the key to India's future lay in
constructive village work.

Of course, everything in politics hangs on the specificity of pro-
grammes, and in this Rabindranath and Gandhi would differ in virtually every particular, especially after the former's withdrawal from the
nationalist cause in 1908. One cannot but agree in general with Sumit
Sarkar's observation that 'Anti-traditionalism in fact was to pervade
virtually all of Tagore's post-1907 writings,'[13] a commitment that would
separate him from the cultivation of traditional clothing, handicrafts,
and Hindu customs so powerfully invoked in the popular imagination
of Gandhism.[14] At the same time, one is compelled to register the considerable complexity of the problem, particularly as Rabindranath's
attitudes altered in the shifting political and ideological winds that
swept across the nationalist movement between 1908 and 1920. Sarkar
points directly to the final pages of *Gora* (1907–10) to indicate Rabindranath's 'vision of an India united on a modern basis transcending all
barriers of caste, religion and race . . .'[15] But this text was written in the
midst of the poet's recoil from the communal violence of 1906–7, and
it is quite understandable for him to have emphasised modernity as the
ideological counter-weight to Hindu revivalism. For the latter, he felt
(and he was not wrong), was in large measure responsible for commu-
nalism's resurgence. With the advantage of distance from the immediate
events, he would come to judge somewhat differently the emergent
nationalism of the swadeshi movement he himself had embraced. It
is to his laconic portrait of the swadeshi era, *The Home and the World*,
that we must now turn.

* * *

For readers unfamiliar with the novel, a schematic recounting of the plot and the substantive ideological issues it presents may be useful at the outset. The story, which is told alternately in three voices, Bimala's Nikhilesh's, and Sandip's, opens with Bimala, wife to a prominent zamindar Nikhilesh, addressing her mother (in a letter? in her diary?) and recalling the events of her marriage, including her husband's insistence that she be educated and liberated from many of the purdah restrictions. Her narrative quickly shifts to the arrival on the scene of Sandip, long-time friend to Nikhilesh and currently a swadeshi leader. Nikhilesh insists, against Bimala's initial resistance, that his wife meet his friend, and in so doing he sows the seeds of disunity in his home. Sandip seduces Bimala (quite literally in the Satyajit Ray film of the novel; more on the divergences between novel and film below) into involvement in swadeshi, exhorting her to purloin some money from her husband to support the cause. Nikhilesh, who has backed swadeshi industry in the past—much to his own disadvantage—consistently resists Sandip's attempts to be enlisted in the current struggle, maintaining that the movement has turned into a coercive campaign that unfairly victimises the poor, especially his predominantly Muslim tenants. Sandip's perfidy is ultimately exposed, in part by the minor character Amulya, who apprises Bimala of his master's hypocrisy, but too late for Bimala to repent successfully of her betrayal of her husband. The novel ends with Sandip's banishment from the household, Amulya's shooting death, and the probably mortal wounding of Nikhilesh, who has ridden off to prevent further violence against his tenants.

On first inspection, the novel would seem unproblematically aligned with the forces of modernisation. Nikhilesh's insistence that his wife Bimala receive a Western education, and that subsequently she come out of purdah to meet his friend Sandip marks the text with the modern reforming social vision with which Rabindranath clearly identified and which was one legacy of his Brahmo heritage. Moreover, to the extent that the text unequivocally condemns extremist nationalism in the morally dubious Sandip, it rejects all the trappings of Hindu revivalism that played a significant role in extremist ideology.[16] It has often been thought that Rabindranath's views can be identified with Nikhilesh's, and certainly there is warrant for this claim. But the text's ideological structure is far from stable, its conclusions highly troubled. That *The*

Home and the World condemns nationalism, no one can seriously doubt; that is recommends a thorough programme of modernisation and universal humanism—which is how Tagore's post-swadeshi thought is customarily understood[17]—is less certain.

To begin to come to terms with this text's ideological specificity, we may turn to Sumit Sarkar's lapidary judgement on the trajectory traced by Rabindranath between 1907 and 1915: 'The unity of humanist values and socially effective action which had been Rabindranath's ideal in *gora* has broken down, and we are faced instead with the stark *ghare-baire* dichotomy of Nikhilesh and Sandip.'[18] This characterisation has the merit of posing the text's basic ideological opposition clearly and without equivocation, and yet it does not quite capture the manifest complexity of the home–world tension as this is figured in the narrative. To the extent that Sandip is associated with political activism and is the principal agent disrupting the household, Sarkar's description holds. But as we learn early on, the domestic space of the home is itself sharply divided between the purdah quarters of the women and the household's public spaces where only men are allowed. Nikhilesh's insistence that Bimala, who resists at first (p. 23), come out of purdah and thereby complete her liberation from the traditional woman's role suggests that 'the world' is not just the domain of political action, but equally the site in the home itself where the affairs of men are discussed and conducted. Later on, Nikhilesh himself presents a further complication of the home–world dichotomy when he explicitly opposes the domestic realm, where commerce occurs, to the inner life, where he believes truth and authenticity properly reside (p. 65). At stake here is a familiar inside–outside opposition that, after Derrida and de Man, we readily recognise as a powerful tropological structure, reversible, flexible, and ultimately totalising.

The power of this figure is dramatically realised in Nikhilesh's meditation near the centre of the text (pp. 109–10), the upshot of which is his decision to let the cards fall where they may. The passage is too long to quote or explicate in detail here, but the main thrust can be grasped economically enough. It opens with the stark opposition between morality and politics, seemingly that posed in the characters of Nikhilesh and Sandip respectively though in this context Bimala embodies political values against her husband's commitment to ethical right. Nikhilesh asserts that correct political action can only issue from sound moral principles; Bimala claims that political necessity overrides ethical duty. As is apparent, the opposition can only be overcome by privileging one term over the other, thereby foreclosing a truly dialectical resolution of the tension. But the text continues, as Nikhilesh experiences a sudden illumination—his recognition that Bimala has been dressing up in order to seduce him into ordering his tenants and dependants to support swadeshi—that liberates his soul and concomitantly transforms the world (here, nature). Nikhilesh's illumination is a liberation from the self (that is, from his selfish passion for his wife) to a recognition of his proper place in the world: 'I seemed to have come closer to the heartbeats of the great earth in all the simplicity of its daily life.' Nikhilesh thus apparently reconciles the two antagonistic values, proclaiming: 'an anthem, inexpressibly sweet, seemed to peal forth from this world, where I, in my freedom, live in the freedom of all else.'

By the end of the passage, Nikhilesh is satisfied that he has at last found the true path in life, and that in doing so he has attained freedom, while acknowledging the freedom of others—specifically, the world. But this ostensible liberation of the self, accomplished through introspection, retains some curious features that render Nikhilesh's untroubled acceptance of his new-found wisdom more fragile than he knows. Nikhilesh's discovering the secret of self-liberation discloses that the subject, which is the agent of its own freedom, depends on the world to realise its freedom: 'In my work will be my salvation.' The means to personal salvation turns out to be the instrument by which the world itself must be transformed in such a way that freedom (presumably the same freedom Nikhilesh attributes to himself) is equally available to all. As Nikhilesh puts it: '. . . I shall allow freedom to others.' On the testimony of this very passage, however, freedom is that which cannot be given by one to another; one can only achieve it for oneself. Nikhilesh never notices the contradiction, and for good reason: the ideology of liberation he embraces here and throughout the text is no Kantian kingdom of ends where all are equally empowered to realise their freedom; it is, rather, the paternalist ideal of the enlightened and wise patriarch extending freedom to others—even when, as in Bimala's case, to do so violates their explicit wishes in the matter.

Sumit Sarkar and others are surely correct to counterpose Nikhilesh

to Sandip. The latter's first appearance *in propria persona* clearly
establishes him as the ideological foil to the former's moral integrity
(pp. 45–6). The text overloads the ethical charge on Sandip by imaging
the revolutionary brigandage he advocates (and later authorises when
he convinces Bimala to purloin a large sum of money from her husband's
treasury) as a rape, an overturning by violence of domestic tranquillity.
And of course he does just that, for Nikhilesh's and Bimala's marriage
is permanently disrupted with his arrival. At the same time, it would
seem that Sandip is intended to represent less an ordinary criminal or
sinner than the quite different figure of the Nietzschean superman,
the transvaluer of all values who, in this instance, subordinates morality
to political necessity. It is therefore not immorality that he figures, but
amorality.

One interpretive commonplace of *The Home and the World* is to
identify Bimala with India (or Bengal), the female figure in nationalist
iconography of the period leading up to swadeshi.[19] Sandip makes the
connection explicitly and often, so there can be little doubt about Tagore's
having consciously mobilised this ideologeme in his portrayal of Bimala.
But the figure itself was far from uncomplicated, as a splendid article
on the subject by Tanika Sarkar demonstrates.[20] Symbolising the nation in its mission to overthrow British rule, woman was at the same
time the repository of traditional values. In fact, in so far as nationalism
was deeply imbricated in traditional Indian (or, more narrowly and not
infrequently, Hindu) values and practices, its ideological programme
was less revolutionary than restorative, to invoke the useful categories
Sumit Sarkar hazards in his study of the relations between elite leaders and the popular masses during the independence struggle. As
Tanika Sarkar argues, there was little recognition of any conflict in this
figure prior to the emergence of Gandhian mass movements. But in
Rabindranath's novel, one cannot ignore the tension between the
modernising values associated with the world, the nation, and politics
and the traditional commitments of women to family, husband, and
home, in a word, to a conventional concept of wifely and motherly
duty. Despite her momentary embrace of nationalist politics (and, in
the magnificent Satyajit Ray film, her literal embrace of Sandip), Bimala
remains tied to many sanctioned forms of domestic subservience,
symbolised most powerfully in the text by her continually brushing the

dust from her husband's feet. And, as the plot reveals, she regards her theft of six thousand rupees as sinful (pp. 138–40); her ultimate repentance is represented by her willingness to undergo 'public humiliation' (p. 186) after having once again subordinated herself to her husband. (In the Ray film, her reversion to the traditional woman's role is brilliantly figured in the film's final image, when Bimala appears with her hair shorn and attired in the Hindu widow's plain white sari.) Seduced into politics by Sandip, Bimala cannot entirely free herself from conventional moral bonds; in the end she is ashamed of what she has done and attempts, vainly it would appear, to rekindle her husband's love by submitting to his will.

While the novel surely projects an ideal resolution of the antinomy between home and world, nothing could be plainer than that the transcendence demanded by its system of values is undermined by the plot's final destiny. Although the novel remains ambiguous in this regard (Ray's film is more explicit), it seems likely that Nikhilesh has been mortally wounded in attempting to quell communal violence in the neighbourhood. This raises a decisive problem: to wit, what are we to make of the ending? For, strictly speaking, the diagram represents only the initial state of the system, not its ultimate disposition.

The novel's conclusion has several components. First is the projected abandonment of the home as this latter has generally been defined in the text: namely, Nikhilesh's household and his rural estates. Prior to his wounding, Nikhilesh has announced his intention to leave the estates and to repair to his house in Calcutta, which latter can be taken to symbolise the world at large—as indeed it did for Rabindranath himself, who never felt comfortable in any modern urban environment. Nikhilesh's decision to go to the city is therefore an admission of defeat, a flight from home to the world. Moreover, there is no indication, despite his wife's desire for it, that Nikhilesh is in any useful sense now reconciled with Bimala.

Second, and directly relevant to the last point, is the rekindling of Nikhilesh's relationship with his sister-in-law, which was prior to and now would seem to take the place of his marital bond (pp. 188–9).[21] This disposition of the two otherwise contradictory semes of world and not-world reverses the ideological trajectory that would carry

Nikhilesh from his rural home to the urban world. Through his sister-in-law, he recovers a previous state of the home, albeit one that is manifestly not in tune with his own values. Moreover, the loss of his wife—for it would appear he no longer loves her (p. 199)—signifies the failure of his educational plans and the incapacity for home and world to be reconciled in a higher synthesis incorporating both.

Third, and a consequence of what has just been said, Sandip has been effectively banished from the household. While Nikhilesh concedes Sandip's freedom to visit them in Calcutta, the latter's residence in the home will no longer be tolerated. In order to recover the formal propriety of his marriage, Nikhilesh is forced to expel the immediate threat to domestic peace. Sandip's rootlessness is simply too disruptive, a force that the home cannot tolerate.

Finally, we have the communal violence itself which, there is every reason to believe, was the cause for Tagore's withdrawal from active political involvement in 1908.[22] It is responsible for the death of Amulya, Sandip's disciple and Bimala's devotee, and, as I've observed, probably Nikhilesh's as well. If I am correct in assuming this latter, then the main narrative action might be crudely summarised as follows: by inviting the antithesis of the home (Sandip; politics) into the household, the representative of progressive humanism (Nikhilesh) has destroyed any possibility for domestic harmony, leaving both the domestic space of the household and the public environment of the estates ultimately bereft of patriarchal authority.

But why should things have to turn out this way? Why could Rabindranath not realise any other than the tragic solution to the tensions thrown up by swadeshi and by the nationalist movement generally? What, in short, is the objective blockage in the text's ideological system that forecloses any alternative dénouement to this episode in the eventual overthrow of British rule?

One possible answer would be that this is just how history went, that *The Home and the World* is no more than a perspicuous accounting of swadeshi's demise and Indian nationalism's degeneration into senseless (and for the most part ineffectual) terrorism. Sumit Sarkar's massive study of the period would in part bear out such an inference. Sarkar unstintingly criticises the movement's middle-class leadership, who signally failed to strike roots in the peasant masses and mobilise them in favour of political resistance.[23] His conclusion is that, because an effective alliance between mostly urban intellectual leadership and the rural masses was never forged, swadeshi could not seriously challenge British rule. Its defeat left the middle-class elites with only two options: return to previous forms of Congress mendicancy; or resort to terrorism. That the latter was not without its positive role Sarkar concedes,[24] but he is quick to point out that ultimately it was a dead end. He cites favourably Rabindranath's terse judgement on the political limitations of such a revolutionary strategy: 'My impatience never makes any road in the world shorter, nor does time lessen itself for my special benefit.'[25]

Sarkar goes on to observe, however, that 'it would be wrong to credit Tagore with an alternative entirely cogent or satisfactory . . . Rabindranath could not really suggest any concrete social or economic programme with which to rouse the uneducated masses. His constructive rural work amounted to little more than humanitarianism, the appeal to zamindars was surely utopian, and the basic problems of land relations remained untouched.'[26] There was, in short, a fundamental contradiction in nationalist ideology at this period that Rabindranath was unable to overcome or circumvent, save by utopian appeals to morality and enlightened humanitarianism.

One strand in recent debunkings of Tagore attributes this impasse to the poet's objective class position. Thus Hitendra Mitra writes:

Tagore was born in a social class which collaborated with the imperialist rulers and acted against the anti-imperialist struggles of the people. He was conscious of the fact and tried to fight against it in his own way when he was young, not socially rooted and practically neglected by his close relatives. He could not succeed to go beyond his class position because he imbibed the thought and perception of his feudal family which appropriated him to its own use after his initial success as a poet.[27]

Mitra later locates the shift in Tagore's ideological position from anti-imperialist to *comprador* at the moment when the poet was sent off to manage his father's estates in 1891.[28] The difficulty with this account is not so much its methodological crudity, which draws a direct line from an objective class position to a set of ideological beliefs. Such examples are not difficult to find. Sarkar himself makes much the same point about the educated *bhadralok* who comprised the bulk of the nationalist movement's leadership during swadeshi.[29] Rather, the weakness in this critique lies in its failure to come to terms with the genuine complexity of Rabindranath's thinking, which was composed of a curious amalgam of different ideological positions, not all of which derived from his remaining a substantial landholder throughout his life. Ideologies, we may say with some assurance, always ultimately serve certain class interests, but they rarely are shaped unilaterally by economic considerations.

To begin to sketch out a more satisfactory explanation of the ideological impasse figured in *The Home and the World*, we need to return to an issue that has hovered on the margins of this essay but which I have not yet fully articulated. It is, to be brief, the question of gender. I referred earlier to the article by Tanika Sarkar on the function of female iconography in Bengali literature and in images of Indian nationalism on the eve of swadeshi. It will be recalled that woman's position in this discourse as an embodiment at once of perdurable traditional values and revolutionary hope created a tension, evident in the figure of Bimala, between the domestic sphere and political activism. But this opposition was not just the 'natural' outcome of gendered social relations in Hindu households. (We can omit for the moment the question of the conditions obtaining among Muslims, since swadeshi nationalism was overwhelmingly a Hindu affair, as the communal riots of 1906–7 would make plain enough.) The contradiction in woman as ideologeme resulted from a quite specific set of historical circumstances imposed by the colonial situation.

The *narrative* problem in that text is determined by the extent to which Bimala can be brought out of the confines of the traditional home into the modern world without destroying her distinctively female virtues. Or, if we follow convention and read Bimala as a figure for India itself (and after Tanika Sarkar's work it seems entirely legitimate to do so), then it can be said that the novel is about just that puzzle which nationalist discourse as a whole set for itself: the possibility for the strengths of indigenous culture to be maintained while altering the traditional functions and forms of female identity in order to signify the resistance to colonial rule. The difficulty, as the novel presents it, lies in the conflict, irresolvable in principle, between the honourable but ineffectual Nikhilesh and the powerful but unprincipled

Sandip. Bimala's initial choice in favour of the latter signifies on one level Rabindranath's negative judgement on the nationalist movement's turn towards extremism. At a deeper level, that of the ideological system which governs the text from the outset, Bimala's choice is to some extent unavoidable. The text cries out for but cannot produce the combination of power and justice that is the ideal figure demanded by the semiotic system: the authoritative, wise, and powerful patriarch. By splitting the necessary qualities for its ideal resolution between two male protagonists, the novel acknowledges the impossibility of fulfilling its own ideological fantasy.

* * *

Something of the contemporary relevance of Tagore's novel can be gleaned by briefly considering Satyajit's film version. In his informative, if overly hagiographic study of Ray, Andrew Robinson observes: 'If non-Bengalis know Tagore at all today, it is mainly by virtue of Ray's interpretations of him on film . . .'[30] These include film versions of the three short stories strung together in *Three Daughters* (*Teen Kanya*), of the novella *Nastanirh* (*Charulata*), and, most famously, of *Ghare Baire* itself, as well as a documentary (sponsored by the Indian government) on Tagore's life. Ray's lifelong fascination with Rabindranath extends well beyond the familiar forms of Bengali piety for the national poet. Both men were reared in prominent Brahmo households and rebelled against the sect's more puritanical practices. Rabindranath was a close family friend, a great admirer of Sukumar Ray's (the filmmaker's father) nonsense verse, and a frequent visitor to the household in which Satyajit was raised. After he graduated from Presidency College in 1939, Ray's mother sent her son to Santiniketan to study art.[31]

Ray contemplated making a film of *The Home and the World* as early as 1948,[32] and he seems to have kept the idea alive over many years.[33] By the time the project was finally realised in the 1980s, Tagore's novel had been overlain in Ray's imagination with a great deal of political history, including the Naxalite episode that had torn Calcutta apart in the early 1970s. When Ray describes Tagore's attitudes towards the nationalist movement in the first decade of the century, one cannot help but hear the echo of Ray's own sentiments about the political violence he himself had lived through:

Tagore's essays on the terrorist movement and some of the other things that he wrote are actually put in the mouth of Nikhil—exact sentences even. He represents Tagore's attitude to the terrorist movement and its ultimate futility. It's a very valid viewpoint, very rational. It was really a middle-class movement with no connection with the lower strata of society at all. So ultimately it just fizzled out, and in other cases it turned into very violent riots between Hindus and Muslims. It was failure and Tagore could see it was going to be a failure, although the political leaders didn't see it his way.[34]

In the film, communal violence figures much more prominently than it does in the novel. In addition, there is an unmistakable allusion to Naxalbari when Amulya justifies his theft from the local treasury to Bimala by reference to the Naxalite slogan that money is 'mine one day, the moneylender's the next'. In general, the politico-ethical allegory projected by Rabindranath is displaced into the purely erotic: Bimala has a real love affair with Sandip, punctuated by those scandalous kisses about which Ray was so nervous that he didn't even reveal his intentions to the actors until shooting the scene. There are some other notable differences between film and novel—a much greater role for the Bara Rani in the former than is warranted by Tagore's text; the clear reconciliation between Bimala and Nikhilesh just before the latter's death in the film; the complete excision of Nikhilesh's transformation from the film—but in general, Ray has captured much of the novel's spirit, not to mention carefully reconstructing its period atmosphere in dwellings, furnishings, and clothing.

*   *   *

To return to *The Home and the World*, it may be said that its narrative of swadeshi's failure speaks to a deeper historical and ideological impasse shared by swadeshi and the Gandhi Congress alike. The latter successfully mobilised peasant masses to overthrow British rule, but without altering the basic structures of agrarian exploitation and domination that were the ultimate cause for the peasant discontent upon which it was able to draw.[35] Gandhi's appeal was never to the peasantry as a class; on the contrary, as Sabyasachi Bhattacharya has observed, the Congress managed to appear 'as a supra-class entity, an arbitrator or mediator, a consensus-making body'.[36] This prepared Congress for the transfer of power; it did not secure its ultimate authority as a party of the people, since by its very nature Congress could only speak of, not for, them. In maintaining the fundamental class relations bequeathed by the British Raj, Congress reinforced the underlying contradictions, explosive at times, that the Raj had created in the transition from Mughal rule.[37] To recall the image drawn from Conrad at the beginning of this essay, both Rabindranath's exclusive emphasis on constructive swadeshi and Gandhi's appeal to the sanctity of traditional village practices were attempts to 'oil the infernal knitting-machine' of British imperialism on the subcontinent. As one of Gandhi's near contemporaries would have said, the real task would have been to smash the machine itself.

Endnotes

1. Throughout, I refer to Rabindranath Tagore indifferently as 'Rabindranath' or as 'Tagore'. Both are, to my knowledge, acceptable, although in some contexts—where other members of his family are in question—use of his given name is required. I have been told by a knowledgeable friend that custom and decorum dictate that only Bengalis use the given name alone. I hope my own usage will give no offence; none is intended. I merely follow standard practice in the secondary literature.

2. Recently, Tagore has figured among the pantheon of anti-colonial nationalists proposed by Edward Said in his *Culture and Imperialism* (New York: Knopf, 1993), see pp. 215, 219, 232, 264. Such a characterisation is not wholly wrong, of course, but as I shall be arguing at some length, it fails to capture the complexity—and mutability—of Rabindranath's views on nationalism and colonial resistance.

3. Gayatri Spivak has recently drawn attention to Tagore's 'colonial prose', describing how in his fiction composed during the last years of the nineteenth century he 'fashion[s] a new Bengali prose' in a 'stunning mixture of Sanskritized and colloquial Bengali . . .' ('The Burden of English', in Rajeswari Sunder Rajan, ed., *The Lie of the Land: English Literary Studies in India* [Delhi: Oxford University Press, 1992], pp. 280–1).

4. *Joseph Conrad's Letters to R.B. Cunninghame Graham*, ed. C.T. Watts (Cambridge: Cambridge University Press, 1969), pp. 56–7.

5. Rabindranath Tagore, *The Home and the World*, trans. Surendranath Tagore (1919; rpt. Harmondsworth, Middlesex: Penguin, 1985); hereafter cited parenthetically by page number.

6. Rabindranath Tagore, *Nationalism* (London: Macmillan, 1917), p. 135.

7. Ibid., p. 134.

8. David Kopf, *The Brahmo Samaj and the Shaping of the Modern Indian Mind* (Princeton: Princeton University Press, 1979), pp. 287–310. Rabindranath's relation to Brahmo culture was far from straightforward. Perhaps the best indication of his views at this period is to be gleaned from his novel *Gora* (1907–10), where both strict Brahmos and orthodox Hindus are held up to scorn.

9. Tagore's involvement in anti-imperialist politics pre-dates the swadeshi period. He wrote a number of anti-British articles during the 1880s, including an attack on the Chinese opium trade; see Krishna Kripalani, *Rabindranath Tagore: A Biography* (New York: Grove Press, 1962), p. 99; and Hitendra Mitra, *Tagore Without Illusions* (Calcutta: Sanyal Prokashan, 1983), pp. 127–38. Nonetheless, Susobhan Sarkar's overall judgement still stands, fifty years after its initial pronouncement: 'In truth Rabindranath had no firm faith in a radical programme of action, any institution or apparatus for administration; Sudhindranath Datta was quite correct in his remark that even the upheaval at the epoch's end did not provide to Tagore sufficient impetus for liberation from certain traditional values' ('"Progress" and Rabindranath Tagore', in Susobhan Sarkar, *Bengal Renaissance and Other Essays* [New Delhi: People's Publishing House, 1970], p. 141).

10. Tagore, *Nationalism*, p. 29.

11. As Partha Chatterjee argues, however, the project announced in *Hind Swaraj* is less nationalist and specifically anti-Western than 'a total moral critique of the fundamental aspects of civil society'. *Nationalist Thought and the Colonial World—a Derivative Discourse?* (London: Zed Books, 1986), p. 93. On the dialectic between 'traditionalism' and 'Westernism' in Tagore, see Susobhan Sarkar, 'Rabindranath Tagore and the Renaissance in Bengal', in op.cit., pp. 148–83. On the pitfalls of such a schematisation, see Sumit Sarkar, 'Rammohun Roy and the Break with the Past', in idem, *A Critique of Colonial India* (Calcutta: Papyrus, 1985), pp. 15–17; and cf. K.N. Panikkar, 'Culture and Ideology: Contradictions in Intellectual Transformation of Colonial Society in India', *Economic and Political Weekly* (5 December 1987): 2115–20.

12. See Sumit Sarkar, *'Popular' Movements and 'Middle Class' Leadership in Late Colonial India* (Calcutta: Centre for Studies in Social Sciences, 1983), pp. 69, 76–8, 94; and idem, *Modern India: 1885–1947* (Delhi: Macmillan, 1983), p. 112.

13. Sumit Sarkar, *The Swadeshi Movement in Bengal 1903–1908* (New Delhi: People's Publishing House, 1973), p. 85. Cf. Susobhan Sarkar, 'Rabindranath Tagore and the Renaissance in Bengal', pp. 173–83.

14. On Gandhi's appeal to the popular masses, see Chatterjee, *Nationalist Thought*, p. 110; Sumit Sarkar, 'The Conditions and Nature of Subaltern Militancy: Bengal from Swadeshi to Non-Cooperation, c. 1905–22', in Ranajit Guha, ed., *Subaltern Studies* III (Delhi: Oxford University Press, 1984), pp. 307–20; but especially Gyan Pandey, 'Peasant Revolt and Indian Nationalism: The Peasant Movement in Awadh, 1919–22', in Guha, ed., *Subaltern Studies* I (Delhi: Oxford University Press, 1982), pp. 143–97, and Shahid Amin, 'Gandhi as Mahatma: Gorakhpur District, Eastern UP, 1921–2', *Subaltern Studies* III, pp. 1–61.

15. Sarkar, *Swadeshi Movement*, p. 85. The decisive moment, after Gora has discovered the truth about his Irish origins, comes in the hero's speech to Anandamoyi, the woman who has raised him: '"Mother, you are my mother!" exclaimed Gora. "The mother whom I have been wandering about in search of was all the time sitting in my room at home. You have no caste, you make no distinctions, and have no hatred—you are only the image of our welfare! It is you who are India!"' (*Gora*, trans. W.W. Pearson under the supervision of Surendranath Tagore [1924; rpt. Madras: Macmillan, 1980], p. 407). Gora then requests a drink to be brought him by Lachmiya, the Christian servant whose touch he has hitherto shunned for fear of losing caste.

16. Here again, *Gora* provides the relevant gloss, for the titular hero's strict observance of traditional Hindu customs throughout the novel is directly linked to his patriotism. Extremism is not yet on the horizon in the novel itself, which is set in the late 1870s or early 1880s, but Tagore composed it after the demise of swadeshi during the moderate–extremist Congress split. Interpreting the narrative in the light of its contemporary context is surely justified.

17. See, for example, Chatterjee, *Nationalist Thought*, p. 100; and Susobhan Sarkar, '"Progress" and Rabindranath Tagore'.

18. Sarkar, *Swadeshi Movement*, p. 502.

19. See Anita Desai's introduction to the novel, op. cit.; and R.P. Bhaskar, 'The Novels of Tagore', in *The Genius of Tagore: Tagore Centenary Volume*, Part I, ed. Mahendra Kulasreshta (Hoshiarpur: V.V.R. Institute, 1961), p. 100.

20. Tanika Sarkar, 'Nationalist Iconography: Image of Women in 19th Century Bengali Literature', *Economic and Political Weekly* (21 November 1987): 2011–15.

21. It is generally agreed that the relationship between the Bara Rani and Nikhilesh was in part determined by Rabindranath's relations with his own sister-in-law, his companion in youth who committed suicide. But the central issue in the text is less the psychological charge this situation

bore for the author, than the structure of familial relations representing the political problematic.

22. See Sumit Sarkar, *Swadeshi Movement*, pp. 82–7.

23. Ibid., pp. 78, 90, 333, passim. Cf. Rajat Kanta Ray, *Social Conflict and Political Unrest in Bengal 1875–1927* (Delhi: Oxford University Press, 1984), who argues that the dependent position of landed and professional elites in the colonial economy held these latter hostage to the existing mechanisms of surplus extraction that exploited rural cultivators, thereby rendering the objective interests of elites and masses necessarily contradictory. Tagore himself seems to have understood this situation perfectly well: 'In the realm of politics [Rabindranath] bitterly criticised from the beginning habits of "mendicancy"; the "atmashakti" (self-help) which he invoked is indeed of priceless value in political life. He grasped the main shortcoming of our earlier political efforts—the lack of contact between our educated classes and the common people' (Susobhan Sarkar, '"Progress" and Rabindranath Tagore', p. 146).

24. Sumit Sarkar, *Swadeshi Movement*, pp. 89–90.

25. Ibid., p. 90.

26. Ibid., pp. 90–1.

27. Mitra, op.cit., pp. 51–2.

28. Ibid., p. 138.

29. Sumit Sarkar, *Swadeshi Movement*, pp. 334–5.

30. Andrew Robinson, *Satyajit Ray: The Inner Eye* (London: Andre Deutsch, 1989), pp. 47–8.

31. Ibid., pp. 13–55. The comparison between Ray and Tagore is one of the leitmotifs of Robinson's study.

32. Ibid., p. 66.

33. See ibid., p. 270, for details about Ray's thoughts during the 1960s on casting this film.

34. Cited in ibid., p. 267.

35. See Rajat K. Ray, op.cit.; Ravinder Kumar, 'Class, Community, or Nation? Gandhi's Quest for a Popular Consensus in India', in idem, *Essays in the Social History of Modern India* (Delhi: Oxford University Press, 1983), p. 68; and Sumit Sarkar, *Modern India*, passim.

36. Sabyasachi Bhattacharya, 'The Colonial State, Capital and Labour: Bombay 1919–1931', in S. Bhattacharya and R. Thapar, eds, *Situating Indian History* (Delhi: Oxford University Press, 1985), p. 192.

37. See Chatterjee, *Nationalist Thought*, pp. 124–5.

Gora and *The Home and the World*: The Long Quest for Modernity*

MALINI BHATTACHARYA

The idea of 'modernity' is an important component of the ideological matrix in which both *Gora* and *The Home and the World*, novels written by Rabindranath at a crucial point in the nationalist movement, are embedded. But modernity itself assumes multiple dimensions in these novels. Both were written after the author had become critical about some of the tendencies manifesting themselves in the swadeshi movement that gathered force in Bengal from the early years of the twentieth century. Yet as far as the 'world-view' of the two novels is concerned there is a crucial difference.

Sumit Sarkar has succinctly referred to this difference in passing in his *Swadeshi Movement in Bengal: 1903–1908*:

... when after a significant silence on political subjects for nearly nine months (Bhadra 1313–Sravana 1314) Rabindranath came out with a series of immensely important essays during 1907–8, we see a decisive break with his own earlier swadeshi writings and a return (on a higher plane one is tempted to add) to a basically anti-traditionalist and modernist approach.[1]

According to Sarkar, the last pages of *Gora* signal this break and foreground the 'vision of an India united on a modern basis transcending all barriers of caste, religion and race'. He points out how subsequently *Ghare Baire* represents a fracturing of this vision:

*References to *Gora* are to the text in *Rabindra Rachanabali*, vol. 7 (Calcutta: 1986).

The unity of humanist values and socially effective action which had been Rabindranath's ideal in *Gora* has broken down, and we are faced instead with the stark *Ghare Baire* dichotomy of Nikhilesh and Sandip.[2]

What Sarkar does not mention is that the approach to 'modernity' itself appears to be deeply riven with contradictions in *Ghare Baire*. It is the amoral swadeshi leader Sandip who becomes the spokesman for modernity rather than the humanist Nikhilesh, although the latter had started by introducing innovations in a traditional household that combined the manners of the 'Moghuls and Pathans' with the 'customs of Manu and Parashar'. It may be recalled here that Pramatho Choudhury, Rabindranath's close associate and the editor of *Sabuj Patra* where *Ghare Baire* was being published in serialised form in 1915–16, somewhat whimsically described the novel as an allegory with Nikhilesh representing 'ancient India' and Sandip 'modern Europe' while Bimala, 'India today' is poised between them and suffers from their opposing pulls on her life.[3] Of course Rabindranath did not accept this interpretation which generated a storm of controversy; he said it was made in 'a lighter vein' and asserted that the novel was 'merely a narrative with no conscious allegorical intention'.[4] Yet it cannot be denied that Rabindranath's critique of modern Western nationalism, voiced in the 1916 lecture 'The Cult of Nationalism' and delivered during his tour of the US,[5] is anticipated in the characterisation of Sandip. Nikhilesh, with his quiescent humanism, on the other hand, represents true indigeneity. Nationalism as a modern phenomenon, as a derivative category that does not have its roots in the Indian soil, is implicitly critiqued through the characterisation of Sandip. Sandip's modernity itself is rendered questionable. But the fact remains that a few years earlier in *Gora*, the relationship between Gora's anti-colonial nationalism and his modernity had been posed in a much more positive way.

If we read *Gora* as a *bildungsroman* in which the eponymous protagonist explores his own identity, what attracts our attention as the central narrative device is the implicit irony. The reader is aware of Gora's non-Hindu origin when Gora himself is not. Gora's advocacy of 'Hindutva' as the touchstone of national identity is continuously undercut by this awareness of the reader. When Gora eventually discovers the truth about his origin, his attitude changes and a broader perception of his own relationship with his world dawns upon him.

The transition is something that happens over time—as the difference between a pre-anagnorisis and a post-anagnorisis state. But there is also a spatial transition. By being cast out, by becoming an outsider, Gora comes to a realisation that had not been possible for him when he had a 'home'. He finds his natural place with other outsiders, such as Anandamoyee, Pareshbabu, Benoy and Lalita, Lachhmiya the 'untouchable' maid and the rural poor whom he encounters on his itinerary of the districts of Bengal. His engagement with the issues that such outsiders represent—issues that cannot be contained or resolved within the parameters of a revivalist nationalism—is what constitutes his modernity. But this engagement takes place alongside the emergence of the consciousness of colonial domination that is developed very carefully, mainly through the persona of Gora, but also through others like Lalita. The denouement in *Gora* leaves this theme hanging like an indelible question mark over the universalist conclusion. How will Gora's new universalist humanism relate to his growing anti-colonial consciousness? It is a question that is left unanswered. But even then, in *Gora*, the possibility of a positive relationship between the two is not rejected.

That Gora was born in the year of the 'Sepoy Mutiny' is not just a clever narrative device. The reference to that period of anti-colonial upheaval has a thematic relevance in the novel. Gora is born of Irish parents. The Irish example of resistance against British domination had an important part to play in the evolution of a nationalist agenda among the middle classes in Bengal. The mention of Gora's Irish parentage may be an oblique reference to this. The time-frame within the narrative may thus be a signifier of the actual time when *Gora* was being written.

In *Gora*, the action in the text is set in the early 1880s when Gora and Benoy are in their twenties. At this time, the educated middle class of Bengal was actually just *beginning* to articulate, through social–cultural practices, the shame of subordination and the need for a national identity. *Gora* was being written and published in serialised form in *Prabasi* during 1907–9, right in the middle of the swadeshi upsurge. Even as *Gora* was being published, armed extremist groups including activists like Khudiram Bose and Prafulla Chaki, under the leadership of Barindrakumar Ghosh, made their mark in the political arena with violent interventions (1908). While the court proceedings on the Alipur bomb case were going on, *Gora* was being published in book form. There can be no doubt that Rabindranath's perception of the contemporary upsurge against the British government constitutes an important subtext in the novel despite the novel itself being situated years earlier in time.

There are two episodes in *Gora* which, from the point of view of narrative relevance, may seem to be minor but which are crucial as moments in the development of the theme of anti-colonial consciousness mentioned above. The first relates to Gora's encounter on a steamer with an Englishman and a 'modern' Bengali gentleman who acts as the former's sidekick in laughing and joking at the sorry plight of the poor 'natives' travelling on the deck. What hurts and shames Gora is the way in which the educated modern Bengali 'babu' connives with the Englishman in exercising power over the ordinary poor Indian. When Gora next visits Pareshbabu's family, in reaction to this experience, his whole appearance 'embodies defiance against modern times'. In the second episode, Gora sees a poor Muslim nearly being run over by a 'babu' in a carriage; the 'babu' hits the man with his whip for coming in his way. While Gora's anger, in this episode too, is directed against the cruelty and highhandedness of some of his own countrymen towards others, the colonial context of this inequitous system is deliberately underscored in each case. The old Muslim, hit by the 'babu', was carrying on his head the raw materials of his British master's dinner. The 'babu' in the other episode too, basks or wilts under the favour or the implicit insult of his British patron. The white man in this latter episode does show more sensitivity than the babu, but the two episodes taken together make it quite clear that Rabindranath seeks firmly to locate oppression within the context of colonial hierarchy.

Both episodes are signposts towards one of the climactic moments in the novel when Gora, as self-appointed spokesman for the oppressed villagers of Char-Ghoshpur, confronts the British magistrate, who subsequently takes advantage of an insignificant pretext to send him to jail. The inequity embedded in the renowned British system of justice, the punitive measures imposed on recalcitrant villagers and the magistrate's harsh treatment of the schoolboys—all these though not unknown in the earlier history of British rule, were inscribed deeply in the middle-class consciousness of the period when *Gora* was actually written. Such incidents were also continually publicised in the 'native' newspapers. The overdetermining presence of colonial oppression in the novel and Gora's increasing awareness of it complicates and enriches the universalist ideal of modernity that Gora approaches towards the end of the novel. This universalism can best be described as a radical universalism, which resists the inequitous colonial hierarchy by seeking to identify with the lives of those whom this hierarchy marginalises and oppresses.

This suggestion is not embodied in the character of Gora alone. The discourse in *Gora*, the novel, includes the question of the status of middle-class women in the colonial hierarchy. Within this hierarchy, such a woman is allowed a degree of modernity; but it becomes evident very soon how constricted this space is. Sucharita and Lalita, from the opening chapters of the novel, combat Gora's conservative 'Hindu' position that the woman's place is in her home. They take pride in their relatively free status. But what is particularly interesting in the novel is that Lalita's moment of actual defiance against the norms of womanliness imposed on her by her family and her community coincides with her defiance of colonial norms of servility dressed up as good-fellowship. She stubbornly refuses to participate in the performance hosted by the magistrate who has put Gora in jail so unjustly; in protest she rejects the hospitality of the magistrate and leaves for Calcutta unchaperoned in the company of Benoy, thus setting the gossip-mills of Brahmo Samaj in motion. She deviates from both the norms of the 'good subject', and the norms of the 'good woman'. She takes a significant step away from the sanitised notion of 'modernity' propagated within contemporary Brahmo Samaj towards a modernity which defies all the inequities of the colonial hierarchy.

The thrust of the larger vision in *Gora* is not towards a 'hybridity' that proposes an in-between level of consciousness that can commute between the two worlds; it is rather towards a 'syncretism' that symbolises a community of interests among the oppressed, the 'outsiders', against the dominant groups, a commonality that may sometimes overcome discriminatory rites and practices. One recalls here the striking passage at the end of the novel, where Gora, just enlightened about his origins, looks at the white doctor who has come for Krishnadayal's treatment and thinks to himself: 'Is this man then my closest kin in this room?' Obviously, his racial similarity with the European doctor does not give him any automatic sense of bonding. The only bonding he still feels is with marginalised people like Anandamoyee, her low-caste Christian servant Lachhmiya, the ostracised Benoy and Lalita and Pareshbabu who has been boycotted by the Brahmo community. The novel had opened with a 'baul', a rural singer belonging to the heterodox syncretic tradition, standing in front of a shop on a Calcutta street and singing a mystic song about an unknown bird that flits in and out of the cage: if only one could capture it one would put mind-forged chains around its feet! The relevance of this (the sight may not have been uncommon on the city street in those days) becomes clear to us only at the end of the novel—the 'baul', rejected both by colonial 'babu' culture and Hindu nationalist culture, still carries the message of an indigenous syncretism that might serve as a bond for all those left out by the dominant culture; it might offer glimpses of an alternative concept of 'modernity', free from colonialist associations.

The question of 'modernity' in relation to a colonial situation is thus woven into the texture of the narrative although the final resolution brushes it aside to some extent. Gora's 'modernity' lies in his efforts to establish contact with those outside the pale of the Hindu revivalists who constitute his immediate community. His regular visits to the 'lower-class' homes in his neighbourhood and his acquaintance with them gives him an idea of the poverty and superstition that darkens their lives, but it also convinces him of the fact 'that our country will one day be free, that it will not remain enmeshed in superstitions and the British will not be able to carry us forever manacled at the back of their trading vessel'. In his revivalist days, Gora had a following of fanatic admirers led by Abinash. They went one better than him and put loving pressure on him to emerge as a new leader resuscitating Hindu glory. Gora becomes more and more aware of their obstreperousness, and distances himself from them in embarrassment. He is deserted by them when he decides to rest at an untouchable's house during his journey; they abandon him when the British magistrate sends him to jail. It is only after he is released that they congregate around him once more, clamouring for a celebration of the release through an ostentatious ritual of penance (*prayaschitta*). Thus the narrative indicates clearly that the evolution of Gora's vision of freedom from the British coincided with his growing conviction about the ineffectuality of the revivalist euphoria. During his wanderings through rural Bengal, this conviction is reinforced by his discovery of the hidden strengths of poor rural people like the old man of the barber caste who shelters a Muslim boy whose father has been unjustly thrown into jail. When asked by Gora and his companion whether he is not afraid of losing his caste, the old man says: 'Sir, we take the name of Hari, they of Allah. There is really no difference' (p. 654). This is the voice of popular reason born of confrontation with harsh reality. The Muslim peasant 'Faru' who would go to jail, but would not submit to the tyranny of the local indigo planter, is for Gora another example of the undying spirit of ordinary people. These are the little 'flickers of light' that give him reason to hope. Such flouting of caste superstitions, such resistance against colonial and class oppression among the rural poor might form the possible basis of a modernity with which the anti-colonial consciousness of Bengali middle-class youth like Gora could establish some correspondence.

This anti-colonial modernity arising out of resistance against oppression might also provide a space for the anguished search of women like Anandamoyee, Lalita and Sucharita for their own identity. This space is not to be found either within the sanitised modernity of Brahmo Samaj or within the reactive Hindu ideology that Gora initially propagates. Anandamoyee's decision on the turbulent night of 1857 to adopt Gora as her own son is not a private, instinctive decision taken out of an innate motherliness. It is taken with full consciousness of its public consequences. She is led by anti-traditional reason rather than a nurturer's instinct. The same thing can be said of Lalita's decision to come away with Benoy. It is not a purely individualistic, emotional decision, but one taken in full awareness of its public implications. Although they keep their decisions to themselves, both Anandamoyee and Lalita take public positions and are prepared to face the social consequences of their action; however in the world in which they live, they are not allowed any public space where a discourse on these decisions is possible. The only space they have is outside their own community. The values that the 'home' represents have thus grown redundant for them. Their modernity lies in the outgoing tendency they stand for.

When we turn to *The Home and the World* (*Ghare Baire*), explorations of the ideas of the 'nation' and of 'nationalism' again constitute an important aspect of the text (it may be noted that in this essay I have referred to more than one version of the Bangla original, apart from the translated text, in order to illustrate my point). We find more than one model of nationalism here embodied in the personae of Sandip and Nikhilesh. We also find more than one model of 'modernity'. The 'modernity' of Nikhilesh creates ruptures in the feudal household with its traditions of libertinism outside and oppressiveness within. Because of him, Bimala, his wife, is 'educated and introduced to the modern age in its own language'. The alternative posed by Nikhilesh to the traditional feudal set-up is based on tolerance and a sense of inner integrity which is compatible with his quietist schemes of rural development. Sandip's militant nationalism stands in an oppositional position to this; but instead of developing this situation as a genuine contradiction it is watered down by frequent suggestions that Sandip's militancy is a mere disguise for personal opportunism. Of course there are other dimensions to Sandip's character too. I have said earlier that Sandip's nationalism resembles in some respects modern Western nationalism as critiqued by Rabindranath in his 1916 lectures. Some critics have seen Sandip as a Nietzchean character, the charismatic individual who is 'amoral' rather than 'immoral' and who can dispense with social and ethical considerations to achieve his own goals. The nationalism of such a character is but an extension of his aggressive individualism. About this brand of nationalism Rabindranath said: 'The idea of the Nation is the most powerful anesthetics that man has invented. Under the influence of its fumes the whole people can carry out its systematic programme of the most virulent self-seeking, without being in the least aware of its moral pervision.'[6] In his subsequent lecture on 'Nationalism in India', Rabindranath asserted that 'India has never had a real sense of nationalism' but that the ideals of the Indian extremists were based on Western history. 'They had no sympathy with the real problems of India', and did not realise that if England were to go away 'we would be victims of other nations', that the same social weaknesses like the caste system and the authority of traditions would continue.[7] Apart from Sandip's added personal kinks like his womanising (details of which are omitted in the English version)[8] or his dishonesty with money (which obviously Rabindranath did not think of as general characteristics of the extremists), there can be no doubt that the character of Sandip anticipates Rabindranath's subsequent assessment of extremist nationalism.

Yet the treatment of Sandip is not entirely unambiguous. For all his darker aspects his presence describes a space that Nikhilesh cannot cover, in spite of the constructive 'swadeshi' schemes through which he tries to reach out to the public sphere. Sandip represents the world outside that Nikhilesh instinctively withdraws from.

Nikhilesh may be contrasted in this respect with Gora, or even with Anandamoyee or Lalita in the earlier novel. Gora's dissatisfaction with his own situation and his marginalisation leads him outwards, beyond the pale of his own society and community, to find alliance with others who are marginalised and oppressed; the women, particularly Anandamoyee and Lalita, also reject the values imposed on them by their home and their community. They too are outcasts and their definition of their own position starts from this. But in *The Home and the World*, Nikhilesh's failed modernity makes him turn inward; he seeks to retrieve his '*ghar*', home, which would give him spiritual integrity. Life at his country seat has become too complicated and full of conflict—'*bahir*' or the outside world of politics keeps impinging upon it. As a consequence, he wishes to retreat to Calcutta and Bimala too chooses to do the same. Nikhilesh rejects the swadeshi ritualism which seeks to construct a social bonding and a sense of community around the revived cult of a mother-goddess. He refuses to agree with Sandip's strident demand that a visual image of the 'motherland'—may be 'one of the current images' (of Hindu deities)—is necessary, because 'the worship of the people must flow . . . along the deep-cut grooves of custom' (*The Home and the World*, p. 159). Nikhilesh's refusal to go along with this stems from his perception that: 'So long as we are impervious to truth and have to be moved by some hypnotic stimulus, we must know that we lack the capacity for self-government. Whatever may be our condition, we shall either need some imaginary ghost or some actual medicine man to terrorise over us.' He cannot be a party to swadeshi being made into an instrument of terror or oppression, any more than Gora can tolerate the demand made by Hindu conservatives that the old barber who has given shelter to a Muslim boy must be shunned. Nikhilesh takes up the cause of Muslim and lower-caste tenants who are being victimised in the name of swadeshi.[9] Yet nowhere is he shown relating to them as Gora does. His position is always that of a landowning patron, and his intervention fails miserably in the case of

Panchu. These interventions do not give him any sense of freedom; freedom lies ultimately in attaining spiritual integrity and withdrawing from the public space. Nikhilesh's position is portrayed with a complete lack of irony. The author's conscious privileging of Nikhilesh's viewpoint goes against the inner logic of the narrative, weakening it. His critique of 'nationalism' tends to lapse into a tacit acceptance of the colonial status quo. Superficially, Nikhilesh's modernity has the same universalist character as the mature Gora's. But it is actually devoid of the radical, heterodox quality that Gora's modernity has. In fact, the last chapters even suggest a demise of modernity.

In 'The Nationalist Resolution of the Women's Question', Partha Chatterjee analyses the significance of the polarised metaphor of 'ghar' and 'bahir' in the discourse of nationalism in the late nineteenth and the early twentieth century and points out that 'bahir' or the world signifies 'the treacherous terrain of the pursuit of material interests, where practical considerations reign supreme', while the 'home' represents our 'inner spiritual self, our true identity'. This space is perceived as still unviolated by colonial domination and the emancipated woman is conferred a new role in the project of nation-making, that is, of maintaining the purity of the home and the inner world thus binding them to 'a new, and yet entirely legitimate subordination'.[10] Michael Sprinker, who regards Nikhilesh as a representative of this 'new patriarchy' and its contradictions, describes him as a patriarch *manqué*:

The text cries out for but cannot produce the combination of power and justice that is the ideal figure demanded by the semiotic system: the authoritative, wise and powerful patriarch. By splitting the necessary qualities for its ideal resolution between two male protagonists, the novel acknowledges the impossibility of fulfilling its own ideological fantasy.[11]

It is true that some lineaments of the new patriarch, both with respect to social hierarchy and gender hierarchy, can be found in the modern, enlightened landowner Nikhilesh. His modernity remains ineffectual in the face of the extremist upsurge, yet it is his guidance that Bimala seeks in her predicament. Nikhilesh's implicit acceptance of Bimala's submission to him ('her hands groping for my feet grasped them and drew them to herself, pressing them against her breast with such force that I thought her heart would break'), can be contrasted with Gora's final abdication of his claim to be Sucharita's 'guru'; it is only Pareshbabu whom he is willing to accept as 'guru' in common with Sucharita, because 'all communities have closed their doors' upon Pareshbabu; Nikhilesh on the other hand, even as he rejects revivalist aspirations and propagates a broad humanism, still fits, to some extent within traditional hierarchies that the nationalist discourse adopted and revitalised.

But in the character of Sandip there is more space for ambiguity. Sandip represents the dubious terrain of political, material power— power without principle. His approach to Bimala, as to his other objects of desire, is marked by an aggressive will to possess and master. His modernity is deliberately underscored as a tainted modernity that may be attractive, but is not to be trusted. The novel altogether excludes the adversary Sandip is fighting, and represents the British Empire by the innocuous Miss Gilby. Swadeshi thus comes to be seen as an instrument the feudal hierarchy uses mainly to oppress Muslim and 'low-caste' peasants.

Yet in spite of all the negative markers with which Sandip is in- vested, he also brings with him certain possibilities of liberation. Unlike the nationalist in Partha Chatterjee's essay who would retain in his construction of sovereign nationhood a somewhat revised form of earlier power structures, Sandip subverts such structures. He not only disrupts Bimala's home life, he also communicates to her ideas which have the capacity to turn her whole world upside down. Although in practice he gangs up with reactionary landowners and petty intellec- tuals propagating revivalism, the power of the ideas he represents ac- quires a different dimension. This power is often described in the text through the problematic metaphor of 'intoxication' that we find Nikhil withdrawing from. It refers not only to Sandip's personal hypnotism, but also to the power of a disruptive moment in history. Bimala says:

This moment of our history seemed to have dropped into our hand like a jewel from the crown of some drunken god . . . we were led to hope that all our wants and miseries would disappear by the spell of some magic charm, that for us there was no longer any boundary line between the possible and the impossible. . . . (*The Home and the World*, p. 116)

Bimala's illicit attraction for Sandip is often found to broaden and merge into her awed awareness of a great historical change that is imminent—'the unthought of, the unknown, the importunate stranger'. Sandip's betrayal of this trust, at a very personal level, cannot altogether destroy the value of the perception he generates. In one striking episode Bimala stands alone on the terrace at night and perceives the darkness like the 'vague embryo of some future creation':

In that future I saw my country, a woman like myself, standing expectant. She has been drawn forth from her home corner by the sudden call of some unknown. . . . She is no mother. There is no call to her of children in their hunger, no home to be lighted of an evening, no household work to be done. No; she hies to her tryst, for this is the land of the Vaishnava Poets. She has left home, forgotten domestic duties; she has nothing but an unfathomable yearning which hurries her on. . . . (*The Home and the World*, p. 120)

In fact, images of the 'Shakto' as well as the 'Vaishnav' esoteric forms of devotion are woven into the text to suggest the subversive, destructive power of the historical changes that are taking place. Nikhilesh's quietist humanism can hardly cope with it; but Sandip's romantic rhetoric, for all the sordid designs of material gain that it conceals, focuses on the revolutionary possibilities of the moment as well. The mother-icon of the 'Shakto' faith was privileged as the image of the motherland in nationalist discourse. Tanika Sarkar notes that the Bengali nationalist appropriation of the female icon causes a metamorphosics in the icon. There is a transformation of 'traces of militancy and sexuality into something more "innocent"', so that 'Kali reverts back to Durga, Durga becomes a household drudge', or so that 'Devi Choudhurani' returns to fulfil her household obligations.[12] We can find quite a few examples of this in different texts.

In *The Home and the World*, the Sandip–Bimala relationship evokes images of Kali, 'the shameless, pitiless goddess', as its presiding deity (Bimala is also sometimes compared to Devi Choudhurani by her sister-in-law); Tanika Sarkar finds this image diluted in other contemporary texts, but in this novel it is intensified through Sandip's rhetoric. His rhetoric eroticises the mother-icon as in the famous passage in which the geographic features of the motherland assume an anthropomorphic form and is identified with Bimala in her 'universal aspect'. Later, when Sandip takes leave of Bimala, there is a more deliberate and explicit transformation of the mother-image into the image of an erotic passion that destroys. Sandip tells Bimala:

My watchword has changed since you have come across my vision. It is no longer 'Bande Mataram' (Hail Mother), but Hail Beloved, Hail Enchantress, . . . The mother's day is past. O love, my love, you have made as naught for me the truth and right and heaven itself. All duties become as shadows: all rules and restraints have snapped their bonds. . . . (*The Home and the World*, p. 241)

or again,

I salute you, Queen Bee, Queen of the bleeding hearts, Queen of desolation! (*The Home and the World*, p. 277)

While the author's sympathies lie with Nikhilesh's creed of universal humanism, the failure of this creed here also indicates certain historical exigencies that are represented through Sandip. This is a moment of self-realisation by the colonised from which there can be no going back. The centrifugal pull that Sandip represents in relation to Bimala is quite different from the outward movement of characters I have referred to in connection with *Gora*. In *Gora*, this is all about commonality of interest among oppressed and marginalised people, about the possibility of new alliances in the face of the social–political hierarchy created by colonialism.

In *The Home and the World*, however, the horizon has darkened and Bimala is isolated in the quest for her own identity. It is her desperate retreat from the modernity she had discovered and her abdication of the public space that was opening up for her, that is traced in the second half of the novel. Her response to the storm of new ideas that Sandip brings with him goes far beyond her rather superficial attraction for Sandip as an individual. Yet through her retreat she is cutting herself off from the inexorable course of history—the evolution of the anti-colonial struggle and the woman's changing role in it. She is withdrawing altogether from playing any part in nation-building except under the guidance of her husband. The possibility at the end of the novel that he might die of his injuries makes her fate even more uncertain.

But Bimala's retreat does not signify a total negation of the wide, though dangerous, spaces that had opened up for her through her association with Sandip. It is not Sandip's borrowed jargon on man–woman relationships but Bimala's awareness of newly available political and sexual spaces through the accentuation of the anti-colonial movement, that becomes the signifier of modernity in the novel. She is unable to bear the uncertainties of this upheaval and retreats from it altogether; her creator, too, even as he weaves these suggestions into the text, seems to retreat from his own perceptions.

In the original serialised version of *Ghare Baire* in *Sabuj Patra*, the novel starts straightaway in the first person as told by Bimala as if the author had initially intended to tell the story through one first person narrator, Bimala. The narration is split up later to accommodate the two male narrators. It is only in the book version of 1916 that the narration starts with the caption, 'Bimalar Atmakatha' (Bimala's story), thus making space for the other two storytellers. That Bimala's perception is only a fragmentary perception which has to be balanced by Nikhilesh's version of the story, that it is necessary for Sandip to soliloquise so that the reader sees him not only through Bimala's fascinated eyes, but can gauge his hidden intentions—all these are perhaps later arrangements made by the author to privilege his own critique of the swadeshi movement.

The text does not wholly fulfil the author's design upon his readers. Reading *The Home and the World* side by side with *Gora* helps us to understand that 'ghar' and 'bahir' in the novel do not only refer to the question of woman's emancipation from the patriarchal system within her family, with the anti-colonial movement providing a kind of background to it; it is also about a woman's awareness of the anti-colonial struggle and the evolution of her political as well as sexual subjectivity as a participant in it. The woman's anti-colonial consciousness need not invariably be seen as trapped within the patriarchal scheme of nationalist discourse and submitting to its restricted agenda. Very often there may be a disjunction between an ideological construct and real practice. In *Gora*, Lalita's community allows her a degree of modernity, but she makes it a launching-pad for a kind of dissenting social–political practice that goes far beyond it. In *The Home and the World*, too, Bimala's exploration of her own modernity, by its very logic, leads her towards her involvement with Sandip and with the swadeshi movement, although this makes the circumscribed nature of this modernity very evident. For her, the swadeshi movement is not merely a pretext for her relationship with Sandip; rather her relationship with Sandip has, in the text, the possibility of opening out towards an engagement with larger historical upheavals, a possibility that the text cannot fulfil.

One must not, however, conclude from this that *Ghare Baire* represents Rabindranath's final position on the anti-colonial struggle of which the swadeshi movement was a phase. His relationship with the nationalist creed continued to be troubled and as *Char Adhyay*, written in the turbulent 1930s shows, his perception of the role of women in the anti-colonial movement was deeply riven by internal contradictions. The perspicacity that we find in *Gora* really belongs to a less troubled earlier phase. Here he constructs a model of modernity which opens out to form alliances against both the traditionalist and the colonialist status quo. The possibility of such alliances is perhaps diminished as the swadeshi movement enters a more rigid phase. Rabindranath's own reaction to it also reflects this rigidity in the reverse. But the questions that *Gora* had raised regarding the problem of redefining modernity in a situation where anti-colonial awareness is on the rise is not completely lost in *Ghare Baire* or in any subsequent work of Tagore.

Endnotes

All the references from *The Home and the World*, translated by Surendranath Tagore, are from the Macmillan edition (1919). The short passages from *Gora*, quoted in this essay, have been translated by me.

1. Sumit Sarkar, *The Swadeshi Movement in Bengal, 1903–08* (New Delhi: People's Publishing House, 1973), pp. 82–3.
2. Ibid., p. 502.
3. '*Shikshar Naba Adarsha*', *Sabuj Patra*, Magh, 1322 (Bangabda).
4. Letter to Amiya Chakraborty, 29 Phalgun, 1322 (Bangabda). Translation mine, from original at Rabindra Bhawan archives.
5. Prosanto K. Pal, *Rabijibani* (Calcutta: Ananda, 1977), vol. 8, p. 239.
6. 'Nationalism', 1927, pp. 42–3.
7. Ibid., pp. 106–7, pp. 112–13.
8. *Rabindra Rachanabali*, vol. 8. West Bengal Government 1986, p. 38. Sandip, scheming to achieve mastery over Bimala, recalls his own near-hypnotic power over women and gives the examples of a young widow and an Anglo-Indian girl who had succumbed to the magic of his personality.
9. In several articles written in 1907–8, Rabindranath underscores the alienation of the Muslim and 'lower-caste' peasants from the swadeshi ideal and the flaw that this creates in the movement. This theme is to be found in 'Byadhi O, Pratikar', 'Deshahita', (1314: Parishishta: Rajapraja, Samuha); 'Sadupaya' (1315: Samuha), etc.

10. Partha Chatterjee, 'The Nationalist Resolution of the Women's Question', in *Recasting Women: Essays in Colonial History*, eds Kumkum Sangari and Sudesh Vaid, (Delhi: Kali for Women, 1989), pp. 233–53.

11. See 'Homeboys: Nationalism, Colonialism and Gender in Rabindranath Tagore's *The Home and the World*,' in this book.

12. Tanika Sarkar, 'Nationalist Iconography: Image of Women in Nineteenth Century Bengali Literature', in *Ideals, Images and Real Lives: Women in Literature and History*, eds Alice Thorner and Maitreyee Krishnaraj (Hyderabad: Orient Longman, 2000), p. 164.

Ghare Baire in its Times*

SUMIT SARKAR

Ghare Baire (*The Home and the World*) has not been a comfortable text for many of its readers. Its author's freshly enhanced stature as winner of the Nobel Prize (in 1913) did not prevent sharp criticism when it was being serialised monthly in *Sabuj Patra* (Baisakh/Falgun, 1322/1915–16), even before the novel was published in book form in 1916. There is even a report that the novel was withdrawn for a time from the Calcutta University Library.[1] One would expect many to have been shocked by the novel's depiction of Sandip, the unscrupulous swadeshi-extremist politician seeking to seduce Bimala, wife of his old friend Nikhilesh, at whose house he had been staying. Sandip's politics of aggressive Hindu nationalist demagogy, combined with coercion, through landlord pressure, of Muslim and lower-caste peasants unwilling to boycott British goods, are shown to lead to communal violence. A charge of unfair criticism of patriots engaged in heroic anti-colonial struggle probably still lingers, and many readers feel, even now, that Rabindranath in *Ghare Baire* betrayed a certain softness towards colonial political–cultural domination. That, one presumes, was Lukacs's assumption when he accused Tagore of having failed in *The Home and the World* to write even a proper 'counter-revolutionary novel', unlike Dostoevsky in *The Possessed*.[2]

*This essay owes much to the comments and criticisms of its initial draft by Pradip Kumar Datta and Tanika Sarkar.

It is interesting, though, that contemporary criticism of the novel seems to have related primarily to the portrayal of Bimala, her adulterous passion for Sandip being thought intolerable for a Hindu wife, a gross violation of the Sita model. Gender then seems to have been given a centrality which it largely lost in subsequent discussions of the novel. But a cultural–nationalist subtext was clearly present not far from below the surface: perhaps the open espousal of extremist nationalism that a denunciation of Sandip as slanderous caricature would have involved, had been thought unwise in 1915–16, a time of war and internal repression. Rabindranath's reply to his critics indicates a full awareness of this submerged dimension. Shakespeare's heroines, he reminded his readers, are seldom judged in terms of their conformity to Christian values or to standards appropriate for good 'English' womanhood. But, 'Bengalees today take great pride in having in India what does not exist anywhere else . . . and so literary debate turns around whether or not a character fits in with the ideals of the "true Hindu woman".'[3]

Criticism on the grounds of insufficient patriotism implies an assumption, still often encountered today in different forms, that the entire field of early-twentieth-century Bengal (and Indian) history was, or at least should have been, occupied by a single colonial–anti-colonial nationalist binary. Everything else—questions of gender or caste, for instance—is either marginalised or, if studied, tends to be evaluated in terms of 'contribution' or otherwise to the process of political or cultural emancipation from Western domination. I find this quite unacceptable, for nationalism then gets valorised without qualification, so long as it appears sufficiently anti-colonial in its politics and/or its affirmation of cultural authenticity. But I have some problems also with the alternative reading put forward by Ashis Nandy in his influential study of Tagore.[4] By hailing the author of *Ghare Baire* as a great critic of conventional forms of nationalism, this study in effect inverts the value judgements implicit in charges made against Rabindranath of having been insufficiently patriotic. I would go along with Nandy for a part of the way, as I certainly share his distrust of aggressive, state-centred nationalism. The novel, along with numerous other writings of Tagore around that time, does represent a valid and still highly relevant critique of the many dangers of chauvinistic forms of nationalism, whether of the West or the non-West.

What I find difficult to accept is the attempt to assimilate Tagore—despite the well-known debates with Gandhi—into Nandy's favoured kind of anti-modernism, to locate him as ultimately 'a critic . . . by implication, of modernity'. For Nandy, Tagore, like Gandhi, was among the 'dissenters among dissenters', who sought the alternative to nationalism not in a 'homogenised universalism' still grounded in some version of the 'Enlightenment concept of freedom', but in a 'distinctive civilisational concept of universalism embedded in the tolerance encoded in various traditional ways of life in a highly diverse, plural society.'[5] The stress on 'civilisational' authenticity leads Nandy back towards cultural nationalism, and does less than justice to a very significant change in Rabindranath's trajectory in his post-swadeshi phase, embodied notably in *Ghare Baire*. It also fails to adequately comprehend the new elements in the handling of gender relationships and images, in the novel as well as in certain near-contemporaneous short stories of Tagore.

A fuller understanding of *Ghare Baire* demands some exploration of a fairly dense web of other, related texts and events. Constituted primarily by a number of other writings of Tagore around this time, this exercise at locating *Ghare Baire* intertextually and contextually has to include an examination of other kinds of documentation, both official and unofficial, about the swadeshi and the immediate post-swadeshi years. A glance at some contemporary gender debates and narratives will also be necessary, for the political debate in the novel is intricately interwoven with the triangular relationship of Nikhilesh–Bimala–Sandip. *Ghare Baire* has to be located in a crucial era of transitions—for both Tagore and his times.

Like his hero, Nikhilesh, Tagore had tried, without success, to promote swadeshi (indigenous) habits and enterprises long before they became popular. He had also been one of the earliest and sharpest critics of the policy of 'mendicancy'—that is, of merely begging for concessions from the rulers without avail—for which the moderate Congress had becomes notorious. Where the novelist differed from his hero was in his initial enthusiasm—during 1905–7—for the new agitational methods, involving the boycott of foreign goods and schools and other forms of passive resistance, adopted by Bengal's middle-class nationalists as a reaction to the partition imposed on their province by Lord Curzon.

A movement, predominantly of upper-caste Hindu *bhadralok*, gentlefolk who tended to have rentier interests in land cultivated mainly by lower-caste Hindus or Muslims, swadeshi often sought mass contact through a highly emotional Hindu revivalism, particularly as it turned more militant or extremist.[6]

A parting of ways between Tagore and the swadeshi movement came with the shock of Hindu–Muslim riots in some villages of East Bengal in the early months of 1907. The evident ebbing away of hopes in a mass movement led some extremists towards methods of individual terror, accompanied by an intensification of Hindu revivalism. For Tagore, in sharp contrast, the riots demanded deep introspection and self-criticism. These were first expressed through a series of essays around 1907–8, some passages of which would be echoed in the reflections of Nikhilesh eight years later.[7] The internal shift through which Tagore was passing also found vivid embodiment in the pages of *Gora* (1907–9), and traces of it are discernible, in more oblique ways, in the novel that immediately preceded *Ghare Baire*, that is, *Chaturanga*, which was serialised in *Sabuj Patra* in 1914 and published the year after. This was followed by an onslaught on nationalism through lectures in Japan and the USA during 1915–17, published in book form as *Nationalism* (1917).

In addition, there was another, related, but little-noticed evolution. Revivalist nationalism was often associated with certain conceptions of ideal Hindu womanhood that, once again, Tagore seems to have briefly shared but then sharply repudiated. This critical attitude to Hindu nationalist notions of femininity deepened between 1914 and 1917 in a spate of short stories, published like *Chaturanga* and *Ghare Baire* in *Sabuj Patra*, itself an experimental, in some ways deeply iconoclastic, monthly which Tagore helped Pramatha Chaudhury to start in 1914.[8] There were ten such *Sabuj Patra* stories by Tagore, among them the remarkable, proto-feministic, *Streer Patra* (The Wife's Letter, Shravan, 1321/1914). In keeping with the evocation of youth and novelty in the title of the monthly,[9] *Streer Patra* and *Ghare Baire* were the first works of Tagore written in the *chalit* (colloquial) Bengali prose. As contrasted with the prevalent, more Sanskritised, *sadhubhasha*, this must have been intended as a democratising move.

I propose to analyse *Ghare Baire* at two levels. A novel—even one as specifically contextualised as this—has of course no obligation to accurately report its times, and therefore the question of the 'fairness' of Tagore's account of extremism is not a vital one. But the issue of Tagore's politics and the understanding of swadeshi that flowed from it cannot be avoided. I begin therefore by briefly juxtaposing *Ghare Baire* with other documentation from the swadeshi years, highlighting, as I had done many years ago in my research on that era, its considerable relevance for an adequate understanding of the limits of the movement in terms of mass involvement. Continuing my analysis of the novel's manifest content, looking upon it as one kind of 'source' among others, I turn to the deeper aspects of Tagore's critique of extremist nationalism, that is, its fetishising of the Nation and the subordination of morality to its worship.

The elaboration of Tagore's nationalism is however a preliminary to the problems of gender and domesticity that I will examine. I will focus on Tagore's conception of Sandip, specifically the dual character of his masculinism. He combines a hard, aggressive conception of masculinity that relates in a totally instrumentalist and exploitative manner to other men, women and nature alike, with a worship of Bimala as an embodiment of the Motherland, an object of eroticised, patriotic adoration. This is certainly not how Tagore had seen things always. For a time—especially during the swadeshi years—he had been attracted to a kind of home–world divide; with home and the Hindu woman providing a haven of cultural authenticity from the subjection to the colonial regime in public life, something Partha Chatterjee has diagnosed as characteristic of the 'nationalist' resolution of the 'women's question'. The considerable novelty of Tagore's *Sabuj Patra* stories therefore requires emphasis and explication. Here, I suggest, as a tentative part-explanation, the impact of a *cause celebre* of January 1914, the Snehalata case.[10]

Ghare Baire, however, provides an additional and to my mind quite crucial complication, going beyond depictions of the burden of patriarchy and occasional protest by women. It presents a sincerely reformist husband hoist with his own petard. Nikhilesh encourages his wife to come out into the 'world', but then Bimala chooses a trajectory that, for him, his creator and the intended audience alike, is utterly disastrous. We need to ask why Tagore deliberately chose to complicate matters in this way. I suggest that the internal conflicts that ensue in Nikhilesh constitute the real heart of the novel, for through them Tagore seeks to work out an alternative conception of masculinity. Diametrically opposed to the notions embodied in Sandip, this tendency seeks to move, through self-examination and autocritique, towards a non-instrumentalised recognition of the autonomy of the Other. Nikhilesh responds to the crisis through a reaffirmation of his reformist values, but also begins to recognise the limits of a reformism which had paid little heed to the subjectivity of women, to the need, above all, for women to develop their own autonomy, their *atmashakti*. *Ghare Baire*, then, can be read in terms of a conflict between alternative notions of masculinity—meaning, by that term, not just ways of relating to women but the entire cluster of values thought to be most appropriate for true manhood. It is in terms of this problematic that I will finally turn to Bimala, and pose a problem concerning the extent of Tagore's readiness and ability to accept the autonomous subjectivity of women.

II

Let me begin with an essay of Tagore entitled *Sadupay* ('The Right way'), published in *Prabasi* in Sravan (July–August 1908). The parameters of Tagore's rejection of swadeshi extremism are expounded here for the first time with considerable clarity. He began with a reference to the hostility of large numbers of Muslim and subordinate-caste Namasudra[11] peasants to boycott in the East Bengal countryside. Some of them were now sticking to foreign salt and cloth even when their swadeshi substitutes were cheaper. Tagore found this understandable. 'We have demanded closeness and brotherhood from them without ever having tried to be close to them earlier. . . . We imagine that the Mother has become real for the whole country through songs and emotional ecstasy alone.' Tagore felt that the problem of alienation—from the Muslims as well as the peasant masses in general—was being compounded by the easy recourse to force when support was not forthcoming. Herein lay a crucial problem of the movement, going beyond the question of defective mobilisation strategy. 'Our misfortune is that we want freedom, but we do not believe in freedom in our hearts. . . . Threats of consigning forefathers to hell, social ostracism through withdrawing the services of washermen and barbers, burning homesteads, beating-up recalcitrants on village paths . . . all these are ways of making slave-mentalities permanent within us.'[12] The swadeshi experience made Tagore more deeply aware of the divisive and oppressive nature of caste and community barriers and the coercion associated with their maintenance: it led him in this essay to perceive a basic incompleteness in the swadeshi concept of freedom. It is this notion of freedom, or individual human rights, affirmed, if needed, against community disciplines, that lay at the heart of Tagore's more general critique of nationalism. This, it is necessary to add, would also provide the basis for a widening of his horizons concerning gender in the post-swadeshi era.

Ghare Baire enters these problems through the subplot of Panchu. Near-landless, surviving through bartering cheap imported cloth and trinkets for grain from women of Namasudra households living in a segregated area amidst swamps, Panchu has to mortgage the little land he possesses due to his wife's illness; his Brahmin-dominated panchayat imposes a monetary *prayaschitta* (ritual penance) on him when she dies.[13] This particular story recalls and is indeed elaborated by another in *Gora*. The hero of that novel, whose burning patriotism had made him seek communion with the motherland through a rigorous upholding of traditional Hindu rituals and values and wanderings among peasants, comes to discover that the ties of community (*samajer bandhan*) 'provide no help in times of need, no comfort in troubles, they only enforce disciplinary commands that add to the problems. . . . No longer could Gora delude himself with the roseate hues of his own imagination.'[14]

Panchu's woes are compounded by the additional burden of swadeshi. He is bullied by Sandip's student cadres (back home from Calcutta for their vacations) for the crime of petty trading in foreign goods. While Nikhilesh as benevolent and philanthropic zamindar refuses to impose the boycott on his tenants, the notoriously oppressive neighbouring landlord, Harish Kundu, has Panchu beaten up and plans to evict him from his tiny bit of homestead land. Meanwhile, the incessant and aggressive Hindu imagery deployed by Sandip's band culminates in plans for organising a massive Durga puja, for which Harish Kundu levies additional cesses on his largely Muslim tenantry. This leads to a Muslim backlash, encouraged by mullas from Dacca. The novel ends amidst the fires of communal violence.

Tagore's story highlights aspects of swadeshi that were often suppressed by its adherents. Contemporary sources, both archival and non-official—indeed, sometimes of nationalist provenance too—speak of real-life incidents that parallel the stories of Panchu and the Muslims. Government records speak of Hindu shrines that were specially targeted by iconoclastic Muslim rioters during the May 1907 riots in the Jamalpur region of Mymensingh district, because these had been constructed by landlords through levying a special *iswar-britti* cess.[15] In the winter of 1907–8 officials started enquiries into alleged oppression of tenants by big zamindars suspected of swadeshi involvement, notably on the Gauripur estate of the leading swadeshi supporter, Brojendrokishore Raychaudhury, in Mymensingh.[16] Nationalist newspapers were indignant that the government was encouraging, through this manner, the 'withholding of rent' by peasants. They may well have been right in suspecting a divide-and-rule strategy behind the choice of zamindars who were investigated. However what was equally clear was the pro-zamindari bias of swadeshi propagandists. For instance, a mild criticism of absentee landlords made at that time by a nationalist newspaper, the *Daily Hitavadi*, did not fail to add that swaraj required the strengthening of 'social ties' and the recognition that 'zamindars are heads of society'. As for the methods of social boycott, so roundly condemned by Tagore in *Ghare Baire*, this is what the same paper had to say in its 23 February 1908 issue:

It would be easy to convert illiterate and half-educated villagers to Swadeshism, subjecting them to social control and threatening them with social boycott . . . The dread of being deprived of the services of the priest, the barber and the washerman will act powerfully to keep the refractory spirits under control.[17]

The social critique developed in *Ghare Baire*, however, is haunted by a sense of failure and isolation. It does not go beyond showing up the network of a dangerous kind of nationalism composed of unscrupulous politicians like Sandip, their deluded student henchmen, and oppressive landlord and/or their agents. The alternative to Sandip, represented by the paternalist zamindar Nikhilesh (in large part, embodying Tagore himself), is one who goes out alone to fight the communal riot and returns (in all probability) mortally wounded. The sense of failure may not have to do with Tagore's pessimism about nationalism alone, a gloom that was enfolding him after the outbreak of the world war in 1914. It may have sprung from an inability to understand changes in the world of swadeshi Bengal which made the binary framework of evil politician/landlord and paternalist zamindar an insufficient one for grasping its complexity.

The research of the Japanese historian Nariaki Nakazato reveals a certain social conjuncture, that provides a more comprehensive map of the social processes taking place in the swadeshi countryside. Indeed it also accounts for the outbreak of social conflict that is indicated in the story—and which is normally explained only as a structural problem of landlord–peasant antagonism coinciding with the division between Hindus and Muslims as well as upper caste and lower caste. Nakazato indicates a coincidence in time between the swadeshi movement and an important shift in agrarian relations that sharpened tensions in the countryside considerably. Prices were rising and under its pressure, zamindars and the gentry in general (particularly the bhadralok intermediate tenure-holders) were trying to extend the practice of produce rent or *bargadari* (sharecropping). This practice was a convenient one for the landlords, since there were no ceilings on rent enhancements on bargadari of the kind imposed on money rents by the Rent Act of 1885. In any case, relatively inflexible money rents at a time of rising prices obviously meant that it would fetch less grain or jute, a factor that would make bargadari even more popular. Bargadari also became more extensive since many among the bhadralok were getting into trade in agricultural produce at this time and were eager to acquire immediate physical control over the harvested crops. On all these counts, tensions sharpened between the gentry and sections of the peasantry who were a part of the bargadari system. Most of these peasants were upwardly mobile Muslims and in some areas, Namasudras. These groups felt that it would be beneficial for them to switch to money rents. Commutation was legally permissible, if peasants applied for it during settlement operations—which consequently could become a time for sharpened class struggle. And here the coincidence with the swadeshi movement was decisive. Matters came to a head in 1907–8 in the Gournadi region which lay in the northern part of Bakarganj district, and which was the homeland of the prominent nationalist leader, Ashwini Dutt, and a major base of bhadralok swadeshi activity. J.C. Jack, an official with pro-peasant sympathies, was conducting settlement operations there just then. Jack felt it his duty to inform peasants of this particular provision (Section 40) of the 1885 act. This set off a rush of commutation application from many Namasudras and Muslims, which, in turn, aroused violent bhadralok indignation and resistance.[18] In this climate of peasant hostility, abstract patriotic appeals to boycott foreign cloth and salt met with firm refusals. There were even instances of counter-boycotts of rent and services to the bhadralok.

III

Nikhilesh and the ideal of zamindari paternalism—to which Tagore himself subscribed—may have been rendered totally inadequate by a mounting process of social conflict that Tagore may have felt but not fully grasped. At the same time it is equally true to say that the presence of Nikhilesh allows for a profound critique of swadeshi-extremist nationalism, which is centred on its fetishisation of the Nation. Towards the beginning of the novel, Bimala (who, unlike Nikhilesh and Sandip recollects events continuously in retrospect) recalls that her husband had anticipated much of swadeshi, but had 'never been able to accept the mantra of 'Bande Mataram' as the ultimate value. 'He used to say that he was willing to serve the country, but reserved his worship for the Being who is above the land. If we make the country our object of worship, we will be leading it to disaster.'[19] Bankim's hymn, with its indissoluble mingling of devotion to the motherland with the worship of Durga and Kali, is well known for having alienated the Muslims when it was made a central feature of swadeshi nationalism.

But Rabindranath's critique goes much beyond the question of failed patriotic mobilisation and communal rupture alone. The disaster, the novel makes clear, resides in a ruthless instrumentalisation of everything else to the presumed cause of the Nation. Of critical importance here is what Rabindranath puts in the voice of Sandip. 'Sandip's Story' begins with the following assertion:

The impotent man says 'that which has come to my share is mine.' And the weak man assents. But the lesson of the whole world is: 'That is really mine which I can snatch away.' . . . The world into which we are born is the world of reality. When a man goes away from the market of real things with empty hands and empty stomach, merely filling his bag with big-sounding words, I wonder why he ever came into this hard world at all. . . what I desire, I desire positively, superlatively. (*The Home and the World*, pp. 45–6)

What Rabindranath is repudiating here is much more than a specific, extremist form of Indian nationalism. Reduced to those terms alone, Sandip might appear to be somewhat of a caricature in his utter villainy.[20] The target is something much more general, what might be called a creed of political 'realism', based on an assumption of universal and inevitable competitiveness—the methods, we might say, of Social Darwinism. Here Rabindranath seems to be grasping, in embryo as it were, certain possibilities that have become frighteningly manifest in today's India, more so perhaps than in the times of the novel. Resonances with contemporary aggressive, chauvinist religious nationalism of the Hindutva variety are only too apparent now.

Take, for instance, the following conversation between Sandip and Nikhilesh, reported by the former:

. . . though we have shouted ourselves hoarse, proclaiming the Mussulmans to be our brethren, we have come to realize that we shall never be able to bring them wholly round to our side. So they must be suppressed altogether and made to understand that we are the masters . . . 'If the idea of a United India is a true one,' objects Nikhil, 'Mussulmans are a necessary part of it.' 'Quite so,' said I, 'but we must know their place and keep them there, otherwise they will constantly be giving trouble'. (*The Home and the World*, p. 120)

We have heard much about the wisdom of being politically 'realist' in India in recent years, whether in terms of keeping Muslims or Christians 'in their place', or in justifying the Indian Bomb. Further, through his strictures concerning 'the impotent man', Sandip linked up his political-realist creed with a basic notion of hard, aggressive masculinity. And here once again we hear more recent echoes. Nathuram Godse, for instance, in his last speech before the court that sentenced him to death for the murder of the Mahatma, repeatedly accused Gandhi of effeminacy. Godse contrasted him with Savarkar, the real founder of the ideology of Hindutva, who he acknowledged to have been his principal inspiration.

But let us return to *Ghare Baire's* own times. The novel clearly points towards Rabindranath's 'Nationalism' lectures of 1916–17, with their trenchant rejection of the 'endless bull-fight' between nation-states and incipient nationalisms threatening to become mirror images of each other, acting according to the Social Darwinist dogma that 'the unfit must go to the wall'. Sandip's fetishised 'world of reality' as the 'market of real things' is now expanded, with a verbosity and rhetoric which is often burdensome, but which, on occasion, manages to hit its mark with remarkable prescience: an endless 'greed of wealth and power . . . [that] can never come to any other end but a violent death . . . Those who have made the gain of money their highest end are unconsciously selling their life and soul to rich persons or to combinations that represent money. Those who are enamoured of their political power and gloat over their extension of dominion over foreign races gradually surrender their own freedom and humanity to the organizations necessary for holding other peoples in slavery.'[21] For Nandy, *Nationalism*, along with *Ghare Baire* and the other two novels he takes up, constitute testimony to Rabindranath's fundamental rejection of the modern West, through a reaffirmation of the 'civilizational' values of plurality and 'toleration encoded in various traditional ways of life'. Many passages can be found in Tagore that support Nandy's reading, and indeed, they dominate his writings in the early 1900s. His initial swadeshi enthusiasm had led him then to a fairly unqualified justification of the varna system, in an essay entitled *Brahman* (1902). The Santiniketan ashram he started around that time initially even had caste-segregated meals. But I consider it indispensable, when looking at a man who wrote so voluminously and for so long, to remain attentive to the discipline of temporal–historical context. Nandy fails to give adequate weight to the fundamental shift in many of Rabindranath's perspectives that accompanied his disillusionment with swadeshi, around 1907–8.[22] Unlike many others then—or later—his rejection of political nationalism did not involve an espousal of what in effect amounts to cultural nationalism.

In the essay *Nationalism in India* (1916), Tagore did occasionally relate the caste system to what he thought had been the Indian experiment 'in evolving a social unity within which all the different peoples could be held together, yet fully enjoying the freedom of maintaining their own differences'. But he went on to add that India had rightly 'recognized differences, but not the mutability which is the law of life', and so had 'set up boundaries of immutable walls', a 'magnificent cage of countless compartments'. The essay went on to bluntly call for the removal of 'the state of affairs. . . . brought about entirely by the domination in India of the caste system, and the blind and lazy habit of relying upon the authority of traditions that are incongruous anachronisms in the present age'.[23] All this, of course, did not make of Rabindranath an uncritical 'Westernist' or 'modernist': the point is that—like Gandhi, too, at least part of the time—he tried to remain aware of the contradictory dimensions of both indigenous 'tradition' and 'modernity.'

Ghare Baire, at times, is even sharper in this regard, with the novel format allowing for greater concreteness. In a magnificent passage, inexplicably left out of the English version, Nikhilesh sees in the Harish Kundu–Panchu episode an epitome of the connections between rural poverty, landlord exploitation and the power of the high caste-religious establishment:

I recalled, then, Panchu, caught in the toils of poverty and fraud—it seemed as if he embodied all the poor peasants of Bengal. I saw Harish Kundu, bloated of body, ever faithful in his rituals, with all the marks of proper piety on his forehead. . . . One will have to fight till the end this monstrosity of greed and power, which has fattened itself through sucking the blood of the dying, and burdens the earth with its sublime immovability—while below it lie all those who starve, remain blinded by ignorance, worn down by endless toil. This is the task that has remained postponed for century after century. . . .[24]

Another passage in the novel goes further towards a rejection of the hierarchical organisation of society that in nineteenth-century orthodox-Hindu discourses was often termed *adhikari-bheda*—a rejection through the affirmation, in theory, of equal rights for all. Nikhilesh recalls sadly how Bimala had once brushed aside as a joke his suggestion, made while thinking of Panchu, that they both devote themselves to the eradication of poverty in the country:

Though Bimala comes from a poor home, she has queenly assumptions. . . . She thinks that the lower orders . . . are bound to have their woes, but they hardly feel it as wants. In Bimala's blood there is that arrogance which traditionally has cut up Indian society into infinite layers in which every level has had the sense of being at least superior to the level beneath it, and has gloried in that petty superiority. She has the true tradition of Manu in her. While in me it seems that the blood of Guhak and Eklavya still flows: I cannot thrust away as lowly those who today are situated below me in society. My

Bharatvarsha is not made up purely of the bhadralok. I see clearly that it is India that declines and dies, when those below us suffer and die.[25]

Gender in nineteenth-century bhadralok discourses had been the major site where this debate between adhikari-bheda and equal rights had manifested itself.[26] *Ghare Baire* resumes that debate, in terms of conjugal relations and the sharply opposed conception of masculinity of Sandip and Nikhilesh.

IV

Sandip's aggressively masculinist and instrumental conceptions of realism and power extend beyond peasants, Muslims, camp-followers like Amulya. They relate, above all, to women, and to nature:

I have found that my way always wins over the hearts of women. . . . This power which wins these women is the power of mighty men, the power which wins the world of reality. (*The Home and the World*, pp. 47–8)

In a subsequent interior monologue Rabindranath makes Sandip link up patriarchal domination with ruthless conquest over the environment in a manner that sounds utterly contemporary:

We are men, we are kings, we must have our tribute. Ever since we have come upon the Earth we have been plundering her, and the more we claimed, the more she submitted. From primeval days have we men been plucking fruits, cutting down trees, digging up the soil, killing beast, bird, and fish . . . it has all been grabbing and grabbing and grabbing—no strongbox in nature's storeroom has been respected or left unrifled. The one delight of this Nature is to fulfil the claims of those who are men . . . Likewise, by sheer force of our claims, we men have opened up all the latent possibilities of women. In the process of surrendering themselves to us, they have ever gained their true greatness. (*The Home and the World*, p. 16)

The counterpoint, throughout the novel, comes in passages where Nikhilesh describes his own relationships with nature, and with Bimala and other human beings: quiet, contemplative, non-masterful, eager to respect the autonomy of the Other. Two conceptions of masculinity are in conflict, conceptions inevitably involving alternative constructions of womanhood. Here, I think, lies the real core of *Ghare Baire*—and yet gender has figured surprisingly little in readings of the novel.[27]

Sandip's conquest of Bimala takes the form of lavish, excessive praise and apparent adulation, placing her on a pedestal as a virtual symbol of motherland and religion, calling her 'mokshirani', queen-bee of the entire patriotic hive. She does not really come into any public arena, it may be noted, does not address meetings, for instance—but instead is repeatedly assured by her lover that everything in the movement is happening because she is its inspiration. The strong erotic note, displacing the mother-figure with would-be mistress, and the sheer crudeness of the whole manoeuvre is Sandip's alone, but otherwise there remains an affinity with the ways through which swadeshi nationalism simultaneously exalted and subordinated womanhood. The woman was revered as a figure of maternity and selfless service to the family, made to embody the 'mother'-land, but remained at home (a few exceptional figures like Sarala Devi apart), serving the cause by sacrificing foreign luxuries, admiring, usually from behind the curtain, the patriotic oratory of the male leaders. (Bimala came out from the veil, but that had been made possible only by her having a modernist husband who had urged her to do so for years.) The swadeshi years possibly marked the climax of Partha Chatterjee's home–world divide, through which nationalism, in his view, had 'resolved' the woman's question.

Ghare Baire in effect places a strong question mark against this 'resolution', by relating one form of the woman-on-a-pedestal theme to a crudely masculinist game of power. It must be emphasised that coming to such a critical understanding of dominant ways of conceiving women had not been easy for Rabindranath. The novel needs to be located within a fairly long and difficult transition—more difficult, probably, for the author than the break with chauvinistic Hindu nationalism.

In April 1902, the same year that he wrote *Brahman*, justifying varna hierarchy, Rabindranath had been capable of the following statement about women:

In Europe a band of modern women feel ashamed even of being women. They are embarrassed about giving birth and serving their husband and children ... Sweeping floors, bringing in water, grinding spices, serving food to relatives and guests and eating only afterwards—in Europe all this is considered oppressive and shameful, but for us it indicates the high status of the *grihalakshmi* [bounteous goddess of the home], their sanctity, the respect that is shown towards them . . . the more women look upon even husbands without any striking qualities as divine, the more they are invested with purity and true beauty . . . Europe claims that all human beings have the right to have or become everything. But in reality everyone doesn't have the same right, and it is best to accept this profound truth from the very beginning . . .[28]

As with the conjoint political transition, *Gora* marks the beginning of a change through intense internal debate—a process, however, which with respect to gender perhaps remains incomplete in that novel. The two friends, Gora and Benoy, endlessly argue about the true location of womanhood, with Gora repeatedly formulating a home–world type of disjunction, justified, like caste, on the ground that it is authentically national, as well as a thing of beauty and grace in itself. Benoy is much more critical, even suggesting at one point an affinity between the confinement of women to purely domestic functions and the bhadralok tendency to categorise peasants and other plebeian folk by their service to their social superiors alone.[29] The conversations of the two Brahmo girls, Sucharita and particularly Lalita, go much further. The latter in a bold act of rebellion flouts convention to travel alone at night with an unrelated man (Benoy), to avoid participation in a play being staged for the benefit of the British magistrate who has just sent Gora to prison.[30] But the men still seem quite far from any adequate recognition of the autonomous subjectivity of women. Even Benoy, by implication, seems to be thinking primarily in terms of the way allowing women to venture outside domesticity could prove beneficial for men: 'If we become capable of seeing women outside our domestic needs, the beauty and plenitude of our country would have become more evident for *us*' (my italics). Love for Sucharita makes Gora realise the incompleteness of his earlier patriotic vision which had excluded women other than as figures of motherhood. Yet the same passage has him exalting 'the woman who, deserving of worship herself, has revered unfailingly the least deserving among us'.[31] The figure of Anandamoyee, quintessentially maternal but free of all social taboos and prejudices, helps in a way to smooth over an unresolved debate. Gora's final peroration denouncing all sectarian barriers remains silent about gender.

The big change in Rabindranath's views about gender seems to have come a few years after his break with most other aspects of swadeshi nationalism, achieved through the 1907–8 essays, and *Gora*. In his 'Woman's Lot in East and West' (*Modern Review*, June 1912), referring to Russian 'Nihilists,' he was still expressing a fear that women in Europe might soon 'appear as Furies of destruction'. The article went on to declare: 'We are quite happy with our household goddesses and they too have never told us that they are very unhappy.' Indian widows seemed to him happier that European spinsters, for they had the chance of rendering 'loving service' to other members of the joint family. And the wives, in traditional systems everywhere, had reigned as 'queen-bees' over the 'hives' to which the male 'worker-bees' brought honey. The metaphor is important, for it would be used again in *Ghare Baire*, but with a very different, clearly pejorative, intent. It is Sandip who uses the metaphor, seducing Bimala through flattery as preparation for getting money from her on false, patriotic pretences. A passage towards the end of the novel vividly demonstrates the shift in Tagore's views regarding the lot of Hindu widows, too. Nikhilesh, on the eve of leaving his ancestral home, feels nostalgic about the childhood he had shared with Mejorani, his sister-in-law who had come as a bride to the house at the age of nine, lost her husband soon, and lived on in the joint family without a break since then. He expresses a desire to return to those days. The sister-in-law replies, 'with a deep sigh': 'No, brother, never again a life as a woman! Let this one life be sufficient for what I have had to endure, I cannot stand any more.'[32]

What can explain this change, the first literary expression of which came through the sudden outburst of *Sabuj Patra* stories, particularly *Haimanti* (Jaishtha 1321/May–June 1914), *Bostomi* (Asar 1321/June–July 1914), *Streer Patra* (Sravan 1321/July–August 1914), *Aparichita* (Kartik 1321/October–November 1914), *Payela Nambar* (Asar 1324/June–July 1917), and *Patra-o-Patri* (Paus 1324/December 1917–January 1918)?[33] The point requires further research, but I am tempted to suggest at least a partial connection, in the way of a proximate impulse, with an event which became a major newspaper sensation in the early months of 1914. This was the Snehalata case, involving a sixteen-year-old north Calcutta girl who burnt herself to death by kerosene on 30 January, two weeks before her marriage, apparently because she had realised that her parents would be ruined by the excessive dowry the groom's family was demanding from them.[34] Judging from the flood of letters, articles, and editorials in newspapers and periodicals that followed, middle-class public opinion was fairly unanimous that excessive dowry demands needed to be curbed—but there the agreement ended. Two rival meetings were organised, to express divergent, relatively reformist, and conservative views on how the admitted evil of dowry could be fought. A College Square meeting on 13 February, mainly of students, tried to set up an Anti Marriage-Dowry League of young men prepared to take a vow not to demand dowry in their marriage.[35] Some letters and articles went much further, suggesting efforts to raise the age of marriage, and more basically to try to end the stigma suffered by girls who remained unmarried (and the social obloquy heaped on their parents). The *Modern Review* added that if more girls remained spinsters, 'it would be necessary to educate them as would enable them to be economically independent, if necessary'.[36] There were even a few suggestions that priests boycott all marriages associated with dowries, and Hindu law be amended 'to bestow on the daughter a share in the parental property equal to that of the son'.[37] That conservative opinion had become alarmed by the reopening of a range of social reform issues threatened by the Snehalata case is indicated by the parallel efforts to channel the sense of shock into safer, indeed recuperative, channels. A rival meeting, held on 14 February (to be followed by another on similar lines on 24 February attended by many 'well-known Pandits'), also condemned dowry, but only as a modern innovation associated with the spread of commercialised values, and went on to suggest earlier marriages, so that brides would have fewer problems in adapting themselves to their husband's family.[38]

Conservatives followed the standard strategy of elevating Snehalata to the pedestal of heroic martyrdom—her act was even described as akin to the *jauhar* as practised by Rajput women 'from the days of Alladin [sic]'[39]—after which the dangers involved in the suggestions of reformers could be outlined. This was done with exceptional clarity in an *Amrita Bazar Patrika* editorial of 24 February. An anti-dowry vow by unmarried young men might lead them to disobey their parents, which would never do. 'A Hindu will never agree . . . that the marriage of Hindu girls should not be made compulsory', while postponing marriage unduly might lead to girls insisting on 'choosing their own husbands. The parental control over the marriage of their children will necessarily be gone and a Brahmin girl might secretly marry, say, a husband of the carpenter caste.' Gender and caste hierarchies alike were felt to be under threat.

There was nothing particularly unique or exceptional about the Snehalata case,[40] and that, in a way, could have added to its impact. What it managed to do was bring into centre space again the question of reform in gender relations, which had been submerged for a time by the rise of revivalist forms of nationalism. In particular, despite the sympathy lavished on the 'martyr', it helped to expose the crudities of social conservatism in matters of family life and gender. In *Streer Patra*, the rebellious wife Mrinal reports the common reaction of many men to cases of women setting fire to themselves: 'They started saying: "It has become a fashion among girls to die by setting their clothes on fire." You [her husband and in-laws] said: "All this is play-acting" . . . Maybe so, but why is it that what gets burnt are always the saris of Bengali girls, and never the dhotis of the brave men of Bengal?'

What is new and remarkable in the *Sabuj Patra* stories is not the depiction of the woes of women: that had been quite a standard theme for long, and the trope of unjust suffering bravely but patiently borne was eminently open to patriarchal recuperation. More striking is a tone of extreme anger, expressed for instance in the passage I have just quoted, going along often with a considerable degree of male guilt and auto-critique. But middle-class male guilt had been an important element in the constitution of the nineteenth-century social reform project focused upon the 'woman's question' from Rammohan Roy down to the 1880s, although from then onwards it had been superseded by the nationalist emphasis on the values of 'traditional' womanhood. Rabindranath's stories—and, I argue, *Ghare Baire*, on a slightly different but very significant register—not only resume that project. The new note here is the effort to depict independent minded, autonomously-acting, rebellious women—an effort which simultaneously adds a new dimension to the theme of male guilt.

Streer Patra stands out from all the others in being written in the voice of a woman, who, moreover, articulates herself at the height of a total, uncompromising rebellion. Mrinal has just left her husband's house for ever, the joint family home which had been comfortable enough, but where she could never be anything more than 'Mejobou' (wife of the second brother), never a full-fledged human being. She recalls how she had entered the house for the first time, 'while all the skies were weeping to the tune of wedding music': a striking image of the woes of patrilocality from the point of view of women. She traces back the roots of her rebellion, very significantly, to her intelligence, which had refused to internalise her many forms of subservience, and which had for long expressed its defiance through her secret poetry-writing: 'Whatever might have been its worth, there the walls of your andar-mahal [women's quarter] could not reach.' Then Bindu, the helpless relative-by-marriage she had befriended, through whose eyes she had first become aware of her own beauty, had been married off to a madman.[41] Refused shelter when she tried to run away, Bindu killed herself by setting her clothes on fire. That was when 'the mejobou of yours died'. Mrinal has left No. 27, Makhan Baral Lane never to come back, and the letter ends in deliberate, defiant inversion of the standard, humble way a Bengali wife at that time was supposed to end a letter to her husband or elder: 'From Mrinal, who is torn off the shelter of your feet.'[42]

Women striking out for freedom in unexpected and unconventional ways figure prominently in many of the other near-contemporary stories. There is the mature teacher (and possibly, political worker) who has refused marriage in *Aparichita*; a wife who suddenly leaves both her husband and a would-be lover in *Payla Nambar*; the daughter of a low-caste woman who defies social taboos to marry the son of a rich higher-caste merchant in *Patra-o-Patri*. The other crucial feature is that, *Streer Patra* apart, most of the *Sabuj Patra* stories are narrated through the persona of a series of self-critical, yet ineffective men, who witness with amazement and a deep sense of guilt the affirmations of the women. The note of male autocritique is clearest in *Haimanti*, where the wife is ill-treated after her in-laws discover her father was not as rich as they had hoped he was. Her own total integrity adds to her problems. Doctors are not called when she falls ill, her father is not allowed to take her home. Haimanti eventually dies, and her mother-in-law is planning a second marriage for her son when the story ends. Her husband understands everything, feels deeply guilty, yet does literally nothing. It is precisely through this depiction of ineffectiveness that Rabindranath is able to make a statement of remarkable power, which goes considerably beyond the limits of nineteenth-century male guilt to extend into a much broader critique of the culture underlying such injustice and inaction. A statement, moreover, that leaps across decades to seem today utterly resonant for our times as well:

All I had to do is to just leave with my wife. Why did I not take such an obvious, simple step? Why indeed! If I am not to sacrifice my true feelings for what people regard as proper, if I was not to sacrifice my dearest one for the extended family, then what about the ages of social indoctrination running in my blood? What is it there for? Don't you know that on the day the people of Ayodhya demanded the banishment of Sita, I was among them? Those who sang the glory of that sacrifice, generation after countless generation, I was one of them too.[43]

The *Sabuj Patra* stories—and, above all, *Streer Patra*—evoked much conservative anger, with the extremist leader Bepin Chandra Pal even attempting a 'revised' version called *Mrinaler Katha* [Mrinal's Story]. Here Mrinal's leaving home is depicted as a mere temporary aberration. She has a brief affair with a poet in Puri, and then learns that Bindu has not really killed herself, and instead is now reconciled to her fate. Mrinal now begs to be allowed to come back to her husband, and the story ends with a letter signed 'Mrinal, ever in the shelter of your feet'.[44] It seems likely that the attacks on Bimala for slandering the Sita-image through adultery may have had something to do with the fact that her creator had just published stories like *Streer Patra* and *Haimanti*.[45]

It is the theme of male autocritique—though in a significantly different register—that allows us now to rejoin *Ghare Baire*, and, specifically, Nikhilesh. Unlike the male narrator of *Haimanti*, he had been actively reformist, and had tried for years to persuade Bimala to come out of her seclusion, join him in constructing a new kind of conjugality grounded in the recognition of the equality of men and women. He refuses to surrender his principles, even at the moment of greatest challenge, when he realises that Bimala is falling in love with Sandip—though the broken style indicates the depth of his inner struggle against the temptation to draw upon the resources of conventional patriarchy:

'My wife—and so, forsooth, my very own! If she says: "No, I am myself"—am I to reply: "How can that be? Are you not mine?"'

'My wife'—does that amount to an argument, much less the truth? Can one imprison a whole personality within that name?' (*The Home and the World*, p. 64)

Nikhilesh, clearly, is a failure, both in his politics, and in the battle over Bimala with Sandip. He realises that he is so, even when, at the end of the novel, Bimala is coming back to him—for that happens only because Sandip has been exposed so utterly. But it is important to explore where and why exactly he fails, for through that we can perhaps understand why Rabindranath deliberately created a situation where the reformer's initiative—which has full authorial sympathy—rebounds back on himself; the freedom which Nikhilesh has given Bimala ends in all-round tragedy. It would be entirely superficial, of course, to construe Nikhilesh's problem as mildness, a certain lack of 'manly' personality: that would involve acceptance of Sandip's approach to life. Nikhilesh's apparent 'mildness' is really his strength, a determined, sustained effort to respect, through an alternative kind of masculinity, the autonomy of the Other. What he realises, and recognises as his failure, is that the effort had after all been incomplete. It had failed to give sufficient imaginative heed to the autonomous subjectivity of Bimala:

I had been decorating Bimal so long with ideals that have been precious for me . . . But Bimal is what she is; she does not have to become the mistress of all virtues and beauty just because I want her to be so. Why should the Creator act according to my commands?[46]

I feel today that there had been an element of oppression, of power, in my relations with Bimal. I had tried to mould her into a model of what seemed seamlessly perfect to me. But a human being's life cannot be cast in a mould . . .[47]

Through Nikhilesh, I would like to suggest, Rabindranath is seeking to reaffirm the basic values of nineteenth-century male reformism, grounded at its best in notions of equal rights, even as he recognises its inadequacy. In that honourable, but limited, reformism, even the phrase *stri-swadhinata*, often used in the 1860s and 1870s, had really meant the freeing of women by benevolently motivated men, not really the emancipation of women as fully autonomous human subjects. What had been lacking was what Rabindranath, in swadeshi and post-swadeshi times alike, had come to foreground as a supreme value: atmashakti, the need for autonomous self-development. Reform had often been over-dependent on foreign support and patronage—the toadyism of some Brahmos like Panubabu and Baradasundari so mercilessly pilloried in Gora—and plagued by sectarian narrowness.[48] Above all, it had been at its best for, not by, women.

It is within this context that we can begin the difficult task of trying to situate and understand Bimala. She is given a privileged position in the narrative structure, for, alone among the novel's protagonists, she looks back on what has already happened, in a process of remembrance coloured by knowledge of the eventual tragic outcome. Bimala remains a complicated figure, more open perhaps to sharply opposed readings than the others.

The novel begins with a beautifully crafted passage, where Bimala, after the tragedy, seems to be entering a mood that reinvokes the values of maternity, in a kind of womb-reversion: 'Mother, today there comes back to mind the vermilion mark at the parting of your hair, the sari which you used to wear, with its wide red border, and those wonderful eyes of yours, full of depth and peace . . .' She recalls the way her mother had served food to her father, 'a beauty which passed beyond outward forms . . . transcended all debates, or doubts, or calculations: it was pure music' (*The Home and the World*, pp. 17–18).

The passage seems to support the kind of anti-modernist reading of *Ghare Baire* and Tagore that Ashis Nandy has tried to develop, and this is the only point where Bimala, and the question of gender as a whole, enters his discussion. For him, 'in Tagore's world, motherliness questions the dominant consciousness' of what he would like to call 'the principle of egalitarian hierarchy'. In contrast to the 'organizing principle of the Indic civilization', the latter gives 'an absolute priority to conjugality over maternity'.[49]

But Bimala and the heroines of the *Sabuj Patra* stories are not mothers but childless wives, an important point that has been emphasised by Kalpana Bardhan. Thus, for Mrinal in *Streer Patra*, it is the relationship with Bindu that becomes the point for open anti-patriarchal rebellion, whereas motherhood could have tied her down more firmly to the husband's family.[50] Sisterhood, or relating to someone in a sisterly manner, seems in fact to be more crucial than maternity in these stories:

one recalls Bimala's relations with Amulya, through which she becomes aware of the real nature of Sandip. And Bimala, in effect, deconstructs her own initial response. She recalls that she had failed to respond emotionally to her husband's constant insistence on equality in their relationship: 'that was my woman's heart, which spontaneously expresses its love through worship' [puja]. But the reader soon cannot fail to recognise that it is precisely such spontaneity that opened Bimala to the wiles of Sandip. And, immediately after this passage, Bimala recognises that with the changes in her own lifetime, unreflective devotion is no longer a matter of 'simple prose'. 'What had been as simple as breathing now requires rhetoric for sustenance.' 'Poetry' has become necessary now to justify the beauty of the wife's devotion and the widow's austerity—'A separation has taken place between truth and beauty. Can truth be recuperated today by mere insistence on beauty?'[51]

Spontaneity, 'my woman's heart'; perhaps Rabindranath's intent through Bimala is precisely to question this 'naturalness', the absence of autonomous self-development through reason and strenuous effort: the need for atmashakti, once again. Bimala is very different from Mrinal, who preserves and cultivates her inner autonomy through the secret writing of poetry, or for that matter from the other heroines of the *Sabuj Patra* stories. Perhaps the point can be clarified through another glance back at *Gora*, this time at the subplot woven around Sucharita's aunt Harimohini. Her's had been the miserable lot of a woman in a traditional family: child-wife, cooking all day, with little or no time for taking her own meals, and then, widowed and pushed out to Benaras by in-laws. But when Paresh helps her to regain a kind of 'sansar' of her own, Harimohini soon begins to reproduce on her own the contours of a similarly oppressive domesticity, seeking to impose numerous constraints on Sucharita, trying to get her married off without bothering to ask for her consent. In a context, and through a persona, utterly different from Bimala, here already is the emphasis on the need of women's self-development for genuine women's freedom, and the insufficiency of even the best-intentioned male reformist benevolence.[52]

But how far did Rabindranath's vision concerning the autonomous self-development of women really extend? The women in the *Sabuj Patra* stories, *Streer Patra* apart, have a certain externality about them: they are portrayed from the outside, as it were, through the eyes of amazed, ineffective men. There are similarities of pattern here with the unforgettable figure of Damini, in the novel just preceding *Ghare Baire*, *Chaturanga*: she, too, retains an element of mystery for the other three male protagonists.[53] Even Mrinal is a figure caught at the moment of rebellion: no attempt is made to portray what she might be able to make of her independent life. Artistically extremely effective, such retention of externality might also be related to a certain authorial recognition of limits in portraying the freed subjectivity of woman.

Recognition of the autonomy of the Other, of course, does not preclude having preferences among the many forms through which such autonomy could manifest itself. Rabindranath certainly did not like some of the forms that women's emancipation could take, and indeed had already started taking in Bengal. Remarkably ahead of his times in some ways from the post-swadeshi phase onwards—notably, for instance, in introducing coeducation in Santiniketan in the early 1920s within a residential set-up—he seems to have retained an aesthetic, almost physical, revulsion to the figure of the politicised, activist, woman. He would express this in quite an extreme form in the novel *Char Adhyay* (1934), written at a time when women had joined revolutionary terrorist groups as comrade-in-arms. (One might recall the reference to the Russian nihilist women in his 1912 article.)

But the dominant note in *Ghare Baire*, surely, remains Nikhilesh's agonised determination to respect the autonomy of Bimala. Autonomy as a moral value, combined, however, with the other central theme in Tagore, the need for self-development, atmashakti, becoming worthy of true independence through one's own efforts, including, crucially, the cultivation of the intellect.

In an essay written twelve years after *Ghare Baire*, Rabindranath argued that the field of work for men and women in society was fundamentally the same. There were some irredeemable physical differences, among which he mentioned the natural pressure on women to be mothers, for men to be active outside their homes. But he was quick to add that these had been greatly exaggerated. 'Women have been enfolded into the stereotypes of mother and housewife . . . Then came an earthquake in the West which has shaken up this age-old structure of discrimination . . . We will have to recognise the common humanity of women as well as men, beyond all differences . . .'[54] And in 1936, in what was perhaps his last essay on the specific question of women: 'All over the world women today are coming out of the confines of their households into the open arena of the world . . . Let us hope for a new age in the building of civilization . . .' He ended with an appeal to women 'to open their hearts, cultivate their intellect, pursue knowledge with determination. They have to remember that unexamined blind conservatism is opposed to creativity.'[55]

Endnotes

1. Asok Kumar Sarkar, *Sabuj Patra o Bangla Sahitya* (Calcutta: Pustak Bipani, 1994), p. 58.
2. Georg Lukacs, 'Tagore's Gandhi Novel: A Review of Rabindranath Tagore, *The Home and the World*', in *Reviews and Articles*, tr. Peter Palmer (London: Merlin Press, 1983), cited extensively in Ashis Nandy, *The Illegitimacy of Nationalism: Rabindranath Tagore and the Politics of the Self* (Delhi: Oxford University Press, 1994).
3. Rabindranath Tagore, 'Teeka Tippani' (*Sabuj Patra*, Agrahayan, 1322/1915). In 'Sahitya Bichar' (*Prabasi*, Chaitra, 1326/1920), he was still engaged in refuting the charge of having shown disrespect to Sita. His rejoinder now was sharper: so many would like to 'make of national literature a literature of frogs in the well', *Rabindra Rachanabali*, vol. VIII, (Calcutta: Visvabharati, 1941), pp. 525–7.
4. Nandy, *The Illegitimacy of Nationalism*.
5. Ibid., pp. 2, x–xi.
6. Rabindranath had in fact suggested some of the new agitational methods, like appropriating the Hindu rite of *rakhi-bandhan* on partition day, 16 October 1905. He had also composed a series of stirring patriotic songs which at times merged Mother Bengal with the Goddess Durga in a manner not far removed from Bankimchandra's 'Bande Mataram'.
7. For a more detailed account of the changing patterns of the swadeshi movement and of Tagore's responses, see my *Swadeshi Movement in Bengal, 1903–08* (New Delhi: People's Publishing House, 1973).
8. For some discussion of the significance of *Sabuj Patra* and the hostility it aroused, see Asok Kumar Sarkar, op.cit., and Arunkumar Mukhopadhyaya, *Birbal o Bangla Sahitya* (Calcutta: 1960, 1968).
9. Sabuj Patra translates as 'Green Leaves'.
10. This refers to the sensational suicide of a North Calcutta girl shortly before marriage. It was seen to highlight the evils of excessive dowry.

11. 'Namasudra' was the somewhat more prestigious name being claimed by a subordinate-caste cluster, previously described by their social superiors as 'Chandals'. Numerous in parts of south and southeast Bengal, they constituted, along with Mahishyas in the southwest and Rajbansis in the north, the three major lower-caste formations of the province. The particular prominence of Namasudras in Tagore and other bhadralok writings of the time was probably related to a certain militancy on their part around caste status as well as on agrarian issues. For more details, see Sekhar Bandopadhyay, *Caste, Protest and Identity in Colonial India: The Namasudras of Bengal, 1872–1947* (Surrey: Curzon Press, 1997), and my 'Identities and Histories: Some Lower Caste Narratives from Early Twentieth Century Bengal', in *Beyond Nationalist Frames* (New Delhi: Permanent Black 2002).

12. *Rabindra Rachanabali*, vol. X, pp. 527–8 (my translation).

13. *Ghare Baire, Rabindra Rachanabali*, vol. X, pp. 466–7, 475–6; *The Home and the World*, trans. Surendranath Tagore, (Macmillan, 1919; Penguin India, 1999), pp. 88, 99. Hereafter cited parenthetically by page number.

14. *Gora, Rabindra Rachanabali*, vol. IX, pp. 318–19. While Gora's ultimate transformation comes about through the fortuitous revelation of his Irish birth, it is made clear that experiences like these had already deeply unsettled his revivalist–nationalist faith. He greets the news, therefore, with exaltation. The gates of all the temples of India have closed in his face, he declares, and it is this that has made him truly Indian ('Bharatiya') for the first time, worthy of bowing to the 'Lord whose temples are ever open to all . . . who is the Lord of Hindus, Muslims, Christians and Brahmos alike, who is the divinity, not only of the Hindus, but of all Indians' (Ibid., pp. 349–50, my translation).

15. 'It is worthy of note that both at Bakshigunj and Dewangunj the rioting began by an attack on the idol which had been erected by the hated Iswarbritti.' Note by R. Nathan, July 1907, Government of India: Home Political A, December 1907, n. 58.

16. 'Conduct of zamindars of Gauripur in connection with political agitation in Mymensingh district', Government of India: Home Political A, February 1908, n. 102–3.

17. *Daily Hitavadi*, 11, 23, 24, February 1908, *Report on Native Newspapers (Bengal)* for the weeks ending February 15, 29, 1908; *Swadeshi Movement in Bengal*, passim.

18. Contrary to what might have been expected, Jack was quickly pulled up by his superiors, and commutations were stopped: race was overridden by considerations of stability of agrarian class structure. For details, see

Nariaki Nakazato, *Agrarian System in Eastern Bengal, c. 1870–1910* (Calcutta: K.P. Bagchi, 1994); J.C. Jack, *Bakarganj Settlement Report, 1900–08* (Calcutta: Government of Bengal, 1915), Appendix g, and my 'Intimations of Hindutva: Ideologies, Caste and Class in Post-Swadeshi Bengal', *Beyond Nationalist Frames*, op.cit.

19. *Ghare Baire*, op.cit., p. 419 (my translation). Here, as in several later instances, the English version inexplicably omits an important passage.

20. The unremittingly dark portrayal of Sandip is redeemed only once, in *Ghare Baire*, pp. 460–3, where Sandip confesses to a certain sense of guilt—which of course he feels is a weakness—about the way he is deceiving his old friend Nikhilesh. Perhaps some awareness of this problem, which does weaken the novel considerably, led Rabindranath to introduce, as a foil to Sandip, the transparently sincere and dedicated young revolutionary Amulya.

21. Tagore, *Nationalism* (New York: Macmillan, 1917; Connecticut, Greenwood Press, 1973), pp. 44–5, 141–4.

22. Nandy does recognise that Rabindranath had once been more Brahmanical in his values, and that 'It was after 1905 that he became open to an inclusive concept of India . . .' (p. 78). I do not think this is precise enough in pinpointing the change, and find it impossible to accept the further assumption that 'Tagore's political concerns did not change' over the twenty-five years that separate *Gora* (1909) from *Char Adhyay* (1934) (p. 10). Such an assumption allows Nandy to ignore the temporal sequence of the novels in his essay, discussing the first among them (*Gora*) last.

23. *Nationalism*, ch. IV, pp. 135, 137–8.

24. *Ghare Baire*, p. 483 (my translation).

25. Ibid., p. 467 (my translation), the English version leaves out some passages.

26. I owe this point to Tanika Sarkar. For some discussion of *adhikari-bhedas*, see my *Writing Social History* (Delhi: Oxford University Press, 1997), ch. 7 and passim.

27. I see now that I had bypassed the question of gender entirely in my discussion of the novel in my *Swadeshi Movement*, op.cit. For Nandy, Bimala is important as embodying a primacy of 'motherliness' over 'conjugality'—a very dubious reading, I intend to argue—and even she is no more than the site, or 'battlefield on which the two forms of patriotism fight for supremacy' (*Illegitimacy of Nationalism*, p. 14). He does not refer at all to the near-contemporary *Streer Patra* and the other *Sabuj Patra* short stories.

28. *Nababarsha* [The New Year], read at Santiniketan on the occasion of

the Bengali New Year, published Baisakh 1309/April 1902. *Rabindra Rachanabali*, Centenary Edition (West Bengal Government, 1961), vol. XII, p. 1024.

29. *Gora, Rabindra Rachanabali*, vol. IX, pp. 78–80.

30. Lalita explicitly rejects the home–world disjunction: 'You [menfolk] think that you'll do the work of the world, while we'll do your work. That won't happen. We too will either do the work, or remain a burden on you . . .' ibid., p. 94. (my translation).

31. ibid., pp. 243–4. (my translation).

32. *Ghare Baire*, pp. 539–40 (my translation).

33. Among these stories, *Haimanti* and *Streer Patra* can now be read in English translation: Kalpana Bardhan, ed. and trans., *Of Women, Outcastes, Peasants and Rebels: A Selection of Bengali Short Stories* (Berkeley: University of California Press, 1990).

34. *Amrita Bazar Patrika*, 7 February 1914, gives some details about the immolation, on the basis of proceedings in the Coroner's Court on 6 February. The headline was: Coroner's Court/Suchalata [sic!] Devi/her heroic death/Saved parents from Ruination/Evils of Marriage Dowry.

35. Ibid., 14 February 1914. The meeting, said to have been attended by a thousand young men, was chaired by the Brahmo nationalist leader Krishnakumar Mitra, and had among its speakers Ramananda Chatterjee, editor of the *Modern Review*.

36. Notes (The Extortion of Dowries), *Modern Review*, March 1914.

37. Letter from S.D. Mazumdar, *Amrita Bazar Patrika*, 27 February 1914.

38. *Amrita Bazar Patrika*, 16 February, 25 February 1914. The editor of this daily, Motilal Ghosh, was prominent at these two meetings, perhaps in part as a consequence of his lifelong rivalry with Surendranath Banerjea, editor of the somewhat pro-reform *Bengalee*, several of whose close associates had been active in the College Square meeting. Unfortunately I have not been able to get access to the files of the *Bengalee* for early 1914 so far.

39. This was at a meeting of the Kalighat Peoples' Association on 15 February, where Snehalata was described 'as our very meek infant Snehas, having no idea of women's suffrage'. *Amrita Bazar Patrika*, 20 February 1914. Periodicals like *Modern Review*, it may be added, had been carrying news fairly often of the suffragette agitation in Britain.

40. Several other similar cases of dowry immolation were in fact reported in the wake of the Snehalata case: see *Amrita Bazar Patrika*, 13 February 1914. Girija Sankar Bhattacharya and four other teachers of Berhampore College mentioned the immolation of Nibhanani soon after Snehalata,

in a long joint letter entitled 'The Dowry System: Its Effect and Cure' (*Modern Review*, April 1914). In 1917, an article in *Bharati*, a monthly associated with the Tagore family, pointed out that the suicide rate among women in Calcutta was four times that among men. Dagmar Engels, *Beyond Purdah? Women in Bengal, 1890–1939* (Delhi: Oxford University Press, 1996), p. 54. A *Modern Review* article of February 1920 was still referring to an 'increasing suicide mania among Bengali young girls'. It did not forget to mention the Snehalata incident, and also described how a particular house in North Calcutta was locally infamous as 'a daughter-in-law killing house' (*bau mara bari*). Sundari Mohan Das, 'The Causation and Prevention of Suicide Among Girls and Women'.

41. There is an interesting note of sisterly solidarity here, at least—and the passage can even be read as hinting at something more.

42. My translations. I have been greatly helped in this brief discussion of *Streer Patra* by Tanika Sarkar, 'Mrinal: Anya Itihasher Sakhshar', *Desh*, 5 August 2000.

43. *Haimanti*, trans. Kalpana Bardhan, op.cit., p. 95.

44. *Narayan*, Sravan 1324/July–August 1917. Pal's version is summarised in Asok Kumar Sarkar, *Sabuj Patra o Bangla Sahitya* (Calcutta: Pustak Bipani, 1994), pp. 56–7, which also refers to another parody of *Streer Patra*: 'Mrinalini Debi', *Streer Prakrita Patra* [The genuine letter of the wife], *Aryavarta*, Aswin 1321/September–October 1914).

45. But Rabindranath seems to have had some unexpected supporters, too. In Magh–Falgun 1321/January–February 1915, a story entitled *Streer Patra* was published in a subordinate-caste woman's journal, *Mahishya Mahila*, depicting the woes of a wife whose husband had married again. The journal, connected with a 'Sanskritising' kind of caste movement, was not usually reformist in its approach towards family and gender issues: it had, however, written bitterly the previous year about the way some were acclaiming the immolation of Snehalata as an act of *jauhar*. 'Bangali Kumarir Jahar-vrata' (*Mahishya Mahila*, Magh–Falgun 1320/January–Feburary 1914).

46. *Ghare Baire*, p. 448 (my translation). I find the English version here (p. 65) inadequate.

47. Ibid., p. 546 (my translation). It needs to be added, however, that the power element in Nikhilesh is far more subtle and nuanced than has been depicted in a recent interesting conjoint study of the novel and Satyajit Ray's film version, by Nicholas Dirks. It is difficult to recognise Nikhilesh—of the novel, at least—in Dirks's ascription to him of a 'relentless and imperious desire to shape Bimala in the image of his own

modern God . . . to shape her in his own terms (he compels her to submit to this plan)'. The essay attributes wrongly to Nikhilesh the key decision, made entirely by Bimala herself, to come out before Sandip. Nicholas B. Dirks, '*The Home and the World*: The Invention of Modernity in Colonial India', in Robert A. Rosenstone, ed., *Revisioning History: Film and the Construction of a New Past* (Princeton: Princeton University Press, 1995), pp. 46, 53; for Bimala's decision, see *Ghare Baire*, pp. 420–1; *The Home and the World*, p. 32.

48. Sectarianism could reproduce within the confines of the 'reformed' community many of the constraints of orthodoxy: this, again, is a theme central to *Gora*. But Nikhilesh's reformist values, and their limits, do not come from any particular religious affiliation, and this allows the problem in *Ghare Baire* to be posed more sharply, independent of religious differences between Brahmos and Hindus.

49. *The Illegitimacy of Nationalism*, pp. 41, 42, 49.

50. '. . . the energy and attention that nurturing requires, tends to diffuse and sublimate the oppression and frustration in conjugal life'. Bardhan, op.cit., Introduction, p. 16.

51. *Ghare Baire*, pp. 408–9 (my translation). Once again, some important passages have been omitted in the English version.

52. *Gora*, pp. 170–6, 198–203, 291–5, 307.

53. One could mention in this context also another of the *Sabuj Patra* stories, *Bostomi*, where Tagore, using his own persona, narrates a tale, apparently based on real life, of a strange encounter he had had with an utterly unconventional Vaishnava sannyasini, who has repudiated husband and religious preceptor alike.

54. 'Nareer manushatva' [The humanness of women] (15 Baisakh, 1335/April 1928; *Rabindra Rachanabali*, vol. XIII, pp. 24, 28).

55. 'Nari' [Woman] (Agrahayan, 1343/November–December 1936; *Rabindra Rachanabali*, vol. XIII, pp. 379–80).

Anandamath and *The Home and the World*: Positivism Reconfigured

JASODHARA BAGCHI

This essay will examine Bankimchandra Chattopadhyay's rendering of positivism in *Anandamath* and its contestatory rereading in Rabindranath Tagore's *Ghare Baire*. Comtean positivism was a Eurocentric ideology that had been assimilated into the class subjectivity and common sense of the elite in colonial Bengal. My analysis will involve a mapping of the ideological field of positivism originally formulated by Auguste Comte in post-revolutionary France in the first half of the nineteenth century, and translated (in its etymological sense of being 'carried across') into colonial Bengal in the second half of the nineteenth century. The fact that this ideology sought to rearticulate man–woman relationships in the context of social regeneration through the active mediation of the *pouvoir spirituel* (a select spiritual elite) was extremely consequential for these two seminal novels. These novels were also engaged in attempts to revise man–woman relationships, although in their own historical context of a profound social crisis, which paradoxically opened up immense opportunities for social regeneration through anti-colonial, nationalist resistance.

I

One of the major 'secular religions' that originated in Europe in the nineteenth century, the positivist 'Religion of Humanity' founded by Auguste Comte in Paris, travelled along extraordinarily varied routes.[1]

It appeared in Bengal in the second half of the nineteenth century as a potent ideology for the upper-class Hindu intelligentsia, poised to apply the fruit of half a century of Western education to a scrutiny of their own history and society.[2] It has been customary to think that the adoption of positivism by the Bengali intelligentsia was simply a process of 'modernising' under Western intellectual influence, hence a fulfilment of the cultural mission of imperial domination. But this would oversimplify matters.

Like the god Janus, Comtean positivism was two-faced—its motto was 'Order and Progress'.[3] On the one side it championed the course of scientific progress; on the other, its professed aim was to restore order and harmony by harking back to an older hierarchical Catholic order.[4] This doubleness can be understood by the circumstances in which it was born. Positivism originated in the social ferment in which the ideas of the Enlightenment were redesigned to suit the period of reconstruction that followed the French Revolution and the Napoleonic era. Progress was the watchword of this era, but there was also a tendency to check the unimpeded ideology of progress by deliberately invoking a past era of stability and order. In England, bourgeois ideologies had a longer run than anywhere else in Europe. But the fears aroused by the French Revolution meant that the dominant bourgeois ideology committed to the idea of progress, had to be tempered by the ideas of 'organic society' and 'clerisy' propagated by Burke and Coleridge respectively.[5] In France, Comte broke away from his master Saint-Simon and tried to strike a harmonious balance between the progressives, including Saint-Simon, Fourier and others on the one hand and revivalists like de Maistre and Chateaubriand on the other. He prepared the complete blueprint of a new society with a specified composition of social groups and 'law of three stages', whereby the entire province of knowledge could be brought up to the 'positive' stage.

In an early youthful 'opuscule' Comte had visualised an agency for bringing about the necessary social transformation. In 1826 he published *Consideration on the Spiritual Power*, the main object of which was to demonstrate the necessity for instituting a *pouvoir spirituel*, distinct from temporal power and independent of it. Unlike Coleridge's 'clerisy', Comte's *pouvoir spirituel* was delinked form the existing power structure. It was to be built on the model of the Catholic priesthood in its ideal moment of intense vigour and complete independence. This is the 'dream of order', an 'invented tradition' which made Comte's 'system' attractive to intellectuals in other transitional societies that went through similar crises of authority.[6]

Like some other nineteenth-century social thinkers, Comte sees society as developing according to a law of three stages. The 'greatest aim of the positive philosophy is to advance the study of society into the third of the three stages to remove social phenomena from the sphere of theological and metaphysical conceptions.' In the final or positive stage, the crisis of transitional society will be alleviated as 'the social facts will be resolved ... into relations with one another'. The conflict-free module of social facts and relations will have two departments, one 'statical' or the laws of order, the other 'dynamical', or the laws of progress. On the progressive side will be the industrial order, comprising capital and labour. Within this order the greater intellectual power of the capitalist, or the 'male patriciate' will provide enough reason for labour to willingly subordinate themselves instead of being coerced into doing so.

Comte tackles not only the rising wave of class warfare but also the possibility of gender warfare that was a part of the landscape of modernising society. Influenced by his intense involvement with Clothilde de Vaux, Comte tempers his earlier admiration for male intellect by emphasising the affective feminine side of human nature in his later thoughts about social regeneration. In his writings after the death of Clothilde de Vaux, from 1848 onwards, he insisted on subordinating the intellect to the heart, because he believed that the springs of social morality and altruism lay in the affective side of humanity. It was from this position that he derived the peculiar positivist cult of Womanhood: the Great Being of Humanity was visualised as a woman. This notion, as we shall see in *Anandamath*, was transmitted to Bengal to provide one of the most important icons of early nationalism.

There was one political area in the life of nineteenth-century Europe in which Comte took a decidedly dissident stand, one that facilitated the transmission of his ideology in colonised societies. This was his stand against colonialism and imperialism. The morally exalted role that he assigned to the great Occidental Republic (France, England, Germany, Italy and Spain including Portugal) made him urge them to give up self-aggrandisement through colonial exploitation. This inspired his English pupil Richard Congreve to denounce British colonialism in India. In 1857, after the 'Mutiny' in India, when British opinion was being roused and whipped up for tightening the imperialist noose around the 'irresponsible' and 'ungrateful' Indians, Congreve proved his loyalty to Comte by writing a polemical piece called *India*, urging the British to withdraw from India. His demand was clear:

It is that we withdraw from our occupation of India without any unnecessary delay, within the shortest period compatible with the arrangements for the security of European life and property, and with such measures as may be deemed advisable in the interest of Indian independence and good government.[7]

While there was an organised positivist movement in Bengal which has been written about,[8] it is the novels and social analyses of Bankim-chandra Chattopadhyay—an intellectual close to the organised posi-tivist group in Bengal—that form an exciting commentary on the possibilities of the reception of positivism in nineteenth-century Ben-gal. Since he was not a camp-follower, his last novels, particularly *Anandamath*, show the way in which a creative mind could destabilise a Western model saddled with deterministic rigidity and galvanise it with the energies of his own novelistic mode, that is, of gothic historicism.

II. *Anandamath*

The late novels of Bankimchandra, far from being a recantation of his early belief in scientific positivism, constitute a fuller response to the positivist ideology of 'order and progress'. This phase saw Bankim transposing the positivist binaries of progress and order in his response to colonial rule. Bankim believed in progress and thought it emanated from British rule. Yet, his nationalist self-respect did not allow him to accept the legitimacy of British rule. This opposition to the British led him to an affirmation of Hindu order—an exercise which also influenced the Hindu upper-class intelligentsia in the redefinition of their self-image. This is the phase of his life when he entered into fresh debates with his positivist friend Jogendra Chandra Ghosh, wrote his *Letters on Hinduism*, rewrote the life of Krishna as a positivist *manqué* and laid down the ethical foundations of a revived Hindu order in the dialogue

Dharmatattva. Using the model of European history, he located the Hindu order in the ancient past. This implied that the rule of Muslims stood for the Dark Ages while the British period marked the beginnings of a renaissance. The ironic implications of the ideal of Hindu order was that it made the Muslims, who were equally victims of British rule, bedfellows of colonial domination.

It is possible to claim that the menacing presence of colonial domination meant that Comte's vision of 'order and progress' when transmitted into nineteenth-century Bengal, did not produce an image of a harmonious transition to a new society. Instead, it produced a situation of tense crisis. This can be seen to leave its impress in the non-naturalistic gothic 'sublime' of Bankim's novelistic diction in his later novels. Particularly in *Anandamath*, order and progress are not discussed in terms of social analysis, nor in naturalistic psychological terms. Instead, a broad historical canvas lit by the lurid glow of a vengeful and mythologised order is set up to be threatened from within and without. Significantly, drawing on the mood and temper of Comte's writings, the idea of Womanhood is used as the emblem of this threatened core of incipient Nationhood. Comte's goddess of Humanity acquires a new dimension in the Devi who is the Motherland.

Much of the appeal of the novel arises from the threatened order symbolised by the Devi/Motherland, an unexpected adaptation of Comte's Goddess of Humanity. With her resplendent past, her wretched present and her radiant future, she is a trope of obvious appeal for a rising nationalist consciousness. The defence of this violated order is assigned by Bankimchandra to the order of the '*santans*' (sons of the Mother) based in Anandamath, the eponymous monastery. Despite many suggested historical origins for this order,[9] it may be seen as a striking adaptation of Comte's *pouvoir spirituel*, a spiritual order, discussed earlier, outside the pale of established priesthood. 'Bande Mataram' originally composed as an innocuous song of praise to the nation visualised as the motherland, and printed to fill a gap in the pages of his journal *Bangadarshan*, ignites an explosive implication within the narrative of the novel[10] where it becomes the anthem of the santans. What is interesting is that their cultivation of violent heroism of resistance is founded on *bhakti* or absolute devotion/submission. The heroic action on which this novel is built is thus ultimately founded on a preponderance of Heart. The extreme vow of renunciation taken by the santans is a manifestation of Comte's altruism, extracted from its European context of piety and put to use in a more fundamentalist defence of Order in its incarnations as both Devi and Motherland. From being a blueprint for a peaceful transition to an industrial society, positivism is transformed by Bankimchandra into the vehicle of a fight for a heroic age that has to be retrieved by sacrifice. Incidentally, in a situation undreamt of by Oscar Wilde, life proceeded to imitate art in the eruption of militant Hindu nationalism nearly two decades after the novel was written. 'Bande Mataram' became the unifying mantra of Hindu militants in the swadeshi movement. In *Ghare Baire*, this phenomenon is picked up by Tagore for his critique of Hindu exclusivism in a struggle that claimed to be nationalist.

Anandamath alternates between settled human habitat and the surrounding forest that contains the monastery. The time indicated is that of the infamous famine of 1769–70. Kalyani, the wife of the householder Mahendra, who clearly belongs to the enclosed space of domesticity, unwittingly becomes the 'temptress'. Whereas Shanti, the outlandish wife, who belongs to the forest, becomes the real *sahadharmini* (partner in *dharma*, or in its Comtean form, the creed of altruism). In the man–woman relationship handled by Bankim in this novel, the figure of the Woman is presented both in the demonic role of a potential temptress and as *daimon* or guardian angel that helps the male santan[11] in the fulfilment of his vow.

It is in creating Shanti that Bankim delinks true wifehood from the enclosed space of a 'home'. Like Kapalkundala, the heroine in an early novel of that title, Shanti belongs naturally to the world outside, in the forest. The heroic struggle to liberate the motherland provides an outlet for Shanti's unusual energy. She is left free to contribute the full strength of her affective self to the heroic life of a sannyasi husband. Brought up outside the pale of domesticity, Shanti decides to play the wife's role by joining her ascetic husband's fight and to this end even dons a male disguise. Bankim transforms the traditionally quietist role of a sahadharmini (a mere performer of domestic rituals) into that of a militant co-fighter. This contributes to the patriotic euphoria of the novel successfully muting the impact of the loyalist message that the author inserted. British soldiers are no match for her: Shanti unhorses

Ensign Lindley and rides away on his horse! It is only after that battle is won that Shanti and Jibananda, man and wife, decide to renounce everything and leave on their 'grand departure', incidentally reminding the reader of Draupadi's last journey.

III. *The Home and the World*

Tagore's *The Home and the World* rewrites *Anandamath*, one may claim, by reverting to the original positivist schema of Auguste Comte. It is a memorable exposition of the notion of sahadharmini in which Bankim's formulations in *Anandamath* are contested and cut down in size to fit the bourgeois 'mentality' latent in the social model constructed by Auguste Comte. By highlighting the family as the area in which the crisis is enacted, Tagore uses his own version of Comtean positivism to critique Bankimchandra's version of it.

Let me recapitulate and elaborate some of the salient features of positivist ideology, for these come into play again in different guises in Tagore's handling of the stresses of the home ('*ghar*') as it confronts the politics of swadeshi militancy ('*bahir*'). In a nutshell, these are:

- A secular 'progressive' outlook that yet retains its sense of validity in 'order'.
- An active male patriciate wielding intellectual hegemony in an industrialising society.
- The altruistic morality of the Occidental Republic that must renounce all imperialist usurpation and exploitation.
- A dedicated secular priesthood, a *pouvoir spirituel*, to disseminate this ideology.
- The supreme importance attached to womanhood, standing for the Heart and the affective aspect of life, without whose active co-operation the positivist utopia may not be attained.
- The family as the area for woman's activity—to be taken as the real viable symbol of order-in-progress.

Tagore's library in Santiniketan contains some of the major works of Comte, presented to him by followers on his trips to Europe. Although in all probability, his exposure to this European ideology was not as great as Bankimchandra's, yet he can be seen to have moved closer to positivism, particularly in its Victorian register. This becomes evident when he takes up Bankimchandra's idea of social regeneration and his essentialising of the man–woman relationship in *Anandamath* for a critical re-scrutiny in *The Home and the World*.

Serialised in Pramatha Chaudhury's *avant garde* periodical *Sabuj Patra* during 1915–16 and published in book form in 1916, *Ghare Baire*, the Bengali original of *The Home and the World*, displays what Harold Bloom has called 'the anxiety of influence'. This anxiety related to the dominant discourse of Bankim, but drew its substantive critical edge from the problems of Tagore's times. The militant Hindu that Bankim had imaginatively visualised in *Anandamath* was translated into political reality by the 'extremists' of the swadeshi movement. For them 'Bande Mataram', which had already found a dynamic context within the novel *Anandamath*, became the electrifying mantra that united the revolutionary energy of the group. Looking back on the movement after it had lost its momentum, Tagore opens up for critical analysis the theme of social regeneration through an activist group (Comte's *pouvoir spirituel*), visualised by Bankimchandra as the 'santans' of *Anandamath*. Further, Bankim had initiated the method of using man–woman relationships as vehicles of historical dynamism. Tagore lifted this mode out of its gothic romance setting and placed it in a familial psychological mode in order to critique Bankim's schema of social regeneration. Bankim subscribed to the refined Victorian ideal of womanhood which possessed two faces—one, the partner in marriage conceived as sahadharmini and its other, the temptress. In these two roles she was made to make or break the home as well as the polity in the social and historical novels of Bankimchandra, including *Anandamath*. This is a model of emplotment that Tagore takes over from Bankim, but places in a more naturalistic setting where his critical powers can be given greater play. Additionally, Tagore deploys the crisis of womanhood—located in Bimala's conflict—as a crisis of nationalism in Bengal at a special juncture.

In his portrayal of womanhood in crisis, Tagore has eschewed the gothic symbolist edge that we find in Bankim's portrayal of the super-woman in the late novels dealing with moments of crisis in the life of a nation. Instead, Tagore uses the model of the bourgeois family which fits in more closely with positivist lineaments. The polarity of 'the home' and 'the world' within which 'womanhood' becomes the focus of the crisis in the social order has a Comtean ring about it as is confirmed by the writings of the great Victorian positivist George Eliot. Eliot's novels show the home as the microcosm of social order and locates it as the proper site for developing the affective powers of the woman. In Tagore's *The Home and the World,* swadeshi nationalism brings about a situation of crisis because the affective empire of the woman's home is suddenly faced with the challenge of the 'world', represented by the *pouvoir spirituel* of swadeshi activists. Interestingly, the entire crisis is visualised in sexual terms. In a typical triangular situation, Bimala is caught between her 'bhakti' for Nikhilesh, her disinterested liberal husband, and her passion for Sandip, the 'Jacobin' swadeshi 'santan'.

Nikhilesh is a proper symbol of the active male patriciate who, as the novel makes clear, tries to combine the demands of order and progress. This is where Tagore comes closest to the paradigm of Comtean positivism. Nikhilesh, we come to know, has paid more than lip service to the 'progressive' demands of his time. Being a master of the liberal arts, he is on record as having tried out for some time the enormous programme of the swadeshi by becoming a benevolent manufacturer. Further, his distinterested liberal culture finds its surest expression in the way he brings the message of progress to legitimise the familial order of his large household. He is seen as a responsible monogamous man who alone can uphold a joint Hindu family. Like a true positivist he believes in educating and enlightening his wife Bimala, because it is only an enlightened woman who can be a fitting 'sahadharmini' to an active 'male patriciate'. He is shown to be perceptive enough to recognise the full affective powers of womanhood in Bimala and prepare her for her new role as a 'modern' woman who will know how to construct a meaningful 'home' only after she knows the 'world' outside.

Bankim's late novels possess a more fluid world. In these, the outside world often means the forests or hazardous roads not yet linked up by the safe public transport that the British were supposed to lay out; nor was the idea of the outside world circumscribed by the norms of the new urban middle class. In *Ghare Baire*, Bimala has to simply cross the threshold to leave the 'enclosed space' of the women's inner chamber and arrive at the man's world of the drawing room and library. But it is not easy for her to make even this transition. In her contentment with the 'home', Bimala builds up her little shrine with a traditional image of the husband as a deity. She identifies the modern clothes that Nikhilesh buys for her and the 'modern' education he organises under the English governess Miss Gilby as the '*leela*' of her god-husband. Even the old grandmother in this big zamindar family accepts Nikhilesh's programme of 'recasting' his wife as a part of a man's whims, certainly a more palatable alternative to the drunkenness and brothel haunting of the older members, who died of an excess of appetite.

The perfect equilibrium of intellect and heart, the positivist utopia of order and progress attempted by Nikhilesh is held in a state of precarious poise by the old grandmother. After her death the brittle order of this home begins to show signs of strain. The world outside breaks in upon this home in the shape of Sandip, the latter-day bhadralok 'santan' of the Great Mother. Sandip is increasingly seen as a travesty of Comte's *pouvoir spirituel*, a false prophet of the false god of nationalism. It is with Bankim's battle-cry of 'Bande Mataram' that Sandip rends the barrier between 'home' and the 'world'—an act that is interpreted by Tagore in predominantly sexual terms. The 'sahadharmini', carefully nurtured by Nikhilesh, is brought down to the level of a temptress by Sandip. Sandip's sexual overtures towards Bimala are made to masquerade as the heroics of swadeshi militancy. Tagore hits out at the reconstructed order of the 'santans' with which Bankim sought to defend the threatened order of Hindu orthodoxy. Tagore, who had entered into debate with Bankim over Hindu supremacism, now points an accusing finger at the swadeshi activists who had not thought twice about exploiting poor peasants, often Muslim, in order to maintain the hegemony of their bhadralok Hindu identity. 'You are well off,' says Chandranathbabu, the voice of conscience in the novel, to the student activists, 'you need not mind the cost. The poor do not want to stand in your way, but you insist on their submitting to our compulsion' (p. 132).[12] It is the use of force that helped to unleash forces of deep communal hatred, thereby giving internal sanction to Curzon's 'divide-and-rule' policy against which the swadeshi activists were supposed to be fighting.

Caught in this interlocking crisis is Bimala's womanhood, increasingly seen in terms of her sexuality. It is difficult not to notice that Sandip's rhetoric is far more effective in pulling down the barrier between the home and the world for Bimala, than the positivist programme of education devised with extreme care and affection by Nikhilesh. When Sandip's eyes discover Bimala's face 'like a star in the Great Bear' among the audience during his first swadeshi lecture delivered in Nikhilesh's house, Bimala thinks, 'Was I then an inmate [*bou*, literally, wife] of an aristocratic family? I was then the only representative of the Bengali womanhood and he was then the hero of Bengal. Just as the rays of the sun had fallen on his forehead, so he needed to be crowned by a woman's heart. How else will he attain fulfilment or his great journey?' (pp. 28–9).

As the story is narrated through the interior monologues of the three main characters, its sexual overtones are expressed without any inhibition. The realisation of the full potential of her womanhood is interpreted in terms of sexual stimulation. This is Bimala again: 'I could feel quite clearly his rhetoric caught fire after looking at my face . . . I said to myself that it was the flame of my eyes that got it ablaze' (p. 29).

Bimala's self-perception is seen as a projection of Sandip's crude egotism, a clear travesty of the altruism of Comte's *pouvoir spirituel*. She blurts out to herself: 'When the hymn to the Nation blends with the hymns to myself, the barriers of hesitation break down, the blood begins to dance . . . It seems to me that my womanhood is a divine glory' (p. 92).

The purpose of representing Bimala in this manner is to embody Tagore's own deep misgivings about the spirit of nationalism, of Hindu nationalism in particular. Sandip betrays the ethics of altruism with which Comte constructs spiritual power. He is identified by Tagore with the demonic power of nationalism, destructive, selfish and mechanistic. With a clever sleight of hand Tagore presents Sandip as 'macho': 'We are men, we are the rulers, we collect revenue. We have plundered ever since we arrived on this earth, the more we have demanded from her, the more she has surrendered' (p. 152). It is as a surrender to this 'machismo' and not to his 'cause' that Sandip sees Bimala's enthusiastic participation in the political programme of swadeshi: 'We men have rent the veil before our women entirely by the force of our demand. The more they have given themselves to us the more they have discovered themselves' (p. 152). The two kingpins of Comte's moral schema— womanhood and *pouvoir spirituel*—are thus brought down with one stroke. Against the aberration of what Tagore called the 'Nation of the

West', there is the 'Spirit of the West'[13] speaking through Nikhilesh: 'It is a symptom of our inherent slave mentality when we have to be intoxicated even though it be with the truth' (p. 171).

Bimala's striving for a womanhood that is larger than the home is ironically vanquished in the world outside: it is aborted in her own site of struggle. She is presented as something of a Sita although for the modern Sita, abduction belongs to the region of mind and passion. In a matching move, Sandip is presented as a modern Ravan—a man motivated by crude materialism, a later-day Darwinian who however feels regret for not going one better on Ravan. Like the Sita of the epic, Bimala has to go through a fire ordeal in her mind. Unlike Ravan, however, Sandip is not destroyed. He flees to save his skin. Bimala, the symbol of Affective Womanhood has to bow to the order of the traditional household. Nikhilesh, the symbol of the active male patriciate, comes home fatally wounded like a true hero.

Rabindranath Tagore's *The Home and the World* may be seen to have used the secular religion of humanity initiated by Auguste Comte in his critique of the essentialised order presented by Bankim's *Anandamath*. His novel is another remarkable expression of the contradictions and fissures contained within the apparently seamless programme of social transformation.

Endnotes

1. For a detailed study of the positivist ideology, see W.W. Simon, *European Positivism in the Nineteenth Century: An Essay in Intellectual History* (Ithaca: Cornell University Press, 1963).
2. G.H. Forbes, *Positivism in Bengal* (Calcutta: Minerva, 1975).
3. 'Comte', *Encyclopaedia Britannica*, vol. VI, ninth edition (Edinburgh: 1877), p. 234. The entry is by John Morley. Curiously enough, this motto is incorporated in the national flag of Brazil.
4. The texts in which Comte talks about the reorganised and secularised Catholic order are *Consideration of Spiritual Power* (1826) and *Positive Philosophy*, vol. V.
5. See Ben Knights, *The Idea of the Clerisy in the Nineteenth Century* (Cambridge: Cambridge University Press, 1978) and Alice Chandler, *A Dream of Order* (London: Routledge & Kegan Paul, 1971).
6. Alice Chandler, op.cit.; Eric Hobsbawm and Terence Ranger, eds, *The*

Invention of Tradition (Cambridge: Cambridge University Press, 1983).

7. Richard Congreve, *India* (London: John Chapman, 1857).

8. G.H. Forbes, op.cit. See also the unpublished Ph.D dissertation by Mridul Bose in the Jadavpur University Library.

9. S.K. Das, *The Artist in Chains* (New Delhi: New Statesman Publishing Company), see especially pp. 140–7.

10. Haridas and Uma Mukherjee, *Bande Mataram and Indian Nationalism* (Calcutta: Firma K.L. Mukhopadhyay), p. 7. The poem may be taken as signifying the very essence of the idealism which permeates the entire novel—a blend of the categorical imperative of the *Gita* and the positivism of Comte.

11. See Nina Auerbach, *The Woman and the Demon: Life of a Victorian Myth* (Cambridge, Mass.: Harvard University Press, 1982).

12. All citations taken from Rabindranath Tagore, *The Home and the World*, trans. Surendranath Tagore (London: Macmillan, 1919, rpt.; Harmondsworth: Penguin, 1976), are given parenthetically in the text.

13. Rabindranath Tagore, *Nationalism* (London: Macmillan, 1985; first published 1917), pp. 3, 11.

Ghare Baire and its Readings

JAYANTI CHATTOPADHYAY

I

'Of all the works of Rabindranath, *Ghare Baire* has probably provoked the largest number of critics, literary or otherwise,' wrote Prabhat Kumar Mukhopadhyay, author of the best-known biography of the poet.[1] Writing in 1936, the veteran Tagore scholar must have been referring to the comments, reviews and articles that began pouring in with the serialised publication of the novel in the journal *Sabuj Patra* (Green Leaves) between 1915 and 1916. The literary furore continued for a few years. In most of them the condemnation of the novel and its author was so severe that, alongside his small group of supporters, Tagore himself felt compelled to write twice during this period in his own defence. However, all this excitement subsided by the end of the second decade and the following years tell a different story. The attention of readers and critics shifted elsewhere, and with the progress of time the number of articles tapered off. Comments on the novel appeared only sporadically in treatises dealing with some larger issues concerning Tagorean thought and literature.

In fact, apart from the initial furore and a few spontaneous responses in between, *Ghare Baire*—or more precisely its film version—became the subject of public debate once more only in 1984. The controversy (heightened no doubt by the fame and reputation of the filmmaker) was caused by the deviations in the film script from the original narrative.

A large number of viewers were irked by Ray's transformation of the somewhat open ending of the novel into a more definite one in the film. The number of Ray's supporters was considerable but the debate did not last long. After that interlude, *Ghare Baire* retreated again from the minds of readers.

Of course, there have been critical writings on *Ghare Baire* in the past decades, produced mainly for the academy. One cannot say that these have been conducive to the development of critical thought. The best among these writings show flashes of brilliance and offer useful insights; the rest—and they form the majority—seem no more than a succession of enthusiastic introductory pieces often reiterating points already made—and made well—by previous scholars. A detailed resume of the plot and the characters is often given, as though *Ghare Baire* is an unknown text. On many occasions critics muffle their individual preferences, abort the natural drive of their argument and flatten out the sharpness of previous debates in a futile bid to settle for an 'objective' presentation. Further, even in the 1990s, these critics have seldom gone beyond assuming a simple and direct relationship between author, text and reader. Most critics have sought out coherence and moral wisdom, overlooking ambiguities, eddies of meaning and disturbing subtexts. Reputed Tagore scholars of our time—such as Abu Sayad Ayub and Sankha Ghosh—whose writings do not strictly belong to the realm of academic criticism, have provided new insights into Tagore's poems, plays, even songs, but have chosen to remain silent about his novels.

The critical evaluations of *Ghare Baire* (or for that matter any book by Tagore) cannot be assessed without placing them in a larger frame of reference. A cultural icon for his language community, Tagore's social, political, moral and even religious positions have always been of enormous importance to his countrymen; but interestingly, these were seldom received uncritically. Tagore on his part was eager to explain his stand and viewpoints to his audience. A survey of the critical comments on his writings, and his responses to them, help us understand the changing patterns of thought in Bengal. *Ghare Baire*, located in a crucial moment in the history of Bengal, is particularly useful to carry out this exercise. Even when they do not deliberately contextualise this novel, critics nevertheless reveal their own social assumptions and anxieties, since it is almost impossible to disengage the different aspects of *Ghare Baire* from some of the wider social and political issues of the time. So while the body of critical writings on *Ghare Baire* remains lean and inadequate, even simple textual exegeses provide a register of key attitudes and preoccupations in Bengal from the time of the novel's first appearance to the present.

II

No other issue in the novel has concerned critics as much as the transgression of Bimala, her passionate involvement with her husband's friend Sandip. Stories of adulterous women were not uncommon in Bengali (like in any other literature). A host of wicked and fallen wives could be found in moral and didactic tales; these apart, the divine and eternal love sport of Radha and Krishna, regarded as 'illicit' in worldly terms, was always very popular.

But *Ghare Baire* is not just the story of an erring wife who repents at the end, nor that of the emotional exuberance of a married woman in love with another man. While the novel may have both these elements (and many others) these need to be located primarily in nineteenth-century representations of upper-caste Bengali women. This will explain what made *Ghare Baire* such a controversial text for its contemporary readers. To make my point clearer, I would like to briefly discuss two texts written before *Ghare Baire* on the same theme.

In Tagore's novella *Nastanid* (The Broken Nest, 1901), Charulata's love for her husband Bhupati's cousin Amal, had broken their home. Saibalini in Bankimchandra Chattopadhyay's novel *Chandrasekhar* (1875) had left her husband and home with an adventurous Englishman in a desperate attempt to be united with her childhood sweetheart, Pratap. Both Saibalini and Charulata were neglected by Chandrasekhar and Bhupati, their respective husbands. Charulata's husband, a busy journalist, has no time for his young wife and her desire for Amal stems both from Amal's recognition of her as potentially equal and from her own sense of being needed by him.[2] On the other hand, Chandrasekhar, a middle-aged Sanskrit scholar who is cold and passive towards his young wife, leaves her dangerously alone: eight years of married life have not been able to obliterate the memory of Pratap from Saibalini's mind.

Both texts question the traditional idea of conjugality, and suggest the need for a closer union based on individual compatibility and companionship, an important part of nineteenth-century discourse on women. But *Chandrasekhar* also reflects the uncertain, oscillating attitude of the nineteenth-century bhadralok. Bankimchandra not only addresses Saibalini as '*papistha*' (sinner) throughout the narrative, but also imposes on her a long and hideous process of self-purification before Saibalini is allowed to return to her home and husband. Tagore's story, on the contrary, does not make any such compromises, and has an open ending.

The story of Bimala, which has been developed on different lines, marks a further step. Nikhilesh, Bimala's husband, has been portrayed as an ideal representative of the nineteenth-century liberal Bengali. A large-hearted and benevolent zamindar, Nikhilesh is a well-educated, modern man, given to scholarship and social work. He believes 'that man and wife are equal in love because of their equal claim on each other' (p. 20).[3] He fulfils, almost in verbatim, the declaration that Kailash Chandra Basu, an advocate of women's education made in 1846, that the Hindu woman 'must be refined, reorganized, recast, regenerated'.[4] Nikhilesh engages an English governess to teach Bimala the English language and English manners. Bimala herself has described his love for her. Addressing him, she writes in a highly charged language:

My beloved . . . you endowed your love by educating me, giving me what I wanted and what I did not. I have seen what depth of love there was in your eyes. When you gazed at me . . . you loved my whole nature as if it had been given you by some rare providence. (p. 20)

Nikhilesh does not stop at this. What he wants is a confirmation of their love in and through experience of the outer world. He tells his wife that, 'If we meet and recognise each other in the real world, then only will our love be true' (p. 23).

Bimala, however, has never been comfortable with her husband's views. She has disliked his friend Sandip from a photograph, thinking his face revealed a lack of character and that 'too much of base alloy had gone into [its] making'. Yet, after nine peaceful years of married life, she falls in love with Sandip when she meets him. Sandip, presented initially as a revolutionary patriot and brilliant orator, turns out to be a man without any moral scruples. Yet even when the baseness in his nature becomes fully apparent to her, Bimala is unable to entirely despise Sandip. She confesses:

I cannot but feel again and again that there are two persons in me. One recoils from Sandip in his terrible aspect of Chaos—the other feels that very vision to be sweetly alluring. (p. 178)

Moreover, she may have come back to her husband, realising he is a better man, but she knows:

that the festive flutes which were played at my wedding, nine years ago, welcoming me to his house, will never sound for me again. . . . God can create new things but has even He the power to create afresh that which has been destroyed? (p. 186)

A later critic described this daring representation of a woman—her passionate outbursts and her frank confessions—as a 'veritable bomb' that hit the genteel society of the early-twentieth-century Bengal.[5] While the more 'progressive' groups were silent, it was the upholders of the sanctity of Hindu religion and customs who reacted strongly to the novel, particularly the characterisation of Bimala. Since its inception in 1914, *Sabuj Patra* and its main contributor Rabindranath Tagore, had been under fire from this group of writers for the journal's 'anti-Hindu stance.'[6] With Bimala represented as the wife of a traditional Hindu zamindar, the revivalists found further cause for ire.

Tagore was deliberately addressing the problems and the tragedies of women in tradition-bound Hindu households in some of the stories he published in *Sabuj Patra* during this period. Some of the women protagonists depicted in these stories revolted against the injustice meted out to them—a fact strongly opposed by a section of society. Mrinal, in Tagore's story *Streer Patra* (The Wife's letter), walks out of her home and marriage leaving behind her completely insensitive husband. At least two stories propagating '*pativrata*' (total devotion to husband) were published as a reaction in periodicals that eulogised the tenets of Hindu orthodoxy.[7] With at least five more instalments of *Ghare Baire* yet to be published, Tagore felt compelled to write a long article in the November 1915 issue of *Sabuj Patra*. He explained that his article was an answer to a personal letter sent to him by an unknown lady. However, he adds that, 'I have reasons to presume that she speaks on behalf of the general readers and expects a public reply.'

Tagore does not quote the original letter, but the lady seems to have asked the author of *Ghare Baire* two questions:

1. What was the intention of the author in writing the novel?
2. Was the story only a figment of the author's imagination or was it based on some actual happening? If the latter was the case, then did the incidents take place in a modern fashionable community proud of its Western education or in a traditional Hindu family?

Tagore's interrogator was making a double insinuation. Such moral lapses, she implies, could only take place in an English-educated Bengali woman belonging to a fashionable section of society; and second, that Tagore deliberately portrays a debased traditional Hindu family.

About the first implication—which was a commonplace in the late-nineteenth and early-twentieth-century Bengal—Tagore did not comment. In fact, he himself would create such stereotypes of Western-educated Bengali woman in some later writings. His reaction to the other insinuation was however quite sharp. Posing a counter-argument, he asked the lady, 'Does that mean that in an orthodox Hindu family, man always follows the commandments of Manu and never goes astray or bids for freedom?'[8]

Tagore, a Brahmo, may have been surmising that the accusing finger of the lady (and of his readers in general) pointed towards the women of his community, considered more independent and emancipated, and consequently criticised and ridiculed by the orthodoxy. While this is conjecture, it is significant that Saratchandra Chatterji, then the most popular novelist in Bengal, whose works are a curious mixture of orthodoxy and radicalism, started serialising one of his most controversial novels, *Grihadaha* (The House on Fire), almost immediately after the publication of *Ghare Baire* as a book. There is little doubt that this novel was written in direct opposition to Tagore's. Achala, the woman protagonist of Saratchandra's novel, is an educated, modern Brahmo woman, who is torn between her desire for two men, one Hindu and the other a Brahmo, both of whom are well educated but differ in character and social status. Her inability to free herself from the attractions of one even after she marries the other of her own accord, brings disaster to Achala's life. 'Her divided emotions,' writes one critic, 'are at once her glory and tragedy.'[9] Meanwhile, there is the young and beautiful Mrinal, once a childhood love of Achala's husband, who was married off to an elderly man and soon widowed. Saratchandra idealises her quiet suffering and shows her to be an anchor and solace for the other characters in the novel.

While upholding the idea of Hindu superiority over the Brahmos, Saratchandra still retained deep sympathy for the plight of a woman attracted to two men simultaneously. Contemporary literary critics (at least a section of them) suffered from no such ambivalence. Rabindranath Tagore, in the article mentioned above, had pleaded that a work of literature should be evaluated as an art form and not as 'a manual of moral instruction'. He argued that 'a story must be taken as a story and not as an opinion of the author'. He had further asserted that 'if at all any classification is done in literature, it should be according to the diversities of human nature, and certainly not on the basis of codified religion'.[10] But his critics thought otherwise. Most of them still favoured the nineteenth-century dictum that the novel was not only a personal communication from the author to the reader, but also a vehicle for delivering a moral message. They had no patience with a work in which the domestic sanctuary of a Hindu home was badly shaken by an 'unchaste woman' while her husband watched and suffered silently. They were still more astounded by the degrading remarks Sandip makes in the novel on the *Ramayana's* Sita. This made them accuse Tagore of immorality, disloyalty to the nation and even sacrilege. 'I am surprised to see,' wrote one of the reviewers, punning on the two words ghar (home) and bahir (outside), 'that Rabindranath, regarded as a saint by many, has in his mature years the desire to paint an obnoxious picture of a Hindu "home" for the "outside world" in such an obscene manner.'[11] Much of the critical writing published between 1915 and 1919 was written in more or less the same vein.[12] And as the language of criticism began flouting the norms of decency, Tagore wrote again on *Ghare Baire*, this time in *Prabasi*, a periodical favourably disposed towards him.

The sole purpose of this short article was to defend himself against the allegations flung at him because of Sandip's remarks on Sita.

Expressing his dismay that the remarks had been regarded as his own, Tagore reiterated his rejection of extra-literary criteria for judging works of literature. He invoked the principle of propriety found in Sanskrit poetics in order to explain the behaviour of Sandip. Bitterly and sarcastically he remarked:

When I introduced the character of Sandip in *Ghare Baire*, I could never have imagined even for a moment that I should be accountable to so many among the important, titled, elite people of our country.[13]

What is intriguing today is not just the loud condemnation of the conservative critics, but the silence of their opponents. The few supporters of Tagore did not put forward their arguments as strongly as the other group. The most interesting case in this regard is that of Pramatha Chaudhury, the editor of *Sabuj Patra* and a close friend of Tagore. Chaudhury had earlier declared that the object of his journal would be to jolt the Bengali mind, to arouse it from its long torpor and to declare a war against all forms of self-deception. However, while defending *Ghare Baire*, Chaudhury took refuge behind an allegory— and not a convincing one at that. He wrote that *Ghare Baire* was not a realist fiction but a poetic allegory: 'Rabindranath has depicted our national problems in *Ghare Baire*, because the novel is nothing but an allegorical poem [in which] Nikhilesh is ancient India, Sandip modern Europe and Bimala present-day India.'[14]

The reasons for this failure may have been many; here I would like to suggest only one. In his essay '*Prachina o Nabina*', Bankimchandra had tried to put forward the proposition that the nineteenth-century discourse on women was male-centric and therefore perpetuated masculine hegemony. He had contended that 'while society looks upon any infringement on the part of the wives as a grievous sin, the moral restrictions on men are rather weak; the biases of the men makes them pay attention to the cause of women's upliftment so far as it suits or serves them, never a jot more'. He did contradict himself on other occasions, for instance when he declared that 'loyalty to the husband is the fundamental duty of all wives',[15] Tagore, to my mind, puts forward an almost similar proposition through Nikhilesh's self-analysis. Nikhilesh speaks in many voices about the Bimala–Sandip relationship. But a number of confessional statements cannot be ignored; for example, Nikhilesh says:

completely, she nevertheless stresses Bimala's final retrieval rather than her initial transgression.

Radharani Devi's article would have been too conservative to be included in *Kallol* but for her estimation of Sandip's character, which is almost identical to that of Bhabani Bhattacharya, down to its language. Though she glorified traditional values in the two women characters of the novel, she was paradoxically fascinated by the 'indomitable virility' of Sandip, and found his honesty (even if only to himself) an important quality.

Both articles were published in *Kallol*. The Kallolians, attracted to Nazrul Islam's 'hot, impetuous, extravagant' verses which betokened 'freedom from bondage',[25] wanted to appropriate Sandip as their idea of a rebel. Apart from portraying low life, the Kallolians 'also thought the uninhibited projection of sex . . . a necessary condition of modernity'.[26] To them, the Tagorean world seemed too sombre and serene.

Troubled by the radicalism of the Kallolians, Sajanikanta Das, an erstwhile anti-Tagore critic, turned supportive and wrote to Tagore in a personal letter in 1927:

I have been pursuing your literary career for at least ten years and I feel that you do not believe in going beyond the limits of decency in literature. I have not come across any such instance in your writing where a character has lost his/her self-control. . . . and I shudder to imagine what shape these modern writers would given to *Ekratri, Nastanid* and *Ghare Baire,* had they been writing them.[27]

Within one and a half decades of its publication the critical opinion on *Ghare Baire* had travelled from one end of the pole to the other. Though the feeling of uneasiness about the characters in *Ghare Baire* would remain in the minds of many, later critics would read them from a different angle.

IV

Even as the Kallolians were expanding the concerns of Bengali fiction, Srikumar Bandopadhyay, the initiator of academic criticism on the novel in Bengali, had begun to write a history of the Bengali novel. He had started the work in 1923 and writing intermittently had produced the chapter on Tagore's novels, by his own admission, sometime in 1928. He ultimately published *Banga Sahitye Upanyser Dhara* (The Novel Tradition in Bengali Literature) in 1938. The book underwent four more editions in the author's lifetime. The last edition, published in 1965, five years before his death, became the most voluminous book on criticism in Bengali.

Bandopadhyay begins by postulating that 'the discussion on *Ghare Baire* should be on two levels—political and socio-ethical'.[28] He elaborates the political theme by observing that 'the emotional high tides in the early days of the swadeshi movement was [sic] at times polluted by a vicious flow of "self-propaganda", loss of moral values combined with a greed for success—all of which was exposed by the author in his characterization of Sandip'. Clearly Bandopadhyay looks at Tagore's depiction of Sandip in a sympathetic manner. But having said this, he hastens to declare almost in the same breath that, 'it will be unfair to consider Sandip as the true representative of the revolutionary leader'.[29]

Bandopadhyay's contradiction may be understood by the fact that he had inherited a long-standing (though, as I have said, subordinate) tradition of critically looking at Tagore's handling of Sandip and swadeshi. In 1916, the *Barisal Hitaishi*, a weekly magazine, had admonished Tagore in harsh terms for his 'ugly attack on the revolutionaries which included showing the hero [?] as trying to seduce another man's wife.'[30] A few months later, the periodical *Upasana*, anticipating Bandopadhyay, wrote, 'To consider the burning of markets or the picketing organised by Sandip as patriotic deeds . . . would be giving a bad name to the patriotic deeds . . .'[31] Clearly, these and other comments have been concerned only with the misrepresentation of the figure of the swadeshi leader in Sandip. Although there were some exceptions[32] the novel's political elements were not given any importance till the end of the 1930s.

In general most critics of the first generation were more concerned with the possible ending of the story and the privations of Bimala. To them *Ghare Baire* was the story of triangular love, or, to be more precise, of immoral love. Looking at half a century of Bengali novels that preceded *Ghare Baire*, it is not difficult to understand why they thought it to be so. Love has been the primary theme of the Bengali novel since its emergence: 'The novel is primarily concerned with love',[33] wrote a critic of the genre in the nineteenth century. Again from his very first novel, *Durgeshnandini* (1865), Bankimchandra, the architect of the Bengali novel, had examined the complexities of man–woman relationships in most of his novels, placing his characters in not only one, but at times, in multiple triangles. In his early novels Tagore had also followed a similar pattern. It was therefore only natural for critics to locate *Ghare Baire* in the tradition with which they were acquainted.

Over time, however, critics changed their assumptions about the love triangle in *Ghare Baire*. Srikumar Bandopadhyay asks a provocative question which opens out a new way of looking at Bimala and love. 'Had Sandip,' he asks, 'been a worthy man, a true rival of Nikhilesh, had he not been a shameless, greedy lecher operating under the cover of patriotism, would then the proposed test of Nikhilesh have ended in the same way?' This is a significant departure from earlier critical stances for he seems to assume that Bimala has a will of her own, but is prevented from exercising it in a free manner by the author himself.[34]

The 'love triangle' critics were primarily concerned with Bimala and saw the swadeshi as providing a mere backdrop to the action. In contrast, the 'political' critics, who emerged at the end of the 1930s, subordinated the issues of the representation of woman and of gender relations to the political concerns of the novel. The second tendency is discernible in two significant studies of the novel.

In his classic study of the swadeshi movement, Sumit Sarkar was one of the first scholars to describe the novel as a study of 'the complexities of the swadeshi age—its grandeur and the pettiness, its triumphs and problems and tragedies'.[35] He has shown how the different components of the movement have been woven into the story of the novel. To Sarkar, Tagore has portrayed the enlightened and progressive zamindar in Nikhilesh who tried to promote self-reliance and swadeshi long before it became fashionable, and pitted his methods against the repressive methods of the political activist Sandip as well as Harish Kundu, the oppressive zamindar-turned-swadeshi hero. But Sarkar has totally marginalised Bimala and simply describes her as the wife of an emancipated man swept off her feet by the virile and nihilistic personality of Sandip.

In the 1990s, Ashis Nandy, who was interested in the psychological biography of the modern nation-state in India, took up the novel along with *Gora* and *Char Adhyay*, to analyse Tagore's nationalism. He read the novel as a symbolic one, deviating only slightly from Pramatha Chaudhury's reading. And when Nandy declared that 'Bimala is the link between the two forms of patriotism the men represent',[36] he harked back to Mohitosh Roychaudhuri's formulation eight decades earlier that 'the author has in Nikhilesh and Sandip presented two different ideals of loving and serving one's country'.[37] Nandy argues that the tragedy of Bimala is not merely personal but possesses wider implications since 'the destruction of her home foreshadows the destruction of society'. Whether or not one accepts the symbolic reading of the novel at any level, it remains a fact that Nandy, by describing Bimala as the country— the battlefield on which two forms of patriotism fight for supremacy— turns her into a passive creature and effectively subverts the question of gender.

In general, the history of discussion on *Ghare Baire* reveals an inability to come to terms with its complexity. It may be remarked that non-Bengali critics too have failed to do so. If anything, their failure has been even more pronounced. Georg Lukacs's caustic review of the novel published in 1922, in which he attacked Tagore for putting himself at the intellectual service of the British police as well as his absurd identification of Sandip as a 'contemptible caricature of Gandhi'[38] (much before Gandhi became prominent in India's politics), is too well known to need elaboration. The same can be said of E.M.Forster's scathing remarks in 1938. 'The Home is not really a home,' he pronounced, 'but a retreat from seemly meditations upon infinity and the world'; it proves to be a sphere not for 'numberless tasks' but for 'a boarding house flirtation'.[39] The faulty translation of the novel has been blamed for such misrepresentations. But this does not seem a persuasive explanation since critical writings in Bengali too have not been able to do justice to the riven and layered structure of *Ghare Baire*. Clearly, the intricacy of this novel awaits its complex reader.

Endnotes

1. Prabhat Kumar Mukhopadhyay, *Rabindra Jibani, 4 vols*, vol. II, *1901–1918* (Calcutta: 1977), p. 546.

2. Rashmi Bhatnagar, 'Genre and Gender: A Reading of Tagore's "The Broken Nest" and R.K. Narayan's *The Dark Room*', in *Woman Image Text* ed. Lola Chatterjee (New Delhi: 1986), p. 174.

3. All citations are taken from Rabindranath Tagore, *The Home and the World*, trans. Surendranath Tagore (London: 1919, rpt. New Delhi: Penguin India, 1999) and are included parenthetically in the text.

4. Kailash Chandra Basu, 'On the Education of Hindu Females' (1846), in *Nineteenth Century Studies*, ed. Alok Roy (Calcutta: 1975), p. 198.

5. Bimanbehari Majumdar, *Heroines of Tagore: A Study in the Transformation of Indian Society 1875–1941* (Calcutta:1968), p. 246.

6. 'From the day Sabuj Patra has sprouted Rabindranath, the incarnation of genius, is writing long and short stories in the periodical. The objective of most of the stories is to undermine or ridicule Hindu society, Hindu beliefs, Hindu scriptures, Hindu customs and the eternal and revered ideals of Hindus.' *Samalochana na Ucchas, Sahitya*, October 1916, cited in *Oheder Aditya Rabindra Bidushoner Itibritta* (Calcutta: 1986), p. 57.

7. Bepin Chandra Pal, *Mrinaler Katha, Narayan*, 1914 and Lalit Kumar Bandopadhyay, *Swamir Patra*, ibid.

8. *Rabindra Rachanabali*, vol. VIII, pp. 521–6.

9. Humayun Kabir, *The Bengali Novel* (Calcutta: 1968), p. 77.

10. Ibid.

11. Cited in Prafulla Chandra Roy, *Oheder Aditya . . .*, op.cit., p. 61.

12. See Ratul Bandopadhyay, *Bitarkita Rabindranath* (Calcutta: 1994), pp. 37–70.

13. *Rachanabali*, vol. VIII, op. cit.

14. Ibid.

15. Bankimchandra Chattopadhyay, *Prachina o Nabina, Bankim Rachanabali*, vol. II (Calcutta: 1954), pp. 249–56.

16. *Rabindra Bidusan Itibritta*, op. cit., p. 61.

17. Jotindramohan Sinha, *Ghare Baire, Rabindra Sagar Sangame*, ed. Bratin Mukhopadhyay (Calcutta: 1962), pp. 263–75.

18. Ibid.

19. (My translation in prose). Achintya Kumar Sengupta, *Achintya Kumarer Samagra Kabita* (Calcutta: 1974), p. 69.

20. Buddhadev Basu, *An Acre of Green Grass* (Calcutta: 1948), p. 81.

21. Bhabani Bhattacharya, *Kathasahitye Rabindranath, Kallol*, July 1927, in *Kallole Rabindranath*, ed. Gautam Bhattacharya (Calcutta: 1987), pp. 67–8.

22. Ibid.

23. Ibid.

24. Radharani Devi Dutta, '*Prakas o Pracchaner Rupmadhurya: Ghare Baire*' in *Kallole Rabindranath*, op. cit., pp. 84–97.

25. *An Acre . . .*, op. cit., p. 48.

26. Sisir Kumar Das, *A History of Indian Literature (1911–1956)* (New Delhi: 1995), p. 215.

27. Cited in Gautam Bhattacharya, *Slilata-Aslilata O Rabindranath* (Calcutta: 1996), pp. 4–5.

28. Srikumar Bandopadhyay, *Banga Sahitye Upanyaser Dhara* (Calcutta: 1965), p. 163.

29. Ibid., p. 165.

30. Cited in Bandopadhyay, *Bitarkite. . . .*, op. cit., p. 44.

31. Ibid., p. 56.

32. Ibid., pp. 56–7.

33. Chandranath Basu, *Novel ba Kathagrantha Uddesya, Bangadarshan*, vol. VII, p. 30.

34. Bandopadhyay's insight has been enormously influential. For instance, while Buddhadev Basu seems overwhelmed by the question of *Ghare Baire's* prose style, nevertheless in a rare moment when he talks of the theme of the novel, he echoes Bandopadhyay's concern about the plot. Buddhadev Basu, *Rabindranath: Kathasahitya* (Calcutta: 1955), pp. 78–87; *An Acre . . .*, op. cit., pp. 31–3.

35. Sumit Sarkar, *The Swadeshi Movement in Bengal 1903–1908* (Calcutta: 1973), p. 91.

36. Ashis Nandy, *The Illegitimacy of Nationalism: Rabindranath Tagore and the Politics of the Self* (Delhi: 1994), pp. 12–14.

37. Cited in *Bitarkite . . .*, op. cit., pp. 56–7.

38. Georg Lukacs, *Reviews and Articles for Die Rote Fahne*, trans. Peter Palmer (London: 1983), pp. 9–11.

39. E.M.Forster, *Abinger Harvest* (London: 1983), pp. 365–7.